Postmillennialism

An Eschatology of
Hope

Postmillennialism

An Eschatology of
Hope

Keith A. Mathison

P&R
P U B L I S H I N G
P.O. BOX 817 • PHILLIPSBURG • NEW JERSEY 08865-0817

Unless otherwise indicated, Scripture quotations are from the New American Standard Bible. Copyright by the Lockman Foundation 1960, 1962, 1963, 1968, 1971, 1973, 1975, 1977.

Composition by Colophon Typesetting

Printed in the United States of America

Library of Congress Cataloging-in-Publication Data

Mathison, Keith A., 1967–
    Postmillennialism : an eschatology of hope / Keith A. Mathison.
        p.   cm.
    Includes bibliographical references and index.
    ISBN 0-87552-389-7 (pbk.)
    1. Millennialism. I. Title
BT891.M37   1999
236´.9—dc21   98-55539

Dedication

This book is dedicated to my daughter, Sarah Faith Mathison.

> *The LORD bless you and keep you;*
> *The LORD make His face shine on you,*
> *And be gracious to you;*
> *The LORD lift up His countenance on you,*
> *And give you peace. (Num. 6:24–26)*

Contents

Acknowledgments

It is a virtual truism that a book like this cannot be written without the help and support of many people. I am especially grateful to my lovely wife, Tricia, and my beautiful daughter, Sarah, who put up with too many trips to the library and too much thinking out loud. They make every day a joyful one for me.

I would also like to extend my heartfelt appreciation and thanks to Mr. Ethan Harris for volunteering to read the first draft of the manuscript. His insightful comments, questions, suggestions, and criticisms improved the text considerably.

Dr. Kenneth L. Gentry, Jr., took time out of his busy writing and preaching schedule to read the second draft of the book. Many of his suggestions were incorporated into the argument of the book. I thank him for his time and his constant willingness to help.

Many others read all or part of the manuscript and offered helpful comments and criticism. I would like to thank Tom Forest, Darren Edgington, Bill Mikler, David Scott, Robert Barnes, Ra McLaughlin, Jay Yang, Jerry Dodson, my parents, and my wife for encouraging me, arguing with me, and all in all helping me to clarify my own thoughts on some very difficult biblical passages.

Everyone at P&R Publishing has been a joy to work with. I thank Mrs. Barbara Lerch for always having an encouraging word, for guiding this project through numerous twists and turns, and for patiently and happily providing me with information. I would also like to thank the editors of the work, James Scott and Thom Notaro, for putting up with my repeated use of the passive voice and for their fine-tuning of the manuscript. Any remaining defects are solely the responsibility of the author.

I thank our Lord Jesus Christ for His unfailing and boundless love, his amazing grace, and His mercy for me, a sinner. I pray that this book, despite its many flaws, will be used in some small way by our Lord to extend His kingdom.

Introduction

*[Postmillennialism is] the view that Christ will return to the earth
after the Spirit-blessed Gospel has had overwhelming success in
bringing the world to the adoption of Christianity.*
—Kenneth L. Gentry, Jr.[1]

A defense of postmillennialism? Who would be optimistic enough to write such a book at the end of the twentieth century? How could anyone actually believe in postmillennialism, especially in light of two world wars, the Holocaust, the atomic bomb, and ethnic cleansing? Just look around you! How can you read today's newspaper and say that the gospel is going to prevail? My response to questions like these is, how can you read the Bible and say that the gospel is *not* going to prevail? Since when did the newspaper become our authority for doctrine?

When God promised to give Abraham a son, everything that his eyes could see told him that he would never have one. Sarah laughed at the promise. Yet Abraham believed God, and God gave him a son. Similarly, God promised Moses that He would use him to lead the people of Israel out of bondage in Egypt. Initially, Moses was doubtful, but when he finally trusted God and believed the promise, God used him to lead the Israelites out of Egypt. Then God promised to give them the land of Canaan. But ten of the twelve spies sent into the land doubted the promise and persuaded the people that they could never take the land. Their faithlessness resulted in forty years of wilderness wandering. But Joshua and Caleb believed God's promise, and they saw God give Israel the land.

God has promised the church that the gates of hell will not prevail against her, that all the ends of the earth will turn to the Lord, and that all the families of the nations will worship before Him. Shall we, like Sarah, laugh at the apparently unrealistic nature of the promise? Or shall we, like Abraham, believe the promise of God? Throughout biblical history, God has promised the seemingly impossible. In response, some have placed their trust in what their eyes could see. "We have to be realistic," they have said. But others, despite the seeming impossibility of fulfillment, have believed the promises of God.

This volume has two purposes. The first purpose is to demonstrate that God has, in fact, promised that the gospel of Christ, through the power of the Holy Spirit, will prevail over the families and nations of the earth. Once the nature and content of that promise are made clear, we must respond by believing what God has said. Today's newspaper is then no longer an excuse for anxiety or apathy.

The second purpose of this book is directly related to the first. It is my sincere hope and prayer that God will use this demonstration of the truth of postmillennialism to encourage preachers and teachers to proclaim this long-neglected doctrine once again, that He will use this renewed faith in His promise as a means to accomplish what He has promised, and that a period of fruitful missions and evangelism, the likes of which the world has never seen, will bring innumerable multitudes into the kingdom of our Lord Jesus Christ.

PART ONE

Hermeneutical Considerations

CHAPTER ONE

Presuppositions and Definitions

If truth exists outside of ourselves, we will not know it by pretending that we have no presuppositions, nor will we attain it by embracing all our presuppositions as unchangeable parts of ourselves; we will achieve it only if we submit ourselves, presuppositions and all, to the One who understands and interprets all things rightly.
—Dan McCartney and Charles Clayton[1]

The way in which we approach Scripture and the assumptions we bring to the text are vitally important matters, especially when we are discussing disputed doctrines like eschatology. These matters are often overlooked, sometimes out of ignorance and sometimes because of the mistaken idea that it is possible to approach Scripture without any biases, theological or otherwise. Of course, during our study of Scripture, our most basic assumptions should become more and more conformed to God's authoritative word, but we must at least be aware that we have these assumptions and make every attempt to recognize what they are. Because of the importance of this subject, the first two chapters of this book will explain some of the most basic presuppositions that the author brings to this study of eschatology.

He Is There

There is no more fundamental truth than the fact that God exists (Gen. 1:1). This should go without saying, but because there are those who mistakenly assume that postmillennialism is a variety of liberalism or secularism, it must be clearly affirmed from the beginning that this volume rests upon the most basic assumption that the sovereign God and Father of our Lord Jesus Christ exists. The Bible itself assumes the existence of God from the first chapter of Genesis to the last chapter of Revelation, and any interpretation that ignores this fact will fail. The Bible also assumes that history is under the providential control of God. As Kenneth Gentry notes, "It means everything to eschatological inquiry whether or not the entire course of world history is under the absolutely sovereign administration of the infinitely personal God of Scripture."[2]

He Is Not Silent

God has definitively revealed Himself and His will to man in the Scriptures of the Old and New Testaments (Isa. 8:19–20; Rom. 15:4; 2 Tim. 3:15–16). He alone is able to define His own nature and His own will authoritatively. Accordingly, He has revealed Himself to man in various ways throughout redemptive history, sometimes in dreams, sometimes in visions, and sometimes through other means. But as the Westminster Confession of Faith explains, "For the more sure establishment and comfort of the Church against the corruption of the flesh, and the malice of Satan and of the world," God committed His revelation to writing (1.1). In other words, we are not left to our own devices to discover the will of God. He has condescended to reveal the truth about Himself, His creation, and His will for that creation in the Bible.[3]

All Scripture Is Inspired

All Scripture is inspired by God (2 Tim. 3:16).[4] As the very word of the living God, Scripture is authoritative, inerrant, and internally self-consistent. An excellent summary of the doctrine of Scripture may be found in the Chicago Statement on Biblical Inerrancy. Because of its importance, the Short Statement is quoted here in full:

1. God, who is Himself Truth and speaks truth only, has inspired Holy Scripture in order thereby to reveal Himself to lost mankind through Jesus Christ as Creator and Lord, Redeemer and Judge. Holy Scripture is God's witness to Himself.

2. Holy Scripture, being God's own Word, written by men prepared and superintended by His Spirit, is of infallible divine authority in all matters upon which it touches: it is to be believed, as God's instruction, in all that it affirms; obeyed, as God's command, in all that it requires; *embraced, as God's pledge, in all that it promises*.

3. The Holy Spirit, Scripture's divine Author, both authenticates it to us by His inward witness and opens our minds to understanding its meaning.

4. Being wholly and verbally God-given, Scripture is without error or fault in all its teaching, no less in what it states about God's acts in creation, about the events of world history, and about its own literary origins under God, than in its witness to God's saving grace in individual lives.

5. The authority of Scripture is inescapably impaired if this total divine inerrancy is in any way limited or disregarded, or made relative to a view of truth contrary to the Bible's own; and such lapses bring serious loss to both the individual and the Church.[5]

In the Image of God

In the creation narrative of Genesis 1, God reveals that He created man in His image and that He gave specific spoken commands to man regarding the creation (Gen. 1:26–30). This reveals that God created the mind of man with the ability to comprehend both His creation and His word. The fact that God continues to communicate and respond to man after the Fall reveals that sin has not annihilated this human faculty. It has corrupted the mind of man, as it has corrupted every other aspect of his nature, but it has not completely destroyed man's ability to think and communicate rationally. This means that it is possible to understand accurately what God has revealed to us in the Scriptures.[6]

Jesus Is Lord

Our understanding of who Christ is and what He has done, is doing, and will do, will also profoundly affect our interpretation of

Scripture. This survey of Scripture is made with the conviction that Jesus Christ is the only begotten Son of God. As all of the orthodox creeds and confessions teach, He became incarnate by the Holy Spirit and was born of the virgin Mary. He is truly God and truly man, having two natures "without confusion, without change, without division, without separation."[7] He was crucified under Pontius Pilate, suffered, and was buried. On the third day He rose from death. He ascended into heaven and is seated at the right hand of God the Father. He will come again visibly with glory to judge the living and the dead.

From beginning to end, Scripture is centered on Christ. The Bible is focused on the redemptive work of God in history, and therefore it focuses on the One sent to be the Redeemer, Jesus the Messiah. Both the Old Testament and the New Testament testify to the person and work of Christ. The Old Testament focuses on the promise of redemption, and the New Testament focuses on the fulfillment of that promise. Both testaments testify that Christ is the central message of the entire Bible.

The Necessity of Faith

The proper interpretation of Scripture requires regeneration, faith, and sanctification in the interpreter. While unbelievers may be able to comprehend the literary message of Scripture, true discernment demands the illuminating work of the Holy Spirit in the heart of the interpreter. Moisés Silva explains that "a right relationship with its divine author is the most fundamental prerequisite for proper biblical interpretation."[8] In other words, knowledge of Greek and Hebrew, while invaluable, does not guarantee a correct interpretation of a particular text of Scripture. The illuminating presence of the Holy Spirit is necessary.

Scripture Interprets Scripture

Scripture is the public revelation of God to man. As such, it may and must be interpreted with great care and caution. Scripture must be interpreted in the normal grammatical sense. This does not mean that every text will automatically be interpreted literally. The question of literalism must be decided on a text-by-text basis.[9] For example, the genre of the particular text must be taken into account. The epistles of Paul are not written in the same way that the Psalms are written and cannot be interpreted in exactly the same way. History must be interpreted as history, allegory as allegory, poetry as poetry. Most importantly, the context, whether canonical, literary, historical, or cultural, must always be taken into consideration.[10] The fundamental importance of the canonical context, of reading every Scripture in light of all of Scripture, is stated in the Westminster Confession of Faith, 1.9:

> The infallible rule of interpretation of Scripture is the Scripture itself: and therefore, when there is a question about the true and full sense of any Scripture (which is not manifold, but one), it must be searched and known by other places that speak more clearly.

As Joseph Braswell explains, "To ignore the *canonical* context is to read smaller textual units out of context and so misconstrue their God-asserted, canonical truth-claims—their Christological meaning."[11]

Scripture, Community, and Tradition

The proper interpretation of Scripture also requires a correct understanding of the role of tradition and community. This simply means that interpretation cannot be done in isolation from the church as the body of Christ. God has been giving the church gifted teachers and interpreters for two thousand years, and it is sheer folly to ignore their testimony. The typical evangelical understanding of the relationship between tradition and biblical interpretation is far removed from the understanding of the orthodox Reformers and the church fathers.

The magisterial Reformers, such as Luther and Calvin, did not reject tradition outright. They rejected the late medieval understanding of tradition, which saw it as a second source of authoritative doctrine. They wanted to return to an earlier view, which understood tradition to be the traditional interpretation of Scripture. The Roman Catholic Church, at the Council of Trent (1545–63), decided firmly in favor of the later view of tradition and accepted it as a second source of doctrine. It was only the radical Reformers, the Anabaptists, who rejected tradition altogether. They claimed that all any Christian needed to interpret Scripture was a Bible and the Holy Spirit. Ultimately, their rejection of the traditional understanding of Scripture led many of them to reject fundamental doctrines of orthodox Christianity, including the Trinity and the deity of Christ.[12]

In order to understand and interpret Scripture rightly, we must utilize the gifts that God has given the church, both today and throughout history. We ignore the insights of those who have gone before us at our own peril. This means that we interpret Scripture within the boundaries of the universally accepted ecumenical creeds of the church. It means that we seek the insights of others who are more gifted than we are, in order to determine whether or not we are reading something into the text that is not there or missing something that is in the text.

This small volume is written by one who stands unashamedly within the Reformed tradition. This means that the great confessions and creeds of the Reformed churches are the framework and boundaries within which this work stands. It is the conviction of this author that the Westminster Confession of Faith is an accurate and faithful summary of the teaching of Scripture. It is also the conviction of this author that, when dealing with a controversial and disputed doctrine like eschatology, it is wise to move from the known to the unknown, from the clear to the less clear. That is, we should first establish the areas of agreement as a foundation, and then, from that vantage point, examine the options. Foundational for this book, providing the vantage point from which we shall proceed, are the Scriptures as the sole source of doctrine, as interpreted by the ecumenical creeds and the Reformed faith.

Definition of Terms

Finally, since this book is an introduction to and a defense of postmillennialism, it is necessary to define it and the other millennial po-

sitions with which it is contrasted.[13] There are basically four millennial positions defended today:

1. *Historic premillennialism* teaches that at the end of the present age there will be the Great Tribulation, followed by the
   second coming of Christ. At Christ's coming, the Antichrist
   will be judged, the righteous will be resurrected, Satan will
   be bound, and Christ will establish His reign on earth,
   which will last for a thousand years and be a time of unprecedented blessing for the church. At the end of the Millennium, Satan will be released and will instigate a rebellion, which will be quickly crushed. The unrighteous will
   at this point be raised for judgment, after which the eternal
   state will begin.[14]

2. *Dispensational premillennialism* is the most popular eschatological position among evangelicals today. It also offers the
   most complex chronology of the end times. According to
   dispensationalism, the present church age will end with the
   rapture of the church, which, along with the appearance of
   the Antichrist, will indicate the beginning of the seven-year
   Great Tribulation on earth. The Tribulation will end with
   the Battle of Armageddon, in the midst of which Christ will
   return to destroy His enemies. The nations will then be gathered for judgment. Those who supported Israel will enter into
   Christ's millennial kingdom, and the rest will be cast into
   hades to await the Last Judgment. Christ will sit on the
   throne of David and rule the world from Jerusalem. Israel
   will be given the place of honor among the nations again.
   The temple will have been rebuilt and the temple sacrifices
   will be reinstituted as memorial sacrifices. At the end of the
   Millennium, Satan will be released and lead unbelievers in
   rebellion against Christ and the New Jerusalem. The rebellion will be crushed by fire from heaven, and Satan will
   be cast into the lake of fire. The wicked will be brought before the Great White Throne, judged, and cast into the lake
   of fire, and at this point the eternal state will commence.[15]

3. *Amillennialism* sees Revelation 20 as a description of the spiritual reign of Christ with the saints throughout the entire

present age, which is characterized by the parallel growth of good and evil. The present "millennial" age will be followed by the second coming of Christ, the general resurrection, the Last Judgment, and the new heaven and the new earth.[16]

4. *Postmillennialism* is probably the most misunderstood of the four millennial positions. Like amillennialism, postmillennialism teaches that the "thousand years" of Revelation 20 occurs prior to the Second Coming. Some postmillennialists teach that the millennial age is the entire period of time between Christ's first and second advents, while others teach that it is the last one thousand years of the present age. According to postmillennialism, in the present age the Holy Spirit will draw unprecedented multitudes to Christ through the faithful preaching of the gospel. Among the multitudes who will be converted are the ethnic Israelites who have thus far rejected the Messiah. At the end of the present age, Christ will return, there will be a general resurrection of the just and the unjust, and the final judgment will take place.[17]

Conclusion

These are the presuppositions and definitions which form the foundation for the remainder of this work. The thesis of the book is simple: Postmillennialism is the system of eschatology that is most consistent with the relevant texts of Scripture, a covenantal approach to Scripture, and the nondisputed doctrines of Reformation theology. The goal of this book is to prove the validity of this thesis.

CHAPTER TWO

Covenant Theology

Magnify greatly whatever you find exceptionally beautiful in order to begin approaching the beauty of God's covenantal work. God's covenantal work involves stunning patterns and silencing choruses, breathtaking landscapes and warm rhythms, tragedy and triumph, and fearful awe. Nothing can really compare to the beauty of God's gracious covenantal work, which He has laid before us magnificently from Genesis to Revelation.
—Douglas Jones[1]

Within contemporary American evangelicalism, there are two major approaches to analyzing the structure of biblical history: dispensationalism and covenant theology. Most books written today on the subject of eschatology are written from a dispensationalist perspective.[2] For this reason, it is necessary to examine each system and explain why this book is written from a covenantal perspective.

Dispensationalism

Definition

Dispensationalism is a widespread and popular system of theology. Its most essential doctrine is that the church consists *only* of those believers saved between Pentecost and the Rapture. Old Testament believers are *not* included in the body of Christ, the church.[3] But dispensationalism's most distinctive doctrines are its eschatological teachings, such as the imminent, pretribulation rapture of the church.

Method of Structuring Biblical History

Dispensationalism, as its name indicates, divides biblical history into self-contained dispensations. According to the prominent dispensational theologian Charles Ryrie, a dispensation is "a distinguishable economy in the outworking of God's purpose."[4] He adds, "If one were *describing* a dispensation, he would include other things, such as the ideas of distinctive revelation, responsibility, testing, failure, and judgment."[5] While there are disagreements among some dispensationalists, they commonly divide biblical history into these seven dispensations:

1. The Dispensation of Innocency (Gen. 1:3–3:6)
2. The Dispensation of Conscience (Gen. 3:7–8:14)
3. The Dispensation of Civil Government (Gen. 8:15–11:9)
4. The Dispensation of Promise or Patriarchal Rule (Gen. 11:10–Ex. 18:27)
5. The Dispensation of the Mosaic Law (Ex. 19:1–Acts 1:26)
6. The Dispensation of Grace (Acts 2:1–Rev. 19:21)
7. The Dispensation of the Millennium (Rev. 20:1–15)[6]

In each of these dispensations, God gives man a particular responsibility or test, man fails, and God judges man. The failure coming at the end of the present age will result in the coming of Christ in judgment; he will then establish the millennial kingdom.

Critique

The most fundamental error of dispensationalism is not its recognition of different dispensations in biblical history. Nondispensationalist Reformed theologians also recognize time periods in biblical history.[7] The most fundamental error of dispensationalism is its unbiblical doctrine of the church, which produces a faulty understanding of the dispensations.[8]

The dispensational doctrine of the church results in an overly strict compartmentalization of the dispensations. For example, do the requirements and promises given in the so-called dispensation of conscience end with the Flood (cf. Rom. 1:16–2:16)? Do not the promise (Gen. 8:21–22) and the responsibility (Gen. 9:1–17) given to Noah continue throughout history? Does the dispensation of promise end with the Mosaic Law, or was the Law *added* alongside the promise (Gal. 3:19)?

Furthermore, the fact that dispensationalism recognizes the covenants as a method of structuring biblical history causes problems.

Dispensationalists have failed to offer a coherent description of the way in which the dispensations and the covenants work together to structure history. A significant tension arises within the system precisely because of the presence of two alternative and often contradictory methods of structuring biblical history.[9]

Finally, the description of the dispensations as periods during which man fails the tests given to him by God is faulty. As the remainder of this book will attempt to demonstrate, this description does not do justice to the promises of God given to Christ and the church during the present age.[10]

Covenant Theology

Definition

Covenant theology teaches that God has structured redemptive history around the biblical covenants. It maintains that the covenantal work of God develops progressively and is unified by God's promise to redeem a people for Himself. Throughout Scripture, we find numerous examples of covenants between men (cf. Gen. 31:44; Josh. 9:15; 1 Sam. 18:3; 2 Sam. 5:3). In these covenants, the parties are equals. Each party to the covenant makes binding promises and negotiates conditions. In the covenants made between God and man (Adam, Noah, Abraham, Moses, and David), however, there is no negotiation between the parties. These covenants are sovereignly imposed, personal bonds.

The elements of a covenant between God and man have been described well by Douglas Jones. He lists four essential elements:

- a mutually binding relationship between the Lord and His servants,
- sovereign administration,
- conditions (commandments, sanctions),
- promises of union and communion.[11]

A covenant between God and man may be defined as a "God-ordained bond of union, peace, friendship, and service between the Lord and His people."[12]

Method of Structuring Biblical History

Covenant theology, as its name indicates, structures redemptive history around the covenants. Traditionally, covenant theologians have understood that the historical covenants are ultimately based upon an intratrinitarian covenant made before the foundation of the world. In this covenant, commonly called the covenant of redemption, God chose to redeem a people for Himself by sending the Son to accomplish their redemption and sending the Spirit to apply that redemption. There are numerous passages in Scripture which point to such a covenant (Ps. 2:8; Matt. 28:18; Luke 22:29; John 10:17–18; 14:31; 15:10; 17:5–6, 21–24; Rom. 5:19; Gal. 3:13; Eph. 1:4; Phil. 2:8–9; Heb. 1:5; 4:15; 12:2; Rev. 13:8; 17:8). The historical covenants between God and man all flow from this initial covenant of redemption.

The Covenant of Works. Immediately after creating man, God entered into a covenant of union and communion with him. As the Westminster Confession teaches, "The first covenant made with man was a covenant of works, wherein life was promised to Adam; and in him to his posterity, upon condition of perfect and personal obedience" (7.2). Although the word "covenant" is not used at this point in Scripture to describe this bond between Adam and God, it is used later to describe it (Hos. 6:7). More importantly, all of the essential elements of a covenant are present: (1) Adam was bound by the command which forbade him to eat of the tree of the knowledge of good and evil, and God bound Himself to continue in intimate communion with Adam on the condition of obedience and to impose the penalty of death for disobedience (Gen. 2:16–17). (2) The covenant was sovereignly and unilaterally established by God. (3) Conditions for continued communion with God were explicitly stated. (4) The union and communion with God that Adam enjoyed would continue forever if he continued to obey the commands of God.

But Adam succumbed to temptation and rebelled against the conditions of the covenant, thereby falling out of the state of union and communion with God (Gen. 3:6–8). Because the covenant was made with all of humanity through Adam as its representative head, his sin did not affect him alone. "The covenant being made with Adam as a public person, not for himself only, but for his posterity, all mankind descending from him by ordinary generation, sinned in him, and fell with him in that first transgression."[13] This fall brought all of mankind into a state of sin and misery and spiritual death (Rom. 5:12–20; 1 Cor. 15:21–22).

The Covenant of Grace. Adam's sin brought upon him the covenant curses of God, and God would have been perfectly just to condemn all of mankind to eternal punishment, but He did not do this. "Man, by his fall, having made himself incapable of life by that covenant, the Lord was pleased to make a second, commonly called the covenant of grace."[14] Within the very curses which God imposed for violation of the terms of the first covenant, we find the promise which would lay the foundation for the covenant of grace and the remainder of redemptive history: "And I will put enmity between you and the woman, and between your seed and her seed; he shall bruise you on the head, and you shall bruise him on the heel" (Gen. 3:15). As O. Palmer Robertson notes,

> The first declaration of the covenant of redemption contains in seed form every basic principle which manifests itself subsequently. God reveals in a most balanced fashion the various elements constituting his commitment to redeem his fallen creation.[15]

In this promise, God established a "holy war" between the seed of the woman and the seed of the Serpent. This war is manifested throughout the pages of the Old and New Testaments, and it comes to a culmination in the person and work of Christ.

The Noachic Covenant. Throughout the remainder of biblical history, God continued to expand and progressively reveal more elements of His covenantal work. He made a covenant with Noah and all of creation that renewed the Adamic covenant commands and added an explicit command against murder (Gen. 9:1–17). In this covenant, God promised to maintain a stable world and keep mankind from destroying itself in order that the work of redemption might proceed.

The Abrahamic Covenant. From the descendants of Noah's son Shem, God chose Abraham as the one through whom His covenantal work of redemption would continue. In Genesis 12:1–4, God calls Abraham to go to a new land and gives him a promise: "And in you all the families of the earth shall be blessed." This is a significant es-chatological promise, which is often overlooked. As Jones notes, "The Lord did not promise that in Abraham a significant minority would be blessed or that a good number of nations would be blessed, but that all families of the earth would be blessed!"[16]

In Genesis 15, God uses an elaborate ceremony to assure Abraham of the truthfulness of the covenant promise. In the usual form of this ancient ceremony, both parties to a covenant would pass through the divided carcasses of the animals and take a self-maledictory oath. The persons taking this oath were agreeing that if the conditions of the covenant were not kept, the blood of the covenant breaker would be shed just as the blood of the animals had been shed. In Genesis 15, however, God passes through the pieces of the animals *alone*. To ensure that the promises of this covenant will be fulfilled, God places the curse of death upon Himself! In Genesis 15, God also makes it clear to Abraham that he and Sarah will have their own son (vv. 1–4), and that Abraham's descendants will inherit the Promised Land (v. 18).

In Genesis 17, God renews the covenant with Abraham. He repeats the promise of a land and numerous descendants, and adds the promise that Abraham's descendants will include kings (vv. 6, 16). At this point, God also adds the covenant sign of circumcision (vv. 11–14). Finally, God specifically declares that Isaac, not Ishmael, is the chosen one through whom the covenantal work will continue (v. 21).

After Abraham died, the covenant promises were renewed with Isaac (Gen. 26:3–5), Jacob (Gen. 28:13–15), Joseph and his brothers (Gen. 50:24), and Joseph's sons Ephraim and Mannaseh (Gen. 48:15–16). From Abraham to Moses, the covenant promises of God were continually renewed. "The covenants progressively elaborated God's promises of triumph over Satan, preservation for redemption, a land for God's people, and a blessing to all the families of the earth."[17] There is a beautiful continuity and unity of purpose in the redemptive work of God throughout these Scriptures.

The Mosaic Covenant. The Mosaic covenant was not unrelated to the covenants that came before it. In fact, it was intimately con-nected with those earlier covenants. In the first chapters of Exodus, we find that God did indeed make Abraham's descendants fruitful.

Their numbers, however, brought fear upon the Egyptians and led to the Israelites' enslavement, and from this bondage they cried out to God for help. God heard and answered their prayers *on the basis of* the Abrahamic promises (Ex. 2:24; 6:1–8). In a magnificent display of His awesome power, God liberated the Israelites from bondage and brought them to Mt. Sinai. At this point, God did not introduce a totally new work. Rather, he renewed the Abrahamic covenant with the people and provided a much fuller revelation of His covenantal work. The Law did not replace the Abrahamic covenant; it was *added* alongside the promise (Gal. 3:19). God also began to dwell with the people by means of the tabernacle. In the centuries following the giving of the Law, the covenant people continually battled the seed of the Serpent, and ultimately failed to find peace and rest.

The Davidic Covenant. The next major development in God's covenantal work was the Davidic covenant. After the period of the Judges, God, in an act of judgment, gave Saul to Israel to be her king (1 Sam. 8:7ff.). Eventually, however, God raised up David to be the king of Israel and chose to renew the covenant promises with him (2 Sam. 7:8–17; 23:5; Ps. 89:3). God promised David an eternal kingdom of peace and stability, but David died, his son Solomon died, and soon thereafter the kingdom was divided and much of faithless Israel was exiled.

During the Exile, Israel was given hope, precisely because of the covenant promises given to Abraham, Moses, and David. The prophets repeatedly appealed to those earlier promises as the basis for hope (cf. Isa. 41:8; 55:3; Jer. 30:9; 33:26; Ezek. 37:24–25; Mic. 7:20; Hos. 3:5; Amos 9:11). The prophets continued to appeal to the promise of a coming Davidic king (cf. Jer. 23:5; 33:17; Ezek. 34:23). And they revealed that this coming "son of David" would be the kinsman-redeemer of his people (Isa. 52:3; 54:5, 8; 61:1–2; 63:4; Jer. 31:11; Ps. 72:14).

A kinsman-redeemer had to be a blood relative (Lev. 25:48–49; cf. Phil. 2:7; Heb. 2:14–17). And, as Douglas Jones explains, he had four primary duties:

1. To ransom a relative who had sold himself into slavery and oppression (Lev. 25:47–55; cf. Luke 4:18ff.; Matt. 20:28; 1 Tim. 2:5–6).

2. To marry the wife of a widowed kinsman (Ruth 3, 4; cf. Isa. 54:3–8; Eph. 5:25–32; Rev. 19:7).
3. To avenge the name of oppressed and/or murdered relatives (Deut. 19:12; Num. 35:16–21, 31; cf. Luke 18:7–8; 1 Cor. 15:25–26; Col. 2:15; Rev. 6:10; 18:20; 19:2).
4. To regain a poor relative's forfeited inheritance (Lev. 25:23–25, 34; cf. Matt. 5:5; 19:29; Rom. 4:13; Gal. 3:16, 29; Eph. 1:11; Heb. 9:15; 1 Peter 1:4).[18]

According to the prophets, each of these duties would be fulfilled by the coming redeemer, the son of David.

The New Covenant. The New Testament opens with the words, "The book of the genealogy of Jesus Christ, the son of David, the son of Abraham" (Matt. 1:1), clearly indicating that the covenant promises were coming to their long-awaited fulfillment in Jesus.[19] The angel Gabriel announced that Jesus was the one who would fulfill the Davidic covenant (Luke 1:31–33). Both Mary and Zacharias declared that the Abrahamic promises would be fulfilled in the birth of Jesus (Luke 1:54–55, 68–74). And Christ Himself declared His continuity with the Mosaic covenant (Matt. 5:17ff.).

In Christ, all of the covenant promises came together in the prophesied new covenant (Jer. 31:31–33; Ezek. 36:25–27). In each of the earlier covenants, God had revealed more of His covenantal work and promise. In the new covenant, these promises were fulfilled and came to fruition.

Several of the continuities between the old covenant and the new covenant have been noted, but the discontinuities are equally important. One of the most significant differences introduced with the new covenant was the outpouring of the Holy Spirit to empower God's people to obey His law. Their lack of power to fulfill the covenantal obligations was one of the reasons for the failure of Old Testament Israel (Heb. 8:7–13). The prophet Ezekiel indicated that one of the primary blessings of the outpouring of the Spirit in the new covenant would be that it would "cause you to walk in My statutes" (36:27). Another significant difference introduced by the new covenant was its finality. The old covenant was never intended to be final. It was always intended to lead God's people to Christ (Gal. 3:24). Even its sacrifices were not able to deal with sin completely and finally (Heb.

10:1). The new covenant, however, was final because the sacrifice of Christ was complete, once and for all (Heb. 9:12).

Conclusion

The dispensational approach to Scripture has resulted in a multitude of erroneous doctrines. Dispensationalism does not adequately portray the unity of God's redemptive work, opting instead for a compartmentalized structure which obscures many of the intricate threads that are woven together throughout Scripture.

The covenantal approach to Scripture recognizes the discontinuities in Scripture without destroying the underlying unifying themes and promises. It maintains that in the person and covenantal work of Jesus Christ, we find the central, unifying theme of Scripture and the fulfillment of all of God's redemptive promises. It is this approach that will be followed in the remainder of this work.

PART TWO

Historical Considerations

CHAPTER THREE

Patristic and Medieval Eschatology

When the sun has come, darkness prevails no longer; any of it that may be left anywhere is driven away. So also, now that the Divine epiphany of the Word of God has taken place, the darkness of idols prevails no more, and all parts of the world in every direction are enlightened by His teaching.

—Athanasius[1]

It is impossible to study any theological subject adequately in a historical vacuum. In order to gain a proper perspective, we must examine what those who have gone before us have written. For almost two thousand years, God has given the church gifted teachers whose insights into Scripture are invaluable. To neglect what these giants of the Christian faith have said is not only presumptuous, but foolish.

Only recently in the history of the church has the doctrine of eschatology become a topic of intensive study. But the church has not been entirely silent on the subject. From the earliest centuries of the church onward, we find numerous statements concerning the coming of Christ and the end of the present age. While these doctrinal statements were often left undeveloped and their implications were left unexplored due to more pressing controversies, they are worth examining.

Patristic Eschatology

The present chapter is not intended to offer an in-depth analysis of the eschatology of the early and medieval church. It is intended to provide an overview of the eschatological teachings of some of the more important figures in the history of the church.[2] It is intended to help us find out where we have been doctrinally in order to see more clearly where we are today. It must also be noted that in any discussion of the history of eschatology, a difficulty arises due to developing terminology. The eschatological categories that are used in the twentieth century do not always apply neatly to the views of Christians in the first nineteen centuries of the church.[3] We will attempt to point out these difficulties as they arise in the course of the following discussion.

The Apostolic Fathers

The apostolic fathers did not have an elaborate eschatology. They had a rudimentary understanding of end-time events. They believed that Christ would return visibly in glory and that the dead would be resurrected for judgment. Very little consensus was reached on anything other than these most basic eschatological points until the time of Augustine in the fifth century. The following paragraphs offer a summary of the prominent eschatological ideas of these early Christians.

Clement of Rome (c. 30–100). Clement was the bishop of the Roman church toward the end of the first century. His eschatological statements are few, and they are largely undeveloped. However, he does provide us with a glimpse of the thinking of this era. He taught that Christ would literally and visibly return (*1 Clement* 23), and that there would be a future bodily resurrection of the dead (*1 Clement* 24–27). In contrast to the Gnostics, he emphasized that this resurrection would be real and bodily. However, he made no mention of the Millennium and made no effort to elaborate on any of his eschatological doctrines.

The Shepherd of Hermas (late first century). The *Shepherd* is a book of intricate, detailed visions. This work expresses the belief that the last day is very near. J. N. D. Kelly explains that, according to Hermas, "the tower, which in his symbolism signifies the Church, is nearing completion, and when it is finished the end will come."[4] Although the exact timing of Christ's second coming is unknown,

Hermas appears to be certain that it will be preceded by the appearance of the Antichrist. Unfortunately, the visions of Hermas are notoriously difficult to interpret and therefore provide little insight into the eschatology of the apostolic fathers.

Barnabas of Alexandria (late first century). The *Epistle of Barnabas* offers an interesting development in patristic eschatology. Barnabas finds a clue to the timing of Christ's second coming in the book of Genesis. He writes:

> Therefore, my children, in six days, that is, in six thousand years, all things will be finished. 'And He rested on the seventh day.' This meaneth: when His Son, coming [again], shall destroy the time of the wicked man, and judge the ungodly, and change the sun, and the moon, and the stars, then shall He truly rest on the seventh day. (Chap. 15)[5]

Barnabas reasoned that because one day with the Lord is equal to a thousand years, human history must last six thousand years in order to correspond with Genesis 1. At the beginning of the seventh millennium, which is equivalent to the Sabbath day, Christ will return to judge the world. A difficulty of interpretation arises here, however, because Barnabas also emphasizes "the eighth day." As Stanley Grenz points out, the *Epistle of Barnabas* "places its focus on the seven millennia giving rise to the eighth day, and not on millenarianism in the strict sense, as in later premillennialism."[6] This means that Barnabas's writings on the subject are not developed enough to place him clearly in any modern eschatological category.

Papias (c. 60–130). Papias is the only subapostolic father whose millennial position can be identified with any degree of certainty. Fragments of his writings can be found only in the documents of other church fathers, but from these we can determine fairly accurately what he believed. These fragments indicate that Papias held to an early form of premillennialism or chiliasm. He looked forward to the fulfillment of many Old Testament prophecies following the return of Christ. He was, however, prone to extremes in his interpretations. His descriptions of the Millennium so abound with crass, exaggerated literalism that Eusebius later referred to his version of millenarianism as "bizarre" (*Ecclesiastical History*, 3.39.11).

The Second- and Third-Century Apologists

The basic eschatological beliefs of the apostolic fathers were accepted by the next generation without question. They continued to believe that Christ would visibly return in glory and that the dead would be resurrected for judgment. However, as J. N. D. Kelly notes, these doctrines "were held together in a naïve, unreflective fashion, with little or no attempt to work out their implications or solve the problems that they raise."[7] Other eschatological issues, such as the Millennium, apparently continued to be a source of discussion and debate.

Justin Martyr (c. 100–165). One of the clearest statements indicating the lack of consensus on the doctrine of the Millennium in the patristic era may be found in Justin Martyr's *Dialogue with Trypho*. In response to Trypho's question about a future millennial kingdom, Justin writes:

> I admitted to you formerly, that I and many others are of this opinion, and [believe] that such will take place, as you assuredly are aware; but, on the other hand, I signified to you that many who belong to the pure and pious faith, and are true Christians, think otherwise. . . . But I and others, who are right-minded Christians on all points, are assured that there will be a resurrection of the dead, and a thousand years in Jerusalem, which will then be built, adorned, and enlarged, [as] the prophets Ezekiel and Isaiah and others declare. (Chap. 80)

The most striking thing about Justin's remarks is that they reveal a lack of agreement among Christians at this point in history concerning the chronology of the Second Coming. As Jaroslav Pelikan observes, "It would seem that very early in the post-apostolic era millenarianism was regarded as a mark neither of orthodoxy nor of heresy, but as one permissible option among others within the range of permissible options."[8] The time and nature of the Millennium was, at this time, a point of doctrine upon which Christians simply disagreed.

Irenaeus (c. 130–202). The eschatology of Justin received its most developed second-century exposition in the writings of Irenaeus, the bishop of Lyons. According to Irenaeus, the end of the present age will be marked by a three-year reign of the Antichrist, who will desecrate the temple in Jerusalem. His reign will be cut short by the return of Christ, who will cast him into the lake of fire. At this point, Christ will inaugurate the millennial age. When the Millennium is over, there will be a general resurrection, the final judgment, and the inauguration of the eternal state (*Against Heresies*, 5.30.4).

Irenaeus grounds his premillennialism upon two primary arguments, according to Geoffrey Bromiley: "First, it is right and fitting that the place of toil and suffering should also be the place of rule. Second, it is right and fitting that God should restore the created order 'to its pristine state,' in which it can 'serve the just without restraint.' "[9]

One aspect of Irenaeus's eschatology that has received little attention is his "contention that the belief in an immediate removal of the soul to the presence of God and Christ at death was a stumbling block to orthodox acceptance of chiliasm, and . . . his counter proposal that the chiliastic hope was properly accompanied and corroborated by belief in a subterranean detainment for the soul until the time of resurrection."[10] His argument was based upon his understanding of the purpose of the Millennium. Charles Hill explains:

> In the Christian chiliasm of Irenaeus this doctrine of an intermediate state under the earth kept man from overstepping the purpose of the millennium—it was the task of the millennium to supply the necessary further training for the entrance into God's spatial presence. To allow that the saints could already be enjoying the celestial life would be to eliminate the need for a future, earthly millennium.[11]

Hill adds that in the first three centuries of the church, virtually every identifiable chiliast shared Irenaeus's view of the intermediate state, in which believers do not go immediately into the presence of God at death. And those who taught that believers went immediately into the presence of God were almost all opponents of chiliasm.[12]

Tertullian (c. 160–220). Tertullian shared the premillennial position of Irenaeus and his understanding of the intermediate state. In perhaps his most well-known treatise, *Against Marcion*, he expresses his chiliasm clearly: "But we do confess that a kingdom is promised to us upon the earth, although before heaven, only in another state of existence; inasmuch as it will be after the resurrection for a thousand years in the divinely-built city of Jerusalem" (chap. 23). Although Tertullian's premillennialism seems clear, there is some ambiguity in his writings. He "also shows signs of a tendency to spiritualize the doctrine, for elsewhere he speaks of the New Jerusalem as really signifying the Lord's flesh."[13] However, the ambiguity does not seem to be widespread enough to call into question his clearer eschatological statements.

Origen (c. 185–254). Although there was a strong apocalyptic and premillennial strain in the second- and third-century church, a belief in the victorious progress of the gospel was not absent. In *Against Celsus*, for example, Origen tells us that

> it is evident that even the barbarians, when they yield obedience to the word of God, will become most obedient to the law, and most humane; and every form of worship will be destroyed except the religion of Christ, which will alone prevail. And indeed it will one day triumph, as its principles take possession of the minds of men more and more every day. (8.68)

Origen was certainly not a postmillennialist in the modern sense of the term. Nonetheless, one of the key tenets of later postmillennialism, a belief in the triumph of the gospel, was clearly present in the early patristic era.

The Nicene and Post-Nicene Fathers

Athanasius (c. 296–373). A note of optimism in patristic eschatology is nowhere more clearly sounded than in the work of the great defender of Trinitarian orthodoxy, Athanasius. His small book

On the Incarnation resounds with faith in the victory of Christ's gospel. He proclaims:

> Since the Saviour's advent in our midst, not only does idolatry no longer increase, but it is getting less and gradually ceasing to be. Similarly, not only does the wisdom of the Greeks no longer make any progress, but that which used to be is disappearing. And daemons, so far from continuing to impose on people by their deceits and oracle-givings and sorceries, are routed by the sign of the cross if they so much as try. On the other hand, while idolatry and everything else that opposes the faith of Christ is daily dwindling and weakening and falling, see, the Saviour's teaching is increasing everywhere! Worship, then, the Saviour "Who is above all" and mighty, even God the Word, and condemn those who are being defeated and made to disappear by Him. When the sun has come, darkness prevails no longer; any of it that may be left anywhere is driven away. So also, now that the Divine epiphany of the Word of God has taken place, the darkness of idols prevails no more, and all parts of the world in every direction are enlightened by His teaching. (Sec. 55)

In Athanasius we find some of the earliest developing expressions of the key doctrines that would later be developed into postmillennialism.

Augustine (354–430). Augustine, who served as bishop of Hippo from 395 to 430, was by far the greatest Christian theologian of the first thousand years of church history. His understanding of world history, and thus of eschatology, was most clearly articulated in *The City of God*, a book written as a reply to those who blamed the fall of the Roman Empire on the Christian religion. One of the central themes of *The City of God*, as Alister McGrath notes, is "the relation between two cities— the 'city of God' and the 'secular city' or the 'city of the world.' "[14] He continues:

> Believers live "in the intermediate period," separating the incarnation of Christ from his final return in glory. The church

is to be seen as in exile in the "city of the world." It is in the world, yet not of the world. There is a strong eschatological tension between the present reality, in which the church is exiled in the world, and somehow obliged to maintain its distinctive ethos in the midst of a disbelieving world, and the future hope, in which the church will be delivered from the world, and finally allowed to share in the glory of God.[15]

Early in his Christian life, Augustine had been attracted to millennialism, but he later rejected it. His rejection of it, it seems, was largely due to some of the excessively carnal versions of millennialism that were current in his day. He changed his position and adopted instead a symbolic approach to the twentieth chapter of Revelation. In *The City of God*, Augustine teaches that the first resurrection mentioned in Revelation 20 is a spiritual resurrection, the regeneration of spiritually dead persons (20:6). In contrast to premillennialism, he teaches that the second resurrection occurs at the second coming of Christ, not a thousand years later.

Augustine offers two options for the interpretation of the "thousand years" (20:7). He suggests that it could refer to the sixth millennium of human history, which would be followed by the eternal Sabbath. Or it could be figurative language representing the entire present age between the advents of Christ. Augustine's rejection of premillennialism and his figurative interpretation of Revelation were profoundly influential and established the exegetical framework for both amillennialism and postmillennialism.[16] As Jaroslav Pelikan observes, Augustine's interpretation "set the standard for most Catholic exegesis in the West" for the next thousand years.[17]

The Early Church and Revelation 20

One often hears the claim that the church of the first centuries was almost unanimously chiliastic or premillennial.[18] However, from the first century onward, there was a nonchiliastic exegesis of Revelation 20:1–8 extant. Charles Hill notes the presence of "the theme, especially popular in Christian preaching, of Satan's binding during the present era (cf. *2 Clem.* 20.4; Melito, *PP* 102; Claudius Apolinarius [Eusebius, *ChronPasc.* Praef.]; Irenaeus, *AH* III.18.6; III.23.1, 7; V.21.3; Hippolytus, *CD* IV.33.4–5; *GospNicod.* 22)."[19]

There were also different interpretations of certain aspects of Revelation 20:4–6. Hippolytus (c. 170–c. 236) taught that the first resurrection was the death of the believer and his rising into heaven.[20] Nonchiliasts also differed with the chiliasts on the state of the "souls" in Revelation 20:4. Hill explains:

> The *psuchai* of 20:4 were to the non-chiliasts "disembodied" souls, pre-eminently those of the martyrs, already in heaven. There they shared in the kingdom of Christ, participating in his ruling and judging and serving the heavenly altar as priests in the heavenly sacerdocy (Clement, *Strom.* VI. xiii.106.2; Hippolytus, *CD* II.37.4; Origen, *ExhMart.* 30 [cf. 28, 37]; Dionysius [Eusebius *HE* VI.42.5]; Cyprian, *Fortunatum* 12; the Roman confessors, Cyprian's *Ep.* XXXI.3).[21]

Chiliasm was clearly present in the first centuries of the church, but the evidence will not support the contention that it was a universally held position.[22]

The Creeds of the Early Church

The Old Roman Creed (late second century). This creed was the most important predecessor of the Apostles' Creed. Its eschatological assertions are very simple. It reads:

> I believe in God the Father Almighty. And in Jesus Christ his only Son our Lord, who was born of the Holy Spirit and the Virgin Mary; crucified under Pontius Pilate and buried; the third day he rose from the dead; he ascended into heaven, and sits at the right hand of the Father, *from thence He shall come to judge the quick and the dead.* And in the Holy Spirit; the holy Church; the forgiveness of sins; *the resurrection of the flesh.*

Like the other patristic documents, this early creed does not go into great detail, but it does assert the two fundamental doctrines that are the hallmark of early eschatological orthodoxy: a literal second coming of Christ and the bodily resurrection of mankind for judgment.

The Apostles' Creed. The Apostles' Creed is the most widely used creed in Christendom because of its concise summary of orthodox Christianity. It states:

> I believe in God the Father almighty, maker of heaven and earth; and in Jesus Christ, His only Son, our Lord, who was conceived by the Holy Spirit, born of the Virgin Mary, suffered under Pontius Pilate, was crucified, dead and buried. He descended into hell, the third day he arose again from the dead, he ascended into heaven, and sits at the right hand of God the Father almighty, from thence he shall come to judge the quick and the dead; I believe in the Holy Spirit, the holy catholic Church, the communion of saints, the forgiveness of sins, the resurrection of the body, and the life everlasting. Amen.

Like the Old Roman Creed, from which it developed, the Apostles' Creed affirms the central tenets of eschatological orthodoxy. And although there are no clear and explicit pronouncements on the time or nature of the Millennium, it does implicitly reject chiliasm or premillennialism. According to the creed, the purpose of Christ's second coming is "to judge the living and the dead," not to establish a thousand-year millennial kingdom.

The Nicene Creed (325). The Nicene Creed also asserts the fundamental doctrines of orthodox Christianity.[23] And it too limits its eschatological pronouncements to the second coming of Christ and the resurrection of the dead for judgment. It also includes the same implicit rejection of premillennialism that is found in the Old Roman Creed and the Apostles' Creed. According to the Nicene Creed, the Lord Jesus Christ "will come again with glory *to judge* the living and the dead."

The Athanasian Creed (c. 500). The Athanasian Creed was not written by Athanasius, but it is one of the three ecumenical creeds used throughout the Western church and is therefore extremely important. The Athanasian Creed concludes with a brief eschatological statement, which teaches that Jesus Christ will come to judge the living and the dead. At his coming all people will arise bodily and give an accounting of their own deeds. Those who have done good will enter eternal life, and those who have done evil will enter eternal fire.

Unlike the other creeds, the Athanasian Creed includes a statement that seems to be something more than an implicit rejection of premillennialism. The statement "At his coming *all* people will arise bodily and give an accounting of their own deeds" connects the second coming of Christ temporally with the last judgment of *all* men.

Summary

From the preceding survey, we have been able to discern several important points about patristic eschatology. First, orthodox Christianity was characterized by two eschatological doctrines: the future return of Christ to judge mankind and the future bodily resurrection of all men for judgment. Second, apart from these two doctrines, there was nothing approaching consensus for the first four centuries. Contrary to the claims of some, both chiliasm and nonchiliasm existed side by side from the beginning. Apocalyptic thought existed side by side with faith in the progressive victory of the gospel. Third, patristic eschatology reached its apex of development in the writings of Augustine, whose views would define orthodoxy throughout the Middle Ages.

Medieval Eschatology

The Middle Ages (c. 1000–1500) were not a time of dramatic eschatological development. A modified Augustinian eschatology, which closely linked the institutional Roman Catholic Church with the kingdom of God, was the predominant position.[24] As Stanley Grenz observes, medieval theologians

no longer interpreted history by means of the image of a cosmic drama—as a drama complete with plot and climax—that lay behind millennialism. In its stead, most had substituted the image of the pilgrim people of God seeking a destination beyond history. Consequently, in the dominant medieval out-look the historical epoch since Christ's advent had no cosmic significance. It was simply the space between the two grand events of history, the Incarnation and the last judgment.[25]

This assessment of medieval theology is echoed by McGrath, who observes that medieval Christianity, which was almost entirely monastic in nature, rejected interaction with society and culture and saw Christians only as "pilgrims on this earth, in the process of trav-eling to heaven."[26] This strongly held belief did not encourage the rethinking of many aspects of Augustine's eschatology. Most me-dieval theologians simply reaffirmed his doctrine or a modified ver-sion of it. A small number did, however, attempt to develop escha-tology in a different direction.

Two Medieval Thinkers

Joachim of Fiore (c. 1132–1202). Joachim was one of the small number of medieval Christians who rejected the commonly held Au-gustinian position.[27] His was a speculative philosophy of history based upon a Trinitarian model. He divided history into three ages:

1. The age of the Father, which corresponds to the Old Tes-tament dispensation.
2. The age of the Son, which corresponds to the New Testa-ment dispensation, including the church.
3. The age of the Spirit, which would witness the rise of new religious movements, leading to the reform and renewal of the church, and the final establishment of peace and unity on earth.[28]

There is some debate as to whether Joachim himself understood these three ages to be strictly sequential. It is difficult, therefore, to state precisely where he stands in the development of millennial thought.[29] Some classify his doctrine as an anticipation of postmil-lennialism; others are not so sure. However, his "age of the Spirit" does seem to sound the optimistic note that would later characterize de-veloped postmillennialism.

Thomas Aquinas (c. 1225–74). Aquinas represented the majority position. His eschatology is found in its most systematized form in the *Supplement* to the *Summa Theologica*, which specifically addresses the doctrine of the resurrection and the end of the world. Although he discusses many issues, the points of Aquinas's eschatology that are most relevant to our discussion are the following:

1. There will certainly be a future bodily resurrection of all men (*Supplement*, Q. 75).
2. There will be a general judgment, at which time Christ will judge all mankind (Q. 88).
3. There will be a future visible coming of Christ in glory (Q. 90).
4. There will not be a future earthly millennial kingdom (Q. 91).

Aquinas, like most medieval theologians, saw no need for any form of millenarianism. Therefore, he can be said to have anticipated modern amillennialism. He discussed many other issues, some of which were unbiblical medieval inventions,[30] but he clearly affirmed the doctrines of orthodox eschatology.

Conclusion

The medieval period did not witness any significant development of Augustinian eschatology. There was doctrinal speculation, but the key tenets of orthodox eschatology remained virtually unchallenged and largely undeveloped. With the beginning of the Protestant Reformation in the sixteenth century, however, the implications of orthodox eschatology would begin to receive renewed attention.

CHAPTER FOUR

Reformation and Modern Eschatology

But our doctrine must tower unvanquished above all the glory and above all the might of the world, for it is not of us, but of the living God and his Christ whom the Father has appointed King to "rule from sea to sea, and from the rivers even to the ends of the earth" [Ps. 72:8; 72:7, Vg.]. And he is so to rule as to smite the whole earth with its iron and brazen strength, with its gold and silver brilliance, shattering it with the rod of his mouth as an earthen vessel, just as the prophets have prophesied concerning the magnificence of his reign.
—John Calvin[1]

On October 31, 1517, Martin Luther nailed his Ninety-five Theses to the church door at Wittenberg. This seemingly insignificant action ignited the flame of the Protestant Reformation. Within only a few decades, the teachings of the Reformers spread across the continent of Europe. With this came a new openness to reexamine some long-neglected doctrines. One of the doctrines that received renewed attention was eschatology. We turn our focus now to the eschatology of the sixteenth through the twentieth centuries. As in the previous chapter, we will provide only a brief summary of the more significant developments.

Eschatology of the Reformation

The eschatological position of the leading Reformers remained generally Augustinian. However, because of the conflict with Rome, several new emphases emerged in their writings. These developments generally focused on the identity of the Antichrist and the method of interpreting the book of Revelation.

The Leading Reformers

Martin Luther (1483–1546). Luther reaffirmed the fundamental tenets of orthodox eschatology. He believed in a visible return of Christ and a bodily resurrection of mankind for judgment.[2] In this respect, his views were simply a continuation of medieval orthodoxy. There are, however, some aspects of his eschatology that mark a clear break with medieval thought. Since the fourth century, the church's eschatology had become more and more focused upon the fate of the individual after death. But, as Paul Althaus notes, Luther's eschatology "once again revives the eager expectation of the coming of Jesus common to the early Christian church."[3] In fact, Luther expected the end to come in the very near future, perhaps in his own day.[4]

Despite his apocalyptic tendencies, Luther agreed with the common Catholic rejection of chiliasm. There were, however, several important developments in Luther's thought which differentiated it from official Catholic doctrine.[5] The most significant of these were:

1. He identified the institution of the papacy as the Antichrist.[6]
2. He interpreted the book of Revelation as a prophecy of the entire history of the church.[7]
3. He believed that the Millennium was fulfilled in the early history of the church and ended either with the rise of the Turks or with the institution of the papacy.[8]

Many of the Reformers followed Luther's lead in identifying the Antichrist as the papacy and accepting a historicist interpretation of the book of Revelation, but there was little agreement on the nature of the Millennium. Their only agreement was to reject premillennialism.[9]

John Calvin (1509–64). John Calvin is considered by many to have been the greatest theologian of the Reformation. Like Luther, Calvin adopted the general tenets of traditional Augustinian eschatology. He also agreed with Luther on the identity of the Antichrist (cf. *Institutes*, 4.2.12). He wrote: "Of old, Rome was indeed the mother of all churches; but after it began to become the see of Antichrist, it ceased to be what it once was" (4.7.24). Unfortunately, Calvin's other eschatological views are not as easily discerned.[10] Like Augustine, he rejected premillennialism, calling it "too childish either to need or to be worth a refutation" (3.25.5). But it would be anachronistic to label Calvin as either amillennial or postmillennial in the modern sense of those terms, since he endorsed central tenets of each position. It is commonly recognized that Calvin focused primarily on the otherworldly aspect of the kingdom of God, which means that his eschatology as a whole is much closer to modern amillennialism than to postmillennialism.[11] Yet a fact that is often overlooked is that he also endorsed one of the central tenets of later postmillennialism, namely, a confidence and hope that a large majority of humanity would be converted to Christ before the Second Coming. And, like biblical postmillennialism, his hope and prayer for a future massive conversion of mankind to the truth did not imply or entail universalism. In his discussion of the second petition of the Lord's Prayer, he writes,

> Now, because the word of God is like a royal scepter, we are bidden here to entreat him to bring all men's minds and hearts into voluntary obedience to it. . . . Therefore God sets up his Kingdom by humbling the whole world, but in different ways. For he tames the wantonness of some, breaks the untamable pride of others. We must daily desire that God gather churches unto himself from all parts of the earth; that he spread and increase them in number; that he adorn them with gifts; that he establish a lawful order among them; on the other hand, that he cast down all enemies of pure teaching and religion; that he scatter their counsels and crush their efforts. From this it appears that zeal for daily progress is not enjoined upon us in vain, for it never goes so well with human affairs that the filthiness of vices is shaken and washed away, and full integrity flowers and grows. But its fulness is delayed to the final coming of Christ when, as Paul teaches, "God will be all in all" [1 Cor. 15:28].
>
> . . . For this is the condition of God's Kingdom: that

while we submit to his righteousness, he makes us sharers in his glory. This comes to pass when, with ever-increasing splendor, he displays his light and truth, by which the darkness and falsehoods of Satan's kingdom vanish, are extinguished, and pass away.[12]

Calvin encourages us to have a zeal for daily progress, but he cautions us that the final and full realization of the kingdom of Christ awaits the Second Coming. These are both key points of postmillennialism. Again, this does not imply that Calvin himself was a postmillennialist in the modern sense; it simply demonstrates that one of the key convictions of postmillennialism was present in the teaching of this great Reformer.[13]

Martin Bucer (1491–1551). Martin Bucer worked closely with Calvin in Strasbourg. In Bucer's work, we find another teaching that would later become a central tenet of postmillennialism—a belief in the future conversion of the Jews to Christ. Bucer believed that Paul, in Romans 11:25–26, guaranteed the future conversion of ethnic Israel.[14] This belief would find widespread acceptance in the Reformed church of the next three centuries.[15]

The Radical Reformation

Thomas Münzer (c. 1490–1525). Münzer, a radical millenarian, revolutionary, and mystic, who claimed that present revelation was more important than the Scriptures, believed that he was inspired by the Holy Spirit to bring in a new age. He taught that Christian believers should join together in a theocratic community and inaugurate the kingdom of God by forcefully and violently exterminating the wicked.[16] He became involved in the Peasants' War in 1525 and incited the people with reports of visions and with apocalyptic sermons. His violent delusions ended, however, when he was captured and beheaded by the German princes.

Münzer's views were adamantly rejected by both Luther and Calvin. The Münster Rebellion of 1534, in which radical Anabaptists led by Jan Matthys took over the city and declared it to be the New Zion, was considered by the leading Reformers to be the logical outworking of such extremely millenarian theology.[17] It discredited millenarianism in the eyes of both Protestants and Catholics for years to come.

Puritan Eschatology

We now turn our attention to the eschatological developments of sixteenth- and seventeen-century England. There is a line of continuity that runs from the first generation of Reformers to the Puritans, yet there is also significant development. Like the continental Reformers, the Puritans continued to employ a historicist interpretation of the book of Revelation. They too saw it as a prophecy of the history of the church. However, the English Puritans thoroughly examined the implications of the optimistic prophecies that had been noted for centuries, but had never been systematized. Indeed, because of this exploration, a large number of Puritans embraced an optimistic eschatology.[18]

Thomas Brightman (1562–1607). Brightman was one of the first Puritan divines to develop some of the optimistic strands of Reformation thought into a concept of what he termed "the latter-day glory."[19] He was also one of the first to write a significant commentary on the book of Revelation. Brightman taught that the Jews would be converted to Christ and that this conversion would usher in a period of even greater blessing to the world. Following this "latter-day glory," Christ would return to judge mankind.[20] Brightman was thoroughly convinced of an optimistic eschatology. His ideas would be taken up and developed further by other Puritan thinkers.

Thomas Goodwin (1600–1679). One of the many Puritans who affirmed Brightman's optimistic eschatology was Thomas Goodwin, the leader of the Congregationalists at the Westminster Assembly. He observes:

> If there be many prophecies and promises in Scripture that are not yet fulfilled, and the fulfilling whereof will bring the church into a more glorious condition than ever it was yet in the world, then there is a glorious time a-coming. Now there are such scriptures, wherein are such glorious things

promised to be fulfilled to the church as yet never were ful-filled.[21]

The faith of Goodwin, like that of Brightman, was not in the in-herent power of man to "bring in the kingdom"; rather, his faith was in the promises of God. If God had in fact promised future gospel suc-cess, then those promises would surely be fulfilled.

John Owen (1616–83). Considered by many to be the greatest English theologian of the seventeenth century, Owen anticipated a time of unprecedented success for the gospel of Christ. In one of his many treatises, he wrote:

> Though our *persons* fail, our *cause* shall be as truly, certainly, and infallibly victorious, as that Christ sits at the right hand of God. The gospel shall be victorious. This greatly comforts and refreshes me.[22]

Owen taught that there were at least six things promised by God for this present age:

1. Fullness of peace for the gospel and the professors of it (Isa. 11:6, 7; 33:20, 24; 54:13; Rev. 21:25).
2. Purity and beauty of ordinances and gospel worship (Rev. 11:2; 21:3).
3. Multitudes of converts, many persons, and indeed nations (Isa. 49:18, 22; 60:7, 8; 66:8; Rev. 7:9).
4. The full casting out and rejecting of all will worship, and their attendant abominations (Rev. 11:2).
5. Professed subjection of the nations throughout the whole world to the Lord Christ (Isa. 60:6–9; Dan. 2:44; 7:26–27).
6. A most glorious and dreadful breaking of all that rise in op-position unto him (Isa. 60:12).[23]

This note of eschatological optimism was repeated in the works of many Puritan and Scottish divines, including such men as Richard Sibbes, Thomas Brooks, James Renwick, John Howe, Thomas Manton, David Dickson, William Gouge, William Perkins, and Samuel Rutherford.

Westminster Confession of Faith and Catechisms (1647). The Westminster Confession of Faith and Catechisms, while not explicitly endorsing a particular millennial view, do include an aspect of hope that is not often recognized. Question 191 of the Larger Catechism asks regarding the Lord's Prayer, "What do we pray for in the second petition?" The Puritan divines answered:

> In the second petition, (which is, *Thy kingdom come,*) acknowledging ourselves and all mankind to be by nature under the dominion of sin and Satan, we pray, *that the kingdom of sin and Satan may be destroyed, the gospel propagated throughout the world, the Jews called, the fulness of the Gentiles brought in;* the church furnished with all gospel-officers and ordinances, purged from corruption, countenanced and maintained by the civil magistrate: that the ordinances of Christ may be purely dispensed, and made effectual to the converting of those that are yet in their sins, and the confirming, comforting, and building up of those that are already converted: that Christ would rule in our hearts here, and hasten the time of his second coming, and our reigning with him for ever: and that he would be pleased so to exercise the kingdom of his power in all the world, as may best conduce to these ends [emphasis added].

The Westminster divines apparently believed that it was God's will and plan to destroy the kingdom of Satan, propagate the gospel throughout the entire world, call the Jews, bring in the fullness of the Gentiles, and exercise His power to bring these things to pass. If they did not believe that this was the will of God, they would not have urged all believers to pray for it.

The Savoy Declaration (1658). The Savoy Declaration was the confession of the independent churches, and in it we find a much more explicit declaration of an optimistic eschatology. In chapter 26, the confession reads:

As the Lord is in care and love towards his Church, and hath in his infinite wise providence exercised it with great variety in all ages, for the good of them that love him, and his own glory; so, according to his promise, we expect that in the latter days, Antichrist being destroyed, the Jews called, and the adversaries of the kingdom of his dear Son broken, the churches of Christ being enlarged and edified through a free and plentiful communication of light and grace, shall enjoy in this world a more quiet, peaceable, and glorious condition than they have enjoyed.

Summary

Our brief survey of Reformation and Puritan eschatology has revealed several important facts. First, the Reformation did not alter the key doctrines of eschatological orthodoxy. The Reformers reaffirmed the visible future coming of Christ and our future bodily resurrection as essential truths of the Christian faith. Second, they introduced a primarily historicist understanding of the book of Revelation. They believed that Revelation was a detailed prophecy of the history of the church and that the papacy was the prophesied Antichrist. Third, and most important for our study, they began to explore the implications of the optimistic strands of eschatological thought that had been expressed in earlier ages, but had never been fully developed. Thus, by the beginning of the eighteenth century, Reformed eschatology had become generally postmillennial in its essential orientation.[24]

Modern Eschatology

The eighteenth century opened with the Enlightenment (c. 1720–80), and witnessed the rise of an antisupernatural rationalism that criticized Christianity as superstitious nonsense. This unbiblical philosophy has influenced every aspect of Christian theology, including eschatology, to the present day. It is beyond the scope of this survey to analyze the eschatological theories of rationalistic theologians.[25] Instead, we will focus primarily on the more important contributions of theologians within the Reformed tradition.

Eighteenth- and Nineteenth-Century Eschatology

Daniel Whitby (1638–1725). One will often, especially in the writings of dispensationalists, see Daniel Whitby erroneously referred to as the originator of postmillennialism.[26] This seems to be an attempt to discredit postmillennialism by association, since Whitby was a Unitarian. While he did indeed hold to a version of postmillennialism, he was not the originator of the essential elements of the doctrine.[27] As the preceding chapters have demonstrated, these elements were present well before the eighteenth century. What is distinctive about Whitby is that he was one of the first to clearly and systematically present what may be termed a *futuristic* postmillennialism.[28] According to his interpretation of Revelation 20, the Millennium is a literal one-thousand-year (or very long) golden age which precedes the second coming of Christ and, more importantly, which commences at some point in the future. The Millennium, in this view, is entirely future, as opposed to an Augustinian postmillennialism which understands the Millennium to be concurrent with the entire present age.

Jonathan Edwards (1703–58). Quite possibly the greatest theologian and philosopher in American history, Jonathan Edwards set forth his postmillennial eschatology most completely in *A History of the Work of Redemption*. He shared the Puritans' faith in the advancement of the gospel in history:

> The future promised advancement of the kingdom of Christ is an event unspeakably happy and glorious. The Scriptures speak of that time, as a time wherein God and his Son Jesus Christ will be most eminently glorified on earth.[29]

Sentiments such as this have earned Edwards the title "the father of American postmillennialism."[30]

Like Whitby, Edwards apparently understood the Millennium to be a distinctive future period of time within the present church age. He argued that although "the kingdom of heaven was in a degree set up soon after Christ's resurrection . . . this [future prosperous state of the church] is the principal time of the kingdom of heaven upon earth."[31] This future millennial age will commence with the fall of the Antichrist and the destruction of Satan's visible kingdom on earth, and it will end with a final great apostasy and the second coming of Christ.[32]

Charles Hodge (1797–1878). Charles Hodge was arguably the most influential Presbyterian theologian of the nineteenth century. His three-volume *Systematic Theology* (1872–73) was a widely used textbook for decades. Hodge explains his optimistic eschatology succinctly in the following passage:

> As therefore the Scriptures teach that the kingdom of Christ is to extend over all the earth; that all nations are to serve Him; and that all people shall call Him blessed; it is to be inferred that these predictions refer to a state of things which is to exist before the second coming of Christ. This state is described as one of spiritual prosperity; God will pour out His Spirit upon all flesh; knowledge shall everywhere abound; wars shall cease to the ends of the earth, and there shall be nothing to hurt or destroy in all my holy mountain, saith the Lord. This does not imply that there is to be neither sin nor sorrow in the world during this long period, or that all men are to be true Christians. The tares are to grow together with the wheat until the harvest. The means of grace will still be needed; conversion and sanctification will be then what they ever have been. It is only a higher measure of the good which the church has experienced in the past that we are taught to anticipate in the future. This however is not the end. After this and after the great apostasy which is to follow, comes the consummation.[33]

As we can see, Hodge expressed faith in the promises of gospel success, but he did not equate this with any kind of utopian universalism.[34] It is also interesting to note that Hodge, although sharing the eschatological optimism of Edwards, appears to have adopted a different understanding of the time of the Millennium. Unlike Edwards, Hodge does not seem to allow for a distinctly future millennial era within the present age. He argues that it "is evident that the

Apostles considered the dispensation of the Spirit under which we are now living, as the only one which was to intervene between the first advent of Christ and the end of the world."[35]

A. A. Hodge (1823–86). A. A. Hodge agreed with his father's postmillennial eschatology. In his *Outlines of Theology*, he argues:

> The Scriptures, both of the Old and New Testament, clearly reveal that the gospel is to exercise an influence over all branches of the human family, immeasurably more extensive and more thoroughly transforming than any it has ever realized in time past. This end is to be gradually attained through the spiritual presence of Christ in the ordinary dispensation of Providence, and ministrations of his church.[36]

It is important to note that Hodge, like every other orthodox postmillennialist, did not believe that the success of the gospel would be brought about by human effort or the "evolutionary progress of man." He taught that it would occur only because of the supernatural work of the Holy Spirit.

James Henley Thornwell (1812–62). James Henley Thornwell was one of the most erudite Southern Presbyterians of the nineteenth century. He was also staunchly postmillennial. In a famous passage, he encourages Christians to have faith in God's promise:

> If the Church could be aroused to a deeper sense of the glory that awaits her, she would enter with a warmer spirit into the struggles that are before her. Hope would inspire ardour. She would even now rise from the dust, and like the eagle plume her pinions for loftier flights than she has yet taken. What she wants, and what every individual Christian wants, is faith—faith in her sublime vocation, in her Divine resources, in the presence and efficacy of the Spirit that dwells in her— faith in the truth, faith in Jesus, and faith in God. With such a faith there would be no need to speculate about the future. That would speedily reveal itself. It is our unfaithfulness, our negligence and unbelief, our low and carnal aims, that retard

the chariot of the Redeemer. The Bridegroom cannot come until the bride has made herself ready. Let the Church be in earnest after greater holiness in her own members, and in faith and love undertake the conquest of the world, and she will soon settle the question whether her resources are competent to change the face of the earth.[37]

Unfortunately, the church was not aroused to a deeper sense of the glory of God and faith in His promise. Instead, she would soon slip into despair and pessimism.

The Decline of Postmillennialism

In the late nineteenth century, several developments led to the decline of postmillennialism. First, the growth of liberal theology undermined the supernaturalistic assumptions that provided a foundation for orthodox postmillennialism. Second, the rise of evolutionary doctrine and its belief in the gradual improvement of man by natural means led many orthodox Christians wrongly to identify all concepts of progress with the atheistic doctrine of evolution. Third, many American Christians began wrongly to equate the cause of Christ with the advancement of the United States. The focus shifted from the preaching of the gospel to social reform and the social gospel. As Stanley Grenz notes, "The American Spirit became saturated with a secularized postmillennialism."[38] Fourth, the dramatic rise in the popularity of dispensationalism resulted in a debilitating pessimism about the future of the church. In the following decades, this would all but eliminate postmillennialism from serious consideration.[39]

Twentieth-Century Eschatology

Postmillennialism did not completely disappear at the turn of the century. But the number of its adherents was rapidly dwindling. With the publication of the *Scofield Reference Bible* in 1909, dispensationalism rose rapidly to become the dominant eschatological position in the United States. In Reformed circles, amillennialism began to be self-consciously differentiated from postmillennialism, and postmillennialism began a steady decline. In the last decades of the twentieth century, however, postmillennialism began to make a comeback.

Benjamin B. Warfield (1851–1921). B. B. Warfield was one of the last defenders of Reformed orthodoxy to teach systematic theology at Princeton Seminary. He was also one of the last staunch defenders of biblical postmillennialism. In one of his many articles defending this doctrine, he declares, "As emphatically as Paul, John teaches that the earthly history of the Church is not a history merely of conflict with evil, but of conquest over evil: and even more richly than Paul, John teaches that this conquest will be decisive and complete."[40] Elsewhere he writes:

> The assumption that the dispensation in which we live is an indecisive one, and that the Lord waits to conquer the world to himself until after he returns to earth, employing then new and more effective methods than he has set at work in our own time, is scarcely in harmony with the New Testament point of view. According to the New Testament, this time in which we live is precisely the time in which our Lord is conquering the world to himself; and it is the completion of this conquest which, as it marks the completion of his redemptive work, so sets the time for his return to earth to consummate his Kingdom and establish it in its eternal form.[41]

Herman Bavinck (1854–1921). Herman Bavinck was one of the leading Dutch theologians at the turn of the century, and his four-volume *Gereformeerde Dogmatiek* (Reformed Dogmatics), published between 1895 and 1901, has influenced Reformed theologians both in Europe and in North America. Bavinck defends a thoroughly amillennial eschatology. He argues, "Nowhere does the New Testament open up to the church of Christ the prospect that they will once more in this dispensation enjoy power and lordship."[42] Bavinck was probably one of those theologians who was most responsible for the rise of Reformed amillennialism in the twentieth century.

Geerhardus Vos (1862–1949). Geerhardus Vos taught biblical theology at Princeton Seminary from 1893 until 1932, and his work has influenced many Reformed expositors. He sets forth his amillennial eschatology in *The Pauline Eschatology*.[43] Vos was one of the first to systematically develop and apply the concept of "the already and the not yet" in explaining the present age.[44] According to this perspective, the age to come has "already" been inaugurated, but is "not yet" fully consummated. The consummation awaits the second coming of Christ. The believer, therefore, can be said to live simultaneously in this age and in the age to come. Vos's important work has influenced postmillennialists and premillennialists as well as amillennialists.

Oswald T. Allis (1878–1973). O. T. Allis was a professor of Old Testament at Princeton Seminary for nineteen years and at Westminster Seminary for seven years. He is perhaps best known for his classic critique of dispensationalism, *Prophecy and the Church,* and is often assumed to have been an amillennialist.[45] However, in the foreword to Roderick Campbell's *Israel and the New Covenant,* Allis defends a strongly postmillennial outlook:

> My own studies in this and related fields have convinced me that the most serious error in much of the current "prophetic" teaching of today is the claim that the future of Christendom is to be read not in terms of Revival and Victory, but of growing impotence and apostasy, and that the only hope of the world is that the Lord will by His visible coming and reign complete the task which he has so plainly entrusted to the church. This claim is rendered formidable and persuasive by the all too obvious fact of the past failures and present feebleness of the church. But it is pessimistic and defeatist. I hold it to be unscriptural. The language of the Great Commission is world embracing; and it has back of it the authority and power of One who said: "All power is given unto me in heaven and in earth. Go ye therefore and make disciples of all nations." The duty of the church is to address herself to the achieving of this task in anticipation of her Lord's coming, and not to expect Him to call her away to glory before her task is accomplished.[46]

While other of Allis's statements could perhaps be read as either amillennial or postmillennial, this passage clearly indicates that Allis believed in the distinctive doctrine which separates postmillennialism from amillennialism.

Louis Berkhof (1873–1957). Louis Berkhof was a professor at Calvin Theological Seminary from 1906 until 1944. In his important and widely used *Systematic Theology*, Berkhof embraced and taught the amillennialism of Herman Bavinck. Berkhof makes the oft-repeated assertion that since the second century, amillennialism has "been the view most widely accepted, is the only view that is either expressed or implied in the great historical Confessions of the Church, and has always been the prevalent view in Reformed circles."[47]

This claim is somewhat misleading for a number of reasons. First, the term *amillennialism* is itself of relatively recent origin. Prior to the late nineteenth century, amillennialism and postmillennialism were not carefully distinguished categories. Second, the twentieth-century understanding of amillennialism carries with it certain connotations that were not always prevalent in Reformed circles. As we have observed in this chapter, much of Reformed eschatology between the sixteenth and the nineteenth centuries was confident and optimistic about the future worldwide success of the gospel prior to the second coming of Christ. This optimism is not shared by modern amillennialists. Third, because it presents an incomplete picture, Berkhof's statement reveals an underlying confusion about the definition of postmillennialism and amillennialism. If amillennialism is defined solely in terms of a particular exegesis of Revelation 20, according to which the Millennium is concurrent with the entire present age, then it is correct to say that amillennialism has been the historic position of the church. However, since many postmillennialists agree with this exegesis, it cannot alone distinguish amillennialism. What Berkhof does not make clear is that the *nature* and the *outcome* of the Millennium, not the *timing* of it, are what distinguish amillennialism from postmillennialism. Furthermore, as we have demonstrated, enough of historic Christianity has been optimistic about the present age to render statements such as Berkhof's highly questionable.

Anthony Hoekema (1913–88). The fullest and most complete defense of modern Reformed amillennialism written in the late twentieth century is Anthony Hoekema's *The Bible and the Future*. Hoekema, who was a professor at Calvin Theological Seminary, admirably ties the older Augustinian foundation together with the contributions made by the Dutch theologians, most notably Geerhardus

Vos. An outline of his developed amillennialism would include the following propositions:

1. Christ has won the decisive victory over sin, death, and Satan.
2. The kingdom of God has both present and future aspects.
3. Although the last day is still future, we are in the last days now.
4. The Millennium of Revelation 20 is the entire present age.
5. The growth of Christ's kingdom in the present age will be paralleled by the growth of Satan's kingdom.
6. The "signs of the times" have both present and future relevance.
7. The second coming of Christ will be a single event.
8. At Christ's second coming, there will be a general resurrection of all men.
9. Immediately after the resurrection, those believers who are alive will suddenly be transformed and glorified in what is commonly called the Rapture.
10. The general resurrection and the Rapture will be followed by the final judgment.
11. After the final judgment, the eternal state will commence.[48]

Hoekema's expression of amillennialism is the predominant position among Reformed believers in the late twentieth century.

The Revival of Postmillennialism

During the greater part of the twentieth century, postmillennialism remained virtually invisible, defended by only a handful of theologians.[49] Beginning in the late 1960s and early 1970s, however, postmillennialism began once again to be seriously studied and taught. Renewed interest in the English Puritans and the simultaneous rise of Christian Reconstructionism led to a rethinking of several areas of theology, including eschatology.[50] This has resulted in the publication of several important works on eschatology by noted postmillennial authors such as Rousas J. Rushdoony,[51] J. Marcellus Kik,[52] Greg L. Bahnsen,[53] Kenneth L. Gentry, Jr.,[54] John Jefferson Davis,[55] Gary DeMar,[56] and R. C. Sproul.[57] Because these works are being read and studied by more and more Christians, this renewed faith in an eschatology of hope shows no signs of slowing down.

Conclusion

Our brief and selective survey of the history of eschatology has revealed several important facts. First, the key elements of Christian eschatology are the belief in the future coming of Jesus Christ to judge mankind and in the future resurrection of our bodies.[58] These are the essential elements of a truly Christian eschatology. Second, there has been little consensus among orthodox Christians on any other eschatological issues. Third, elements of all three millennial positions have been present since the earliest centuries of the Christian church. Fourth, from the sixteenth to the early twentieth century, an optimistic eschatology was predominant among the great Reformed theologians. This fact alone should give pause to those modern Reformed Christians who so cavalierly dismiss postmillennialism. The giants of the historic Reformed faith found something in the Bible which compelled them to believe that God had made glorious promises concerning the future of the church and her gospel preaching. What they found will be the subject of the following chapters.

PART THREE

Old Testament Considerations

CHAPTER FIVE

The Pentateuch and the Historical Books

Now the LORD said to Abram, "Go forth from your country, and from your relatives and from your father's house, to the land which I will show you; and I will make you a great nation, and I will bless you, and make your name great; and so you shall be a blessing; and I will bless those who bless you, and the one who curses you I will curse. And in you all the families of the earth shall be blessed.
—Genesis 12:1–3

We proceed now to ask the most important question of this study: What saith the Scriptures? For once we have discerned what Scripture says, we know what God says. And once we know what God says, our response must be faith in His infallible word. The purpose of the following chapters is to demonstrate that postmillennialism is the eschatological position which is most consistent with the teaching of Scripture.

The Pentateuch

Many Christians assume that our understanding of eschatology is derived only from the book of Revelation and certain passages in the Prophets. But in order to comprehend the goal toward which God's plan of redemption is working, we must begin at the beginning. In fact, some of the most foundational eschatological principles and promises are articulated in the earliest chapters of Scripture.

Creation

In the first chapters of Genesis, we read of the creation of the heavens and the earth, the creation of man in God's image, and the mandate given to Adam (Gen. 1–2). In these chapters, we discover some fundamental truths that are of profound importance for our study of eschatology.

1. *The Purpose of the Creation.* The biblical narrative of creation is important for the study of eschatology because in it we learn that God has a purpose for man and for the world. He created man to have dominion over the earth (Gen. 1:26–28) and to have eternal union and communion with Him in Eden (Gen. 2:15–17). This is relevant to eschatology, as Kenneth Gentry explains, because postmillennialism "expects *in* history what God originally intended *for* history."[1] Throughout the remainder of redemptive history, we see God working toward the accomplishment of His original purpose for the world and for man.

2. *The Goodness of the Creation.* At the end of each day's work of creation, we hear that "God saw that it was good" (Gen. 1:4, 10, 12, 18, 21, 25). And at the conclusion of the six days of creation, we read, "And God saw all that He had made, and behold, it was very good" (1:31). Thus, this created world is not in and of itself bad. It cannot be bad because God created it (1:1). Against all gnosticizing tendencies, which deny the importance or goodness of the created order, postmillennialism reaffirms the truth that God's creation is an essentially good creation that has been marred by man's sin and cursed because of it. This curse, however, is not of the essence of the creation, and it is not permanent.

3. *The Creation Mandate.* In Genesis we also read that God created man in His image and commanded him to rule over the earth and over all of its creatures (1:26–28). Part of what it means to be created in the image of God is to be "God's vice-regent on earth."[2] In other words, man was created to be God's representative, ruling under God and over the creation. This mandate was not annulled by the Fall, and it is still in force (Gen. 9:1–7; Ps. 8:4–8). As redemptive history

unfolds, we shall discover that one of the primary responsibilities of the last Adam, Jesus Christ, will be to fulfill this
mandate by exercising dominion over all of creation (Heb.
2:5–8).

The Fall and the Promise

In Genesis 3, we find the record of the Fall of man into sin and
ruin, and the initial redemptive promise of God. This chapter is also
foundational to a correct understanding of the remainder of Scripture, and it reveals two facts that bear directly on the eschatological
debate.

1. *The Results of the Fall.* The sin of the first man resulted in
   his radical corruption. As the Westminster Confession explains, man became "wholly defiled in all the parts and faculties of soul and body" (6.2), and the guilt of this sin was
   imputed to all of his posterity (6.3). As a result of man's sin,
   all of creation was placed under a curse (Gen. 3:17–18;
   Rom. 8:20–22). However, the narrative does not indicate
   that the Fall would permanently frustrate God's original
   purpose for man and the creation. We will see that as the
   history of redemption progresses, the effects of God's salvation are as worldwide in scope as the effects of His curse. In
   other words, since sin affects more than the soul of man, redemption must affect more than the soul of man.

2. *The Promise of a Seed.* Genesis 3:15 records the first redemptive promise made by God. In the context of cursing
   the serpent, God says, "And I will put enmity between you
   and the woman, and between your seed and her seed; he
   shall bruise [crush] you on the head, and you shall bruise him
   on the heel." At this point, a "holy war" between the seed
   of the woman and the seed of the serpent is established by
   God, and its outcome is known from its inception. In this
   passage of Scripture, we find a promise of certain victory.[3]
   To be sure, the exact nature of that victory is not clearly revealed at this point, but a hint is given by the "bruises" promised. A person is pictured crushing the head of a serpent so
   violently that the serpent bruises his heel. Satan and his peo-

ple get crushed, not Christ and His people. The New Testament will reveal when, how, and by whom this happens.

The Noachic Covenant

In the generations between Adam and Noah, we see the consequences of unbridled sin. In Genesis 4, the warfare between the two seeds begins with a vengeance as Cain ruthlessly murders his brother Abel (4:8). In chapter 5, we are vividly reminded of God's warning to Adam that he would "surely die," for we repeatedly hear "and he died" (5:5, 8, 11, 14, 17, 20, 27, 31). But we are not left without hope, because we are told of Enoch, who "walked with God" (5:22–24). In chapter 6, we find that the ongoing battle has taken its toll, as there is only one righteous man remaining, a man named Noah. The results of mankind's sin are summed up in the biblical evaluation of Noah's generation:

> Then the LORD saw that the wickedness of man was great on the earth, and that every intent of the thoughts of his heart was only evil continually. . . . Now the earth was corrupt in the sight of God, and the earth was filled with violence. And God looked on the earth, and behold, it was corrupt; for all flesh had corrupted their way upon the earth (6:5, 11–12).

Left alone in his sin, man had become utterly wicked. However, as Vos explains, this period of time was not without a purpose in the plan of God. In these chapters, "the downward tendency of sin is clearly illustrated, in order that subsequently in the light of this downgrade movement the true divine cause of the upward course of redemption might be appreciated."[4]

In the midst of this wickedness, God calls the one man who has remained righteous. He warns Noah of His impending judgment on the world and instructs him to build an ark. Genesis 6–9 records God's judgment of the earth by means of a worldwide flood. The only ones who are spared from the judgment are Noah, his family, and the animals he was instructed to bring aboard the ark. In chapters 8–9, after the flood has subsided and Noah has left the ark, God establishes a covenant with him and with the entire earth. God promised before the Flood to establish His covenant with Noah (6:18), but at this point

He actually declares the terms of the covenant. In some ways, the Noachic covenant is a repetition or renewal of the original covenant mandate given to Adam. We find two main similarities:

1. The command to be fruitful and multiply (Gen. 1:28; 9:1, 7).
2. The command to have dominion over the creation (1:28; 9:2–3).

In this restatement of the original dominion mandate, we see again that God has not abandoned His original purpose for His creation.

The new aspects of the Noachic covenant reveal its other intended purpose in the working out of the covenant of grace: its promise of preservation. First, God promises that He will not judge the earth again in such a cataclysmic way until all is accomplished (8:21–22; 9:11, 15). Second, God institutes the death penalty for murder (9:6) in order to curb the widespread violence that had covered the earth before the Flood. Through this covenant, God sets the stage for His future work of redemption by protecting the earth from both divine destruction and human self-destruction.

The Abrahamic Covenant

The Abrahamic Covenant is of paramount importance in our study of biblical eschatology. In it we find the promises that shape the redemptive work of God from this point forward. There are three encounters between God and Abraham (Gen. 12, 15, 17). In each one, more aspects of the Abrahamic covenant are revealed. In Genesis 12:1–3, God calls Abram, giving him a command and a promise:

> Now the LORD said to Abram, "Go forth from your country, and from your relatives and from your father's house, to the land which I will show you; and I will make you a great nation, and I will bless you, and make your name great; and so you shall be a blessing; and I will bless those who bless you, and the one who curses you I will curse. And in you all the families of the earth shall be blessed."

In this initial command, we find four promises:

1. God promises that Abram is to become "a great nation."
2. God promises that He will make Abram's name great.
3. God promises Abram divine protection.
4. God promises Abram that he will be the mediator of divine blessing to all nations.[5]

When Abram arrives in Canaan, God adds an additional and crucial promise to the original promises:

5. God promises to give the land of Canaan to Abram's descendants (12:7).

There are a number of important elements in this passage, especially the nature of the covenant, the promise of land, and the promise of blessing to all nations.

1. *The Nature of the Covenant.* The Hebrew word for *covenant* is *berith*. We have already defined a covenant as a "God-ordained bond of union, peace, friendship, and service between the Lord and His people."[6] The aspect of a covenant that is of special importance here is its *surety*. As Vos explains, "The outstanding characteristic of a *berith* is its unalterableness, its certainty, its eternal validity, and not (what would in certain cases be the very opposite) its voluntary nature."[7] The essential point is that God's covenant will not be abrogated. God's promises to Abram will certainly be accomplished, even if He has to fulfill the conditions Himself.

2. *The Promise of Land.* One of God's promises to Abram is that He will give him the land of Canaan (12:7; 15:18; 17:8). This promise becomes the focal point of future prophecy and a central concern of the Old Testament people of God. As this study unfolds, we shall see how this promise develops and is fulfilled. Although we will discover in the New Testament that it ultimately points to something much greater than the land of Palestine, the fundamental point that must be noted here is that the covenant promise of salvation is integrally tied to the promise of the land. In other words,

the Abrahamic covenant is intimately concerned with *this creation* and with who will inherit it.[8]

3. *The Promise of Blessing to All Nations.* In Genesis 12:3, God promises Abram, "In you all the families of the earth shall be blessed." The first question that immediately arises is, what families? The answer to that question is found in the context preceding the promise. In Genesis 10, we find a record of all "the families of the sons of Noah" (10:32). In choosing Abraham, God chose one of the descendants of Noah through whom He would bless *all* the descendants of Noah. In this, we again see the marvelous continuity of God's covenantal work as He establishes the Abrahamic covenant in order to bless the descendants of His covenanted servant, Noah. In this promise of blessing to all nations, God clearly reveals that His intention is to "bring salvation not only to Israel, but through this people, to all the peoples of the earth."[9]

In Genesis 15, God repeats His earlier promise to Abram and ratifies it in an elaborate ceremony. Early in the chapter, we read that Abram is wondering how God could possibly make him into a great nation when he did not even have one child (v. 2). He suggests that one born in his house be his heir (v. 3), but he is told by God that he would have a son through whom the promise of blessing would be fulfilled (v. 4). Abram places His faith in God's promise, and God assures him again that He will give him the land (v. 7). At this point, Abram asks God, "How may I know that I shall possess it?" (v. 8). God commands Abram to divide several animals in half, and when the sun sets, He assures him that after four hundred years of enslavement in a foreign land, his descendants will return to the promised land (vv. 9–16). In the most unusual part of the narrative, a "smoking oven and a flaming torch," symbolizing God, pass through the divided carcasses *alone* (v. 17). It was not unusual for *both* parties to a covenant to pass through the divided carcasses of animals, thereby promising to fulfill the agreed-upon conditions or else have their blood shed in the same manner. What is unusual about the biblical account is that only God passes through the divided carcasses. By doing so, God takes an unbreakable oath of fidelity to his promises and takes upon Himself the curses symbolized by the dead animals.[10] There can be no greater assurance for us that the Abrahamic promises, including the promise to bless all the families of the earth, will most certainly be accomplished.

In Genesis 17, we read of the third covenantal encounter between God and Abram. In this encounter, God reaffirms His covenant promises (17:1ff.). He also introduces several new elements of the covenant. First, God changes Abram's name to Abraham, which means "father of a multitude" (v. 5). Second, He promises Abraham that his descendants would include kings (v. 6). And third, God institutes circumcision as the sign of the covenant (vv. 10–14). This communicates an important fact to Abraham. "Circumcision," as Vos explains, "teaches that physical descent from Abraham is not sufficient to make true Israelites."[11] Instead, "the uncleanness and disqualification of nature must be taken away."[12]

The Abrahamic covenant lays a strong foundation for a postmillennial eschatology. In it God swears by an unbreakable oath that He will bless all the families of the earth. Through Abraham's descendants, He will bless all the descendants of Noah. Whatever else "all families of the earth" means, it does not mean a minuscule percentage of the families of the earth.

The Exodus

In the years between Abraham and Moses, God repeatedly renewed His covenant with the chosen descendants of Abraham. In Genesis 21:1–3, God fulfills His "impossible" promise by giving Abraham a son. Years later, God renews the covenant with Isaac (26:3–5, 24) and then with Isaac's son Jacob (28:13–15; 35:9–12). Finally, we hear the blessing pronounced over Jacob's son Judah: "The scepter shall not depart from Judah, nor the ruler's staff from between his feet, until Shiloh comes, and to him shall be the obedience of the peoples" (49:10; cf. Ezek. 21:27). As the book of Genesis ends, the descendants of Abraham are in Egypt (50:22–26) as God has foretold (15:13).

In due course, a Pharaoh arose in Egypt who did not remember Joseph (Ex. 1:8). This Pharaoh enslaved the descendants of Abraham and murdered their sons. The people cried out to God in their bondage, and He heard their cry (2:23–25). He began to raise up a leader who would lead the people out of Egypt and into the Promised Land. This leader's name was Moses. Everything that happened from that moment onward was based upon God's covenant promise to Abraham. God reminded Moses and us of this fact repeatedly (3:6, 13, 15; 6:2–7).

After God miraculously led the people out of Egypt and destroyed the pursuing armies, He renewed His covenant with them (19:5–8) and gave them the Law (chaps. 20–23), a greatly expanded statement of His will for His people. The moral law was given specifically to Israel in summary form in the Ten Commandments, but, as Vos points out, "the primary application to Israel in no wise interferes with a world-wide application in all ethical relationships."[13] This is not surprising when we remember that the Mosaic Law was "added" alongside the Abrahamic promise (Gal. 3:19), which clearly has universal application.

One element of the Law that has clear eschatological significance is the Sabbath. The sabbath principle was expressed as early as Genesis 2:3, which states that God rested from his work and sanctified the seventh day. The sabbath principle was also clearly expressed prior to the formal giving of the Mosaic Law (see Ex. 16:23–26). But in the Ten Commandments we find the law expressed in its most recognized form, "Remember the sabbath day, to keep it holy" (20:8). The sabbath principle has eschatological significance since human life and history have been constructed on the basis of it. That is, human history will reach a conclusion, an eternal sabbath rest.

The Jubilee

Brief mention must be made of the law of the Jubilee (Lev. 25). In Israel, a man who incurred a debt that he could not repay could be forced into slavery. The Jubilee year occurred every forty-nine years. In the year of Jubilee, the debtor was released from slavery and regained his lost possessions. During the history of Israel, this law remained, for the most part, an unrealized ideal. We mention it here because one was later promised who would come and inaugurate the ultimate Jubilee (Isa. 61:1–2), one who would "proclaim release to the captives, and recovery of sight to the blind, to set free those who are downtrodden, to proclaim the favorable year of the Lord" (Luke 4:18–19). The Jubilee is eschatologically significant because it looks back to God's redemption of His people from Egypt and forward to the final redemption of all things by the Messiah.[14]

The Wilderness Wandering

An illustrative incident is reported in Numbers 13 and 14. Eleven months after their arrival at Sinai, the people departed and traveled to the wilderness of Paran (Num. 12:16). Moses sent out twelve spies who were to bring back information on the Promised Land and its inhabitants. When the spies returned, they brought this report to Moses and the people:

> We went in to the land where you sent us; and it certainly does flow with milk and honey, and this is its fruit. Nevertheless, the people who live in the land are strong, and the cities are fortified and very large; and moreover, we saw the descendants of Anak there. (Num. 13:27–28)

Apparently the report caused fear, because at this point one of the spies spoke up:

> Then Caleb quieted the people before Moses, and said, "We should by all means go up and take possession of it, for we shall surely overcome it." But the men who had gone up with him said, "We are not able to go up against the people, for they are too strong for us." (13:30–31)

At this point, the people of Israel cried out in fear and despair, and grumbled against Moses and against God:

> "Would that we had died in the land of Egypt! Or would that we had died in this wilderness! And why is the LORD bringing us into this land, to fall by the sword? Our wives and our little ones will become plunder; would it not be better for us to return to Egypt?" So they said to one another, "Let us appoint a leader and return to Egypt." (14:2–4)

Then the two spies who were not fearful, who trusted the promise of God that He would give them this land, spoke up:

And Joshua the son of Nun and Caleb the son of Jephunneh, of those who had spied out the land, tore their clothes; and they spoke to all the congregation of the sons of Israel, saying, "The land which we passed through to spy out is an exceedingly good land. If the LORD is pleased with us, then He will bring us into this land, and give it to us—a land which flows with milk and honey. Only do not rebel against the LORD; and do not fear the people of the land, for they shall be our prey. Their protection has been removed from them, and the LORD is with us; do not fear them. (14:6–9)

But, sadly, the people did give in to fear and did not trust God (v. 10). Because of their faithlessness, God told Moses that none of the people over the age of twenty, except for Joshua and Caleb, would enter the land (vv. 22–24, 29–32). Instead, they would be forced to wander in the wilderness for forty years, until they died (v. 33). God explained that they would suffer for their unfaithfulness until they died in the wilderness (vv. 33–35).

What bearing does this story have on the millennial question? On the surface, very little, until one hears a common amillennialist critique of postmillennialism. It is argued against postmillennialism that the church between the first and second coming of Christ is a wilderness church.[15] This objection will be dealt with fully in Part Six, but it should be observed here that the wilderness wandering was a judgment of God upon a faithless people.[16] To suggest that the church during the present age is essentially like Israel during the wilderness wandering is to suggest that the church is essentially unfaithful and undergoing divine judgment.

The Coming Prophet

A brief comment must be made about a prophecy in Deuteronomy 18:15–19. Moses tells the people, "The LORD your God will raise up for you a prophet like me from among you, from your countrymen, you shall listen to him" (v. 15). God promises Moses:

I will raise up a prophet from among their countrymen like you, and I will put My words in his mouth, and he shall speak to them all that I command him. And it shall come about that whoever will not listen to My words which he shall speak in My name, I Myself will require it of him. (Vv. 18–19)

Moses prophesies here of one who would be raised up as a prophet "like him," one who would mediate a fuller understanding of the normative revelation of God. The coming of this prophet would become a common eschatological expectation in Israel (e.g., see Luke 7:16; John 1:21, 25), and as we shall see, it was fulfilled by the coming of the prophet *par excellence*, Jesus of Nazareth (cf. Acts 3:22; 7:37).

Blessing and Cursing

A final chapter of the Pentateuch that we must note for its prophetic significance is Deuteronomy 28. In the first four chapters of Deuteronomy, Moses recounts the history of Israel after the Exodus from Egypt. In chapters 5–26, he repeats the Law to the people (thus the name Deuteronomy, which means "a repetition of the law"). Finally, chapters 27–30 contain the solemn renewal of the Mosaic covenant.

Chapter 28 is significant because in it we find the covenantal blessings and cursings. God promises Israel that blessings will be the consequence of obedience (vv. 1–14) and that cursing will be the consequence of disobedience (vv. 15–68). Unfortunately, the remainder of the history of Israel was an almost unbroken record of disobedience, with the result that God poured out the covenant curses. But when Israel repented and obeyed God, He always poured out His covenant blessings. The lesson is that God blesses His people when they are obedient—He doesn't curse them. Thus, we can expect God to bless the church if she obediently carries out the Great Commission and takes the gospel to the nations. We have no reason to expect God to do otherwise.

The Historical Books

The Historical Books, Joshua through Esther, span a period of approximately one thousand years. The book of Joshua outlines the conquest of Canaan (c. 1400–1375 B.C.) and the division of the land. The books of Judges and Ruth cover the period of Israel's history between the conquest of the land and the birth of Samuel. The books of 1 and 2 Samuel cover a period of almost 130 years, including the reigns of Saul (c. 1040–1010) and David (c. 1010–970). The books of 1 and 2 Kings relate the history of Israel from the rebellion of David's son Adonijah until the captivity of Judah in 586. It also covers the entire history of the northern kingdom from its secession in 931 until its destruction in 721. The books of 1 and 2 Chronicles summarize the main events from the time of creation to the proclamation of Cyrus in 538 permitting the Jews to return to Palestine. The book of Ezra describes the events that happened between the time of Cyrus's decree and the arrival of Ezra in Jerusalem in 458. The book of Nehemiah tells the history of Israel from the time of Nehemiah's return to rebuild the walls of Jerusalem in 445 until his period of governorship (c. 433).

The purpose of these books, however, is not merely to tell us the fascinating story of an ancient nation. The Historical Books of the Old Testament are intimately tied to what has been revealed in the Pentateuch. Essentially, these books tell Israel's history in terms of her obedience or disobedience to God's covenant with her. Obedience brought blessing, and disobedience brought cursing. For the purposes of our study, we must discuss one crucial text found within this section of Scripture in which God promises further blessing.

The Davidic Covenant

The Davidic covenant marked a major milestone in the development of God's redemptive work. In 1 and 2 Samuel, we read of how God raised up David to be the king of Israel. After securing Jerusalem, David offered to build a permanent "house" for God to replace the tabernacle (2 Sam. 7:1–5). However, instead of accepting David's offer, God promised to build a house for David (7:11). He then promised that He would raise up one from the house of David who would build a house for God (7:13). Finally, God promised that He would establish the throne of this descendant of David forever (7:13). Although this promise is not explicitly described as a covenant in this passage, it is termed a covenant elsewhere (2 Sam. 23:5; Ps. 89:3). David Holwerda notes the interesting irony in this passage: "Two houses would be built, David's house and God's house, and amazingly in the end—in Jesus—these two houses would become one."[17]

There are two aspects of the Davidic covenant that we must briefly discuss. First, the Davidic covenant expands on the earlier promise to Abraham that his descendants would include kings (Gen. 17:6). In the Davidic covenant, we learn that a king would come whose throne would be eternal (2 Sam. 7:16). This promise became the basis for the pronouncements of many of the prophets.

The second aspect of this covenant that is important for our discussion is the nature of the "house" that would be built. David's son Solomon did build a temple for God (1 Kings 6), a temple that lay at the center of Israel's worship. But this temple would not be the final fulfillment of the Davidic covenant (1 Kings 9:8). Later in Israel's history, the temple became an idol and was destroyed by God (Jer. 7:4; Ezek. 10:18–19; 11:22–25). But all hope was not lost. God had promised that he would raise up one whose throne would be established forever, and that this one would also build Him a "house" in which He would dwell in the midst of His people. As we shall see, in one of the most extensive prophecies in the Old Testament, Ezekiel describes a future temple that will be filled with the glory of the Lord (Ezek. 40–48). When we turn to the New Testament, we shall meet One who, in His very person and work, is this prophesied "house" of God and who fulfills all that the temple symbolized: God's presence in the midst of His people, cleanliness, healing, and the forgiveness of sins.

Conclusion

The Pentateuch and the Historical Books of the Old Testament provide us with the history of God's early covenantal redemptive work. They lay the foundation for the remainder of redemptive history. This is what we have discovered in these books:

1. *The Purpose of Creation.* God created the universe and man for a purpose, and the Fall did not destroy that purpose.
2. *The Creation Mandate.* God gave man a mandate to rule over creation, and that mandate was not abrogated after the Fall.
3. *The Promise of a Seed.* God promised that the seed of the woman would crush Satan and his seed.

4. *The Promise of Land*. The foundational covenant made with Abraham was intimately concerned with this earth and with who would inherit it.
5. *The Promise of Worldwide Blessing*. The primary promise of the Abrahamic covenant was that God would, through Abraham's seed, bless "all the families of the earth," a promise that is worldwide in scope.
6. *The Wilderness Wandering*. The wilderness wandering of Israel was a time of punishment for a faithless generation.
7. *The Curses and Blessings of the Covenant*. The obedience of God's covenant people results in blessing; disobedience results in cursing.
8. *The Davidic Covenant*. In the Davidic covenant, God promised that He would raise up one of David's descendants, whose throne would be eternal.

The covenants revealed in the Pentateuch and the Historical Books provide a firm foundation for a postmillennial eschatology, a fact that will be further established as we turn to the poets and the prophets of the Old Testament.

CHAPTER SIX

The Psalms

The LORD says to my Lord: "Sit at My right hand, until I make Thine enemies a footstool for Thy feet." The LORD will stretch forth Thy strong scepter from Zion, saying, "Rule in the midst of Thine enemies."
—Psalm 110:1–2

The Old Testament foundation for a postmillennial eschatology does not begin and end with the Abrahamic covenant. We also find promises throughout the Psalms which, as John Jefferson Davis points out, present "clear pictures of a great king, God's Messiah, ruling over a vast kingdom that far transcends the boundaries of the nation Israel."[1] We turn our attention now to some of the most significant of these Psalms.[2]

Psalm 2

> I will surely tell of the decree of the LORD: He said to Me, "Thou art My Son, today I have begotten Thee. Ask of Me, and I will surely give the nations as Thine inheritance, and the very ends of the earth as Thy possession. Thou shalt break them with a rod of iron, Thou shalt shatter them like earthenware." (Ps. 2:7–9)

Psalm 2 is a "coronation psalm," which was sung at the enthronement of a new king in Israel. It is frequently alluded to or quoted in the New Testament in connection with the life of Jesus, such as at His baptism (Matt. 3:17), at His transfiguration (Matt. 17:5), and with reference to His resurrection (Acts 13:33).

The psalm has a great deal to say about the reign of Christ and thus about the present age. In verses 1–3, we hear utter astonishment at the foolish rebellion of the kings of the earth, and in verses 4–6 we see the contempt that God has for this kind of arrogance. Verses 7–9 then present God's decree. The language of verse 7 points back to the words of the Davidic covenant in 2 Samuel 7:14, in which God promises, "I will be a father to him and he will be a son to Me." When we see how the fulfillment of this psalm is tied to the resurrection of Christ in the New Testament (Acts 13:32–33), its significance begins to become clear.

In verse 8, we read of the privileges that belong to the anointed king, privileges that have to be asked for, but which God promises to grant. The king is promised the "nations" as His inheritance and "the very ends of the earth" as His possession. When we turn to the New Testament, we see that after Christ's resurrection, His commission to the disciples is, "Go therefore and make disciples of *all the nations*" (Matt. 28:19). And immediately before His ascension, Jesus says to His disciples, "You shall be My witnesses both in Jerusalem, and in all Judea and Samaria, and even to *the remotest part of the earth*" (Acts 1:8). Through the sending of the disciples into the world, Christ the anointed king is receiving His rightful inheritance—all the nations of the earth. And since He is the seed of Abraham (Gal. 3:16), this sending out of His church is also the means by which He is bringing blessing to all the families of the earth (Gen. 12:3).

Christians do not participate in Christ's obtaining of His inheritance (Psalm 2:9; cf. Rev. 2:26–27) by conquering the nations by force of arms. As Paul explains in 2 Corinthians 10:3–5, "We do not war according to the flesh, for the weapons of our warfare are not of the flesh, but divinely powerful for the destruction of fortresses." Our weapon is the Word of God, sharper than any two-edged sword (Heb. 4:12; cf. Rev. 19:15). Will all the nations of the earth be conquered by the reigning Christ and His church through the spiritual power of the gospel? According to the apostle Paul, "He must reign until He has put all His enemies under His feet" (1 Cor. 15:25).

Psalm 22

All the ends of the earth will remember and turn to the LORD, and all the families of the nations will worship before

Thee. For the kingdom is the LORD's, and He rules over the nations. (Ps. 22:27–28)

Sometimes called the "Fifth Gospel" account of the Crucifixion, Psalm 22 gives us a prophecy that is fulfilled in minute detail in the death, resurrection, and ascension of Christ. The psalm can be divided into two basic sections. The first section (vv. 1–21) describes the cry of the humble sufferer. When we remember that this psalm was quoted by Christ on the cross (Matt. 27:46), these verses remind us of the punishment Christ bore as He became a curse for us (Gal. 3:13).

The turning point of the psalm comes at verse 22, where the cries and prayers become a chorus of praise and, as Derek Kidner observes, "a broadening vision of God's perfect rule."[3] The verses with which we are specifically concerned are vv. 27–28, which are clearly based upon both the Abrahamic and the Davidic covenant promises. The psalmist declares with confidence that "all the families of the nations will worship before Thee." The psalmist's confidence that this Abrahamic promise will be fulfilled is based upon the fulfillment of the Davidic promise, "For the kingdom is the LORD's, and He rules over the nations." In the New Testament, we learn that both covenants are fulfilled in Jesus Christ, whose own personal cry this psalm becomes.

Finally, we should note that the first verse of the first section of this psalm was quoted by Christ in the context of His suffering and dying. Hebrews 2:12 quotes verse 22, the first verse of the second section, in the context of His resurrection and exaltation. The first section of this psalm was fulfilled to the letter by Christ on the cross. The second section of the psalm will just as certainly be fulfilled by Christ at the right hand of God. As surely as the hands and feet of Christ were pierced, all the families of the earth will remember and turn to the Lord and worship Him.

Psalm 47

Sing praises to God, sing praises; sing praises to our King, sing praises. For God is the King of all the earth; sing praises with a skillful psalm. God reigns over the nations, God sits on His holy throne. The princes of the people have assembled themselves as the people of the God of Abraham; for the shields of the earth belong to God; He is highly exalted. (Ps. 47:6–9)

In Psalm 47, all nations are called to praise God (v. 1), the great King who has subdued His enemies (v. 3). Verses 5–7 picture God ascending His throne with the appropriate call to sing for joy. In the concluding verses of the psalm, the aim of the King is brought into view. The "peoples" and "nations" from "all the earth" will become one—"the people of the God of Abraham." This is a dramatic prophecy of the fulfillment of the Abrahamic covenant. It is elaborated upon by Paul when he describes how Gentiles who believe become the children of Abraham by virtue of their being united to Christ, *the* seed of Abraham (Rom. 4:11; Gal. 3:16, 29). In other words, God's promise to bring blessing to all the families of the earth through the seed of Abraham will be fulfilled by uniting all the families of the earth to Christ. Since union with Christ comes by faith, and faith comes through hearing the gospel, the preaching of the gospel is instrumental in fulfilling the Abrahamic promise.

Psalm 67

God be gracious to us and bless us, and cause His face to shine upon us—Selah. That Thy way may be known on the earth, Thy salvation among all nations. Let the peoples praise Thee, O God; let all the peoples praise Thee. Let the nations be glad and sing for joy; for Thou wilt judge the peoples with uprightness, and guide the nations on the earth. Selah. Let the peoples praise Thee, O God; let all the peoples praise Thee. The earth has yielded its produce; God, our God, blesses us. God blesses us, that all the ends of the earth may fear Him. (Ps. 67:1–7)

This psalm expresses the hope of the Abrahamic promise of blessing in terms very similar to that of the Aaronic blessing (cf. Num. 6:22–27). The primary difference, however, is that here the circle of blessing is ever widening. The hope is expressed that the blessing will extend to all nations, even to the ends of the earth. As Marvin E. Tate explains, "The psalm invites a messianic perspective which looks forward to an age when the relationship between Yahweh's saving-work in Israel and his blessing-work in all creation will no longer be obscure but will lead the peoples of the world to rejoice and sing of his judgments and guidance (v 5)."[4] In another valuable summary of Psalm 67, I. Abrahams writes:

> This psalm is a prayer for salvation in the widest sense, and not for Israel only, but for the whole world. Israel's blessing is to be a blessing for all men. Here, in particular, the Psalmist does more than adopt the Priestly formula (Num 6:22–27); he claims for Israel the sacerdotal dignity. Israel is the world's high priest . . . if Israel has the light of God's face, the world cannot remain in darkness.[5]

Old Testament Israel was unable to fulfill her task as the priestly mediator of God's blessing to the nations of the earth. As we shall see, in the New Testament, Jesus is declared the corporate representative of Israel, and the church, which is His body, is, because of its union with Him, also recognized as such.[6] Jesus is now, therefore, the great high priest (Heb. 2:17; 3:1; 4:14–15; 5:5, 10; 6:20; 7:26; 8:1, 3; 9:11; 10:21), and His body, the church, is given the title of "priests" that once belonged to the nation of Israel (1 Peter 2:5, 9; Rev. 1:6; 5:10; 20:6; cf. Ex. 19:6). But will this High Priest and His kingdom of priests also ultimately fail in their duty to be a mediator of the Abrahamic blessing to all nations? Clearly not, because "as many as may be the promises of God, in Him they are yes" (2 Cor. 1:20).

Psalm 72

> May he also rule from sea to sea, and from the river to the ends of the earth. Let the nomads of the desert bow before him; and his enemies lick the dust. Let the kings of Tarshish and of the islands bring presents; the kings of Sheba and Seba offer gifts. And let all kings bow down before him, all nations serve him. . . . May his name endure forever; may his name increase as long the sun shines; and let men bless

themselves by him; let all nations call him blessed. (Ps. 72:8–11, 17)

Psalm 72 is a "royal psalm," a prayer for the king. It consists of five sections or stanzas. The first stanza (vv. 1–4) consists of a prayer for the king to be one who exercises justice according to the righteous standard of God. The second stanza (vv. 5–7) is a prayer for an endless reign of righteousness. In the third stanza (vv. 8–11), we find the petition that hearkens back to the Abrahamic promise to bless all nations. God is implored to extend the king's dominion over all the nations of the earth. In the fourth stanza (vv. 12–15), the reason for the entire psalm is revealed: the king is compassionate and delivers the poor and oppressed from violence. The final stanza (vv. 16–17) is a prayer that endless blessing may extend to all the nations of the earth. The psalm closes with a benediction (vv. 18–19).

Psalm 72 is never quoted in the New Testament as messianic, but it has direct parallels in prophetic passages that are definitely messianic (Isa. 11:1–5; 60:3–9, 12–14; 61:1–2; 62:1–12; Zech. 9:9–10), and therefore its significance cannot be overlooked. In verses 8–17 of this psalm, the people pray for their earthly king to have worldwide dominion, to have all kings and nations bow before him, and to have all nations call him blessed. They were praying these things for their earthly king. How much more then should this be our prayer for the greater son of David, the King of kings and Lord of lords?

Unfortunately, the two most common millennial positions, premillennialism and amillennialism, effectively deny the legitimacy of this prayer for the present reign of our King. Premillennialism applies the fulfillment of this prayer almost exclusively to the period after Christ's second coming, thereby ignoring to a great extent that Christ is reigning as King now. Amillennialism denies that the things prayed for in this psalm will ever be fulfilled in history, asserting instead that their fulfillment will be in heaven or in the eternal state. Postmillennialism asserts, on the other hand, that Christ has been enthroned as King over the heavens *and the earth*, that He is *presently* fulfilling the promises made to Abraham and to David, and that He *will continue to reign* until He has put all His enemies under His feet. According to postmillennialism, then, this psalm is a legitimate prayer for the present reign of Christ the King.

Psalm 86

> All nations whom Thou hast made shall come and worship
> before Thee, O Lord; and they shall glorify Thy name. For
> Thou art great and doest wondrous deeds; Thou alone art
> God. (Ps. 86:9–10)

Psalm 86 is the lament of an individual in distress. Verses 1–7 and
14–17 contain the prayers of lament, consisting primarily of grievances.
Interestingly, however, these two sections surround the central section
(vv. 8–13), which is a song of praise and thanksgiving. Even in the
midst of distress, the psalmist clings to the promises of God.

Verses 8–13 form the central core of the psalm, and in them we
find a description of the incomparable greatness of the Lord. In the
midst of praising the Lord, the psalmist declares with confidence that
He will fulfill the Abrahamic covenant, proclaiming that all nations
will come and worship the Lord. This promise is, like so many others, worldwide in scope (v. 9). But is such worldwide worship of God
possible? The context is suggestive, appealing to the omnipotent cre-
ative power of God. Our God is the One who has done "wondrous
deeds" (v. 10). As surely as He made the nations (v. 9a), He will convert the nations (v. 9b).

Psalm 110

> The LORD says to my Lord: "Sit at My right hand, until I make
> Thine enemies a footstool for Thy feet." The LORD will
> stretch forth Thy strong scepter from Zion, saying, "Rule in
> the midst of Thine enemies." Thy people will volunteer freely
> in the day of Thy power; in holy array, from the womb of the
> dawn, Thy youth are to Thee as the dew. The LORD has
> sworn and will not change His mind, "Thou art a priest for-
> ever according to the order of Melchizedek." (Ps. 110:1–4)

Psalm 110 is unarguably one of the most significant eschatological passages in the Bible. It is cited or alluded to in the New Testament more than any other Old Testament text (e.g., Matt. 22:41–45;

Mark 12:35–37; Luke 20:41–44; Acts 2:33–35; 1 Cor. 15:25; Heb. 1:13; 5:6; 7:17, 21; 10:13). In the New Testament, this psalm is repeatedly used to challenge the common Jewish misconceptions about the Messiah (Matt. 22:41–45; Acts 2:33–35). It provided the foundation for the apostolic doctrine of the ascension and present reign of Christ as the great Priest-King. For these reasons, this psalm deserves our closest attention.

Verse 1 begins with the oracle of God, "The LORD says to my Lord." The Jews understood this psalm to be referring to the Messiah who was to be David's son. Jesus pointed out to them that the Messiah is much more than David's son, since David himself calls him "my Lord."

Derek Kidner outlines well the New Testament significance of the next line of the psalm, "Sit at My right hand, until I make Thine enemies a footstool for Thy feet." He makes the following five points:

1. He [the Messiah] is not only greater than David (Acts 2:34, "for David did not ascend into the heavens") but greater than the angels (Heb. 1:13, "to what angel has he ever said, 'sit at my right hand . . .'?");
2. God exalted Him as emphatically as man rejected Him (Acts 5:30f., "Jesus whom you killed . . . God exalted . . . at his right hand");
3. It is as Saviour and Intercessor that He reigns (Acts 5:31; Rom. 8:34, "Christ . . . who is at the right hand of God . . . intercedes for us");
4. (*"Sit . . ."*): In token of a finished task, He is seated (Heb. 10:11f., "every priest stands daily . . . , offering repeatedly. . . . But . . . Christ . . . sat down at the right hand of God");
5. (*"till . . ."*): He awaits the last surrender (Heb. 10:13, "to wait until his enemies should be made a stool for his feet"; *cf.* also 1 Cor. 15:25f.).[7]

Furthermore, this psalm emphatically demonstrates that it is *not* necessary, as premillennialism asserts, for Christ to be physically present on earth in order to conquer his enemies. He is perfectly able to accomplish this from the right hand of God.

Verse 2 illustrates the oneness of the Lord and the King. The Lord stretches forth His scepter while commanding the King to "rule." In verse 3, we see a poetic description of the Messiah-King leading a dedicated volunteer army into battle. In verse 4, the Messiah is declared to be a priest forever after the order of Melchizedek. In Melchizedek, kingship and priesthood were united, as they were to be in the coming Messiah. Verses 5–7 describe the enthroned King going forth in world conquest.

The psalm ends with the picture of a battle in progress, with the King pausing before advancing onward into the fight. Is there any doubt in this psalm about the outcome of the battle? The promise in verse 1 leaves us without any question whatsoever. The Lord will make the enemies of the King a footstool for His feet.

The New Testament writers give us the identity of this King. He is Jesus of Nazareth, the son of David (Matt. 1:1), and yet he is also David's Lord (Matt. 22:43). He is the One who ascended into heaven and is now seated at the right hand of God with all authority (Acts 2:34–36). He is the One who will reign from the right hand of God *until* He has put all of His enemies under His feet (Heb. 10:12–13; 1 Cor. 15:25). This is the apostolic doctrine of the exaltation and present reign of Jesus Christ. And this teaching provides us with the reason why we can anticipate the victory of Christ's gospel on earth prior to His second coming.

Conclusion

The book of Psalms is a record of inspired praise and prayer to God. In these songs we find a wealth of material pointing to a future King, a Messiah who would fulfill the covenant promises made to Abraham and David. In each of the psalms we have examined, a different facet of the reign of the Messiah is brought to light:

1. *Psalm 2.* Christ is the rightful heir of all the nations.
2. *Psalm 22.* The same Christ who was crucified and is now exalted will fulfill the Abrahamic promise, and all the nations of the earth will remember and turn to God.
3. *Psalm 47.* All nations of the earth will be united to Christ and will become the one people of the God of Abraham.

4. *Psalm 67*. Although national Israel has failed, Christ will succeed as the mediator of the Abrahamic blessing to the nations of the earth.
5. *Psalm 72*. The people of God should faithfully pray for Christ to have worldwide dominion, to have all nations bow before Him, and to have all nations call Him blessed.
6. *Psalm 86*. The same omnipotent God who made all the nations will convert all the nations.
7. *Psalm 110*. Christ will reign from the right hand of God until He has brought all His enemies into either willing or unwilling submission.

The Psalms continue to expand upon the covenant promises of the Pentateuch and the Historical Books by expressing Israel's faith in the sure fulfillment of those promises. In doing so, they reinforce the postmillennial foundation, even as they begin to build upon it. As we turn to the prophetic books, we shall see even further elaboration and development of this covenantal hope.

CHAPTER SEVEN

The Prophets

*Now it will come about that in the last days, the mountain of the house of the
LORD will be established as the chief of the mountains, and will be raised above
the hills; and all the nations will stream to it.*
—Isaiah 2:1–2

The covenant relationship between God and His people that is
established in the Pentateuch, recorded in the Historical Books, and
used as the basis of prayer and praise in the Psalms, is declared and
defended by the prophets. When the people sinned, the prophets
called them to repentance and reaffirmation of the covenant. When
the judgment of God fell upon them, the prophets explained why it
had happened. And in the face of Israel's continued recalcitrance, the
prophets pointed beyond their own age to a time when the covenant
would be established to the fullest.[1]

Entire books could be written on the eschatology of the prophets,
and several have been. We shall again survey only the most important texts bearing upon our topic. That which was promised in the
covenants and prayed for and proclaimed in the Psalms, was then foretold in the Prophets.

Isaiah

Isaiah was a prophet in Jerusalem from 740 to 701 B.C. His ministry spanned the reigns of four kings of Judah. His book has two main
sections. Chapters 1–39 focus primarily on God's judgment of Israel
through the Assyrians. Chapters 40–66 focus on a number of themes,

including the kingdom of God, the restoration of Israel, and the creation of a new heaven and a new earth. We shall examine several of the most significant eschatological prophecies in this book in order to discover what light they shed upon our study.[2]

The Future Jerusalem

> Now it will come about that in the last days, the mountain of the house of the LORD will be established as the chief of the mountains, and will be raised above the hills; and all the nations will stream to it. And many peoples will come and say, "Come, let us go up to the mountain of the LORD, to the house of the God of Jacob; that He may teach us concerning His ways, and that we may walk in His paths." For the law will go forth from Zion, and the word of the LORD from Jerusalem. And He will judge between the nations, and will render decisions for many peoples; and they will hammer their swords into plowshares, and their spears into pruning hooks. Nation will not lift up sword against nation, and never again will they learn war. (Isa. 2:1–4)

This prophecy, which is repeated almost verbatim in Micah 4:1–3, makes several significant statements that we must examine. First, the time period referred to as "the last days" is a future age or epoch which, in the eyes of the prophet, will alter every aspect of redemptive history. This time period is revealed more fully in the New Testament, when Peter identifies the exaltation of Christ as marking the inauguration of the last days (Acts 2:16–17).

Isaiah records several characteristics of "the last days":

1. The mountain of the house of the Lord will be established as the chief of the mountains during this age, indicating that God will be victorious over all false gods.
2. "All the nations" and "many peoples" will come to the mountain of the Lord, indicating the fulfilling of God's promise to Abraham to bless all the families of the earth.
3. People will come because they are drawn by God to desire the truth.

4. The recognition and worship of the one true God will be followed by the elimination of warfare.

All of this suggests that something that is yet to unfold in this present age will be above and beyond anything we have experienced so far.

A Child Will Be Born

> For a child will be born to us, a son will be given to us; and the government will rest on His shoulders; and His name will be called Wonderful Counselor, Mighty God, Eternal Father, Prince of Peace. There will be no end to the increase of His government or of peace, on the throne of David and over his kingdom, to establish it and to uphold it with justice and righteousness from then on and forevermore. The zeal of the LORD of hosts will accomplish this. (Isa. 9:6–7)

This prophecy of the coming King is one of the richest in all of the Old Testament. Building upon the prophecy in Isaiah 7:14, which promises a child who would be called Immanuel, this passage sheds more light on his identity and reign. He is called "Wonderful Counselor," "Mighty God," "Eternal Father," and "Prince of Peace." These titles indicate that this child will somehow be God Himself. The description of His reign is no less significant. He will reign from the throne of David and "there will be no end to the increase of His government or of peace." As J. Alec Motyer explains, this means that "His kingdom will *increase* and occupy progressively all space until he rules over all."[3] And what assurance do we have that this will occur? "The zeal of the LORD of hosts will accomplish this." The same almighty God who promises that it will surely be done also promises that He will be the One to do it. We cannot ask for greater assurance.

A Glorious Hope for the Future

> They will not hurt or destroy in all My holy mountain, for the earth will be full of the knowledge of the LORD as the waters cover the sea. Then it will come about in that day that

the nations will resort to the root of Jesse, who will stand as a signal for the peoples; and His resting place will be glorious. Then it will happen on that day that the Lord will again recover the second time with His hand the remnant of His people, who will remain, from Assyria, Egypt, Pathros, Cush, Elam, Shinar, Hamath, and from the islands of the sea. And He will lift up a standard for the nations, and will assemble the banished ones of Israel, and will gather the dispersed of Judah from the four corners of the earth. (Isa. 11:9–12)

Motyer explains that Isaiah 11 "is specifically a word of assurance for the dark day of the Assyrian threat but contains in itself clear indications that its fulfillment is for time yet to come."[4] The entire chapter contains several important eschatological themes, but we will focus here on one in particular: the extent of the change that is to come during the reign of the Messiah.

The change described in verses 6–9 is not limited in scope. It is instead a radical change that will affect the entire earth.[5] The created order is to be restored, with the result that the whole earth will be called the Lord's "holy mountain." The extent of the restoration is illustrated further by the expression "as the waters cover the sea." This is not descriptive of a partial effect. As Motyer explains, "Everywhere God is present in holiness, and in every place the knowledge of him is enjoyed to its fullest extent."[6] What we see in these verses is a worldwide restoration that confirms the promises made to Abraham and David.

A New Creation and a New City

For behold, I create new heavens and a new earth; and the former things shall not be remembered or come to mind. . . . No longer will there be in it an infant who lives but a few days, or an old man who does not live out his days; for the youth will die at the age of one hundred and the one who does not reach the age of one hundred shall be thought accursed. . . . They shall not labor in vain, or bear children for calamity; for they are the offspring of those blessed by the LORD, and their descendants with them. (Isa. 65:17, 20, 23)

Among Reformed commentators, there are generally two lines of interpretation for Isaiah 65:17–25. Amillennialists usually interpret it as a prophecy of the eternal state, while postmillennialists tend to interpret it as a description of blessings that are promised for the present millennial age. There seems to be evidence that this particular prophecy describes elements of both without clear distinction.[7]

1. *New Heavens and a New Earth.* This kind of language can be used as a description of ongoing change in the existing state of affairs (cf. 2 Cor. 5:17; Gal. 6:15), but it is also used to describe the state of affairs after the final judgment (2 Peter 3:13). In other words, there is an element of the new creation that is "already" fulfilled in the New Testament age as well as an element that is "not yet" fulfilled. During this period, there is an ongoing work of "re-creation" or sanctification.

2. *Preconsummation Conditions.* This prophecy describes conditions that can hardly apply to the eternal state. For example, birth, death, aging, time, sin, and accursedness are all mentioned in verse 20. Construction and agriculture are mentioned in verses 21 and 22. But although these are all elements of the preconsummation stage of the new creation, they are described as taking place in a radically restored creation.

3. *Edenic Conditions.* Verse 23 describes a state in which the original curse on labor and childbirth has been reversed and God's original purposes for creation are being fulfilled. God originally created man to have dominion over the earth and all the creatures of the earth (Gen. 1:26–28) and to have eternal union and communion with Him in Paradise (Gen. 2:15–17). This prophecy describes the accomplishment of that purpose.

This prophecy focuses on the restoration of God's original purposes for both man and creation. How does this provide support for a postmillennial eschatology? Since God's original purposes were for the human race and the world that exist now, the realization of those purposes requires their fulfillment and actualization in the same human race and the same world. In other words, this earth is the "stage" that God preserved for the outworking of His redemptive promises (Gen. 8:21–22; 9:11, 15). Therefore, unless clear evidence is presented to the contrary, our assumption should be that this earth is where all these promises will be fulfilled.

Worldwide Conversion

> "For I know their works and their thoughts; the time is com-ing to gather all nations and tongues. And they shall come and see My glory." . . . "For just as the new heavens and the new earth which I make will endure before Me," declares the LORD, "So your offspring and your name will endure. And it shall be from new moon to new moon and from sabbath to sabbath, all mankind will come to bow down before Me," says the LORD. (Isa. 66:18, 22–23)

Isaiah's prophecy concludes with a vision of worldwide conver-sion. As Motyer observes, "In New Testament perspective, this final section spans the first and second comings of the Lord Jesus Christ: his purpose for the world (18), his means of carrying it out (19–21), the *sign* set among the nations, the remnant sent to evangelize them (19) and the gathering of his people to 'Jerusalem' (20) with Gen-tiles in full membership (21)."[8] In other words, what we find in Isa-iah is a prophecy of the entire course of this present age. Once again we find the language of the Abrahamic promise fulfilled as we see "all nations and tongues" and "all mankind" worshiping the Lord of glory. And once again we must note that although the biblical word "all" is often used figuratively to mean "many" or "most," it seldom if ever means "few."

Jeremiah

Jeremiah was a prophet during the last years of the southern king-dom of Judah (c. 626–586). The history of God's people had, to this point, been one of repeated and persistent failure to live according to the stipulations of the covenant. By the time of Jeremiah's call, idolatry was widespread. In the midst of such wickedness, he announced the coming judgment of God upon the nation. This prophecy of judgment was fulfilled when Babylon invaded and conquered Judah. The final deportation of the people of Judah into exile was completed in 586. The prophecies of Jeremiah did not end, however, with judgment. He also had a message of hope, but it was a hope that would be realized only after the impending judgment (Jer. 29:11–14). Israel had been unable to fulfill the old covenant because it did not provide the power to produce the internal change necessary for obedience. But God promised to establish a new covenant with His people in which He Himself would bring about the necessary internal change of heart.

The New Covenant

> "Behold, days are coming," declares the LORD, "when I will make a new covenant with the house of Israel and with the house of Judah, not like the covenant which I made with their fathers in the day I took them by the hand to bring them out of the land of Egypt, My covenant which they broke, although I was a husband to them," declares the LORD. "But this is the covenant which I will make with the house of Israel after those days," declares the LORD, "I will put My law within them, and on their heart I will write it; and I will be their God, and they shall be My people." (Jer. 31:31–33)

The prophecy of the new covenant is universally recognized to be of fundamental importance to a proper understanding of redemptive history.[9] In it we find motifs and themes which affect not only our understanding of the events that will fulfill the prophecy itself, but also all of redemptive history leading up to that fulfillment. There are a number of important themes associated with the establishment of this new covenant:

1. *The Fulfillment of All Previous Covenant Promises.* Jeremiah specifically tells us that God's law will finally be obeyed (v. 33). The new covenant passage in Ezekiel 37:24–28 is even more clear, in that it promises the fulfillment of all the ear-

lier promises in the one new covenant. This passage indicates that the new covenant will include the coming of the promised King (the Davidic covenant), obedience to the law (the Mosaic covenant), the possession of the land, and the blessing of the nations (the Abrahamic covenant).

2. *The Internal Change in the Believer.* In the old covenant, God's law was external to the believer, written on tablets of stone (Ex. 31:18; 34:28–29; Deut. 4:13; 5:22) or in a book (Ex. 24:7). The unique aspect of the new covenant is that the law is inscribed on the hearts of the people (v. 33). It transforms a believer from within, rather than from without.

3. *The Finality of the New Covenant.* While the previous redemptive covenants were spoken of as "everlasting," which they are in that they are realized in the new covenant, the new covenant itself is spoken of in terms of finality (Jer. 50:5; cf. Isa. 61:8; Ezek. 37:26). It is not only the new covenant, but the last covenant. As O. Palmer Robertson observes, "Because it shall bring to full fruition that which God intends in redemption, it never shall be superseded by a subsequent covenant."[10]

What is the significance of this for our study of eschatology? The new covenant was inaugurated by Jesus Christ at His first coming and is being fulfilled in and through the church during this present age (Luke 22:20; 2 Cor. 3:4–6; Heb. 7:22; 8:6–13; 9:15; 10:14–18, 29; 12:22–24). It is the covenant of the age between the two advents. The institution of the new covenant does not await the start of the Millennium or the eternal state. Since the new covenant is the means by which God will finally and completely fulfill all previous covenant promises, and since the new covenant is specifically the covenant *of* the present age, these promises must be fulfilled *in* the present age.

Ezekiel

The prophet Ezekiel was one of the captives carried away into exile by Nebuchadnezzar. He witnessed and experienced firsthand the pouring out of the covenant curses upon the people of Israel. His ministry lasted approximately twenty-three years (c. 592–571). The message of Ezekiel focuses on two primary subjects. First, he explains the reasons for God's judgment upon His people. Second, he declares God's promises of future restoration. We shall briefly examine one of the most prominent of his restoration prophecies, his vision of the new temple.

The Temple of the Kingdom of God

After declaring prophecies of judgment on Jerusalem and the nation (chaps. 1–24) and on foreign nations (chaps. 25–32), Ezekiel turns to prophecies of restoration and mercy (chaps. 33–48). In chapters 40–48, he presents an extraordinarily detailed vision of the future reconstruction of the temple. Commentators have suggested several ways to understand this prophecy. The two most common interpretations in conservative eschatological literature are (1) the dispensationalist interpretation, which sees in these chapters a vision of a literal temple that will be constructed by the Messiah during the Millennium,[11] and (2) the figurative interpretation, which sees these chapters as a typological vision of the present church age.[12] The evidence for the figurative interpretation is weighty and has been explained in detail by Patrick Fairbairn.[13] The most decisive evidence in favor of this view may, however, be stated briefly. The vision itself includes numerous descriptions of atoning sacrifices (e.g., Ezek. 40:39; 43:19, 21, 22, 25; 44:27, 29; 45:15, 17, 22, 23, 25; 46:20) and other ceremonial laws whose literal reinstitution would directly contradict the New Testament (Heb. 10:18).[14] If these specific details of Ezekiel's prophecy must be understood symbolically, then the other details of this prophecy should also be understood symbolically.

It is beyond the scope of this book to examine this entire prophecy. We shall, however, focus our attention on one particular element of this vision. Ezekiel 47 contains an extraordinary vision of a river flowing outward from the new temple:

> Then he brought me back to the door of the house; and behold, water was flowing from under the threshold of the house toward the east, for the house faced east. . . . When the man went out toward the east with a line in his hand, he meas-

ured a thousand cubits, and he led me through the water, water reaching the ankles. Again he measured a thousand and led me through the water, water reaching the knees. Again he measured a thousand and led me through the water, water reaching the loins. Again he measured a thousand; and it was a river that I could not ford, for the water had risen, enough water to swim in, a river that could not be forded. . . . Then he said to me, "These waters go out toward the eastern region and go down into the Arabah; then they go toward the sea, being made to flow into the sea, and the waters of the sea become fresh. And it will come about that every living creature which swarms in every place where the river goes, will live. (Ezek. 47:1, 3–5, 8–9)

What is the meaning of this vision? The New Testament provides the keys necessary to understand the references to water in this prophecy. In John 7, Jesus declares that from the innermost being of those who believe in Him "shall flow rivers of living water" (7:38; cf. 3:5; 4:13–14). In the next verse, John explains that this water is a reference to the Holy Spirit. Earlier in John's gospel, Jesus declares Himself to be the true temple (2:19–21).[15] Jesus, then, is the true fulfillment of the temple prophecy of Ezekiel. And He is the One who, after His ascension to the right hand of God, sends forth the Spirit as the river of living water (cf. Acts 2:33). The river in Ezekiel begins as an ankle-deep trickle and gradually deepens until it reaches the depth of a large river. This is an astounding representation of the gradual increase of the Spirit's work in the present age.

Daniel

Daniel was carried into captivity in Babylon in 605. He rose to a position of prominence among the wise men of Chaldea and was ultimately made governor of Babylon. His book has two main sections. The first six chapters are historical narratives concerning Daniel and his companions. The last six chapters contain prophetic visions that were given to him. Within this small book, we find some of the most important eschatological passages in the Bible.

The Stone That Filled the Earth

> You, O king, were looking and behold, there was a single great
> statue; that statue, which was large and of extraordinary
> splendor, was standing in front of you, and its appearance was
> awesome. The head of that statue was made of fine gold, its
> breast and its arms of silver, its belly and its thighs of bronze,
> its legs of iron, its feet partly of iron and partly of clay. You
> continued looking until a stone was cut out without hands,
> and it struck the statue on its feet of iron and clay, and crushed
> them. Then the iron, the clay, the bronze, the silver and the
> gold were crushed all at the same time, and became like chaff
> from the summer threshing floors; and the wind carried them
> away so that not a trace of them was found. But the stone that
> struck the statue became a great mountain and filled the
> whole earth. . . . And in the days of those kings the God of
> heaven will set up a kingdom which will never be destroyed,
> and that kingdom will not be left for another people; it will
> crush and put an end to all these kingdoms, but it will itself
> endure forever (Dan. 2:31–35, 44).

This passage has significant eschatological implications. In Chapter 2 of Daniel, Nebuchadnezzar has a dream that his wise men cannot interpret. Eventually Daniel tells the king his dream and its interpretation. The dream is recounted in verses 31–35. Daniel tells the king about a giant statue made of different materials and about a stone that crushes it and grinds it to dust. In verses 36–45, Daniel interprets the dream. The four different sections of the statue represent four kingdoms, which we understand as follows:

1. *The head of gold*—the Babylonian Empire
2. *The breast and arms of silver*—the Medo-Persian Empire
3. *The belly and thighs of bronze*—the Greek Empire
4. *The legs of iron and the feet of iron and clay*—the Roman Empire

The stone represents the messianic kingdom of God. The fact that it struck the feet means, as E. J. Young explains, that it was "in the days of the last of the four that the kingdom of Messiah was set up."[16]

What are the characteristics of this messianic kingdom, according to Daniel? First, the kingdom of Christ was established during the Roman Empire. Its inauguration does not await some unknown future date. Second, it is a kingdom that will never be destroyed. In the words of Jesus, "The gates of hell shall not prevail against it" (Matt. 16:18 KJV). Third, it is destined to overcome all opposing kingdoms and grow into a kingdom that will fill all the earth. It is characterized by the gradual subjection of all the enemies of God. Fourth, the growth of the kingdom is gradual. The kingdom of God begins as a stone, but does not remain a stone, and it certainly does not shrink into a pebble. Instead, it grows into a mountain that fills the whole earth. This incredible prophecy of Daniel leaves us with solid grounds for faith in the progressive victory of the kingdom of Christ.

The Son of Man

> I kept looking in the night visions, and behold, with the clouds of heaven One like a Son of Man was coming, and He came up to the Ancient of Days and was presented before Him. And to Him was given dominion, glory and a kingdom, that all the peoples, nations, and men of every language might serve Him. His dominion is an everlasting dominion which will not pass away; and His kingdom is one which will not be destroyed. (Dan. 7:13–14)

Another intriguing prophecy is found in the seventh chapter of Daniel. In this vision, Daniel sees a succession of four beasts, which he interprets as four kingdoms (v. 17). These four kingdoms parallel those seen in Daniel 2.[17] After the vision of the four beasts, Daniel sees a vision of the throne room of God (vv. 9–12). He sees God seated upon a throne, and books are opened to pass judgment. That this is not a vision of the final judgment is made clear by two related considerations. First, verses 22 and 26 explicitly declare this to be a judgment against these human kingdoms during the kingdom of the fourth beast. Second, the result of this judgment is that dominion is taken away from the fourth beast and given to the ascended Son of Man

(vv. 12–14, 18, 22, 27). And what does Daniel describe happening in the throne room immediately following this judgment?

The vision recorded in verses 13–14 is claimed by premillennialists to be a prophecy of the second coming.[18] However, the context makes this interpretation impossible. Daniel sees this vision from the perspective of the throne room of God, not from the perspective of one on earth. The Son of Man, in these verses, comes up with the clouds of heaven to the Ancient of Days (cf. Acts 1:9), not down from the heavens. In other words, this is a vision of the ascension of Christ, not of His second coming (cf. Acts 2:30–31, 34–35).

After the Son of Man ascends to the Ancient of Days, He is presented before God and is given "dominion, glory and a kingdom, that all the peoples, nations, and men of every language might serve Him" (v. 14). His dominion will be "everlasting." His kingdom will not pass away or be destroyed.

This prophecy also speaks of the coreigning of the saints with Christ. Verse 18 declares, "But the saints of the Highest One will receive the kingdom and possess the kingdom forever, for all ages to come." Verses 21–22 repeat this truth: "I kept looking, and that horn was waging war with the saints and overpowering them until the Ancient of Days came, and judgment was passed in favor of the saints of the Highest One, and the time arrived when the saints took possession of the kingdom." In verses 26–27, it is made even clearer that Christ reigns simultaneously with His people:

> But the court will sit for judgment, and his [the little horn of the fourth kingdom] dominion will be taken away, annihilated and destroyed forever. Then the sovereignty, the dominion, and the greatness of all the kingdoms under the whole heaven will be given to the people of the saints of the Highest One; His kingdom will be an everlasting kingdom, and all the dominions will serve and obey Him.

The picture presented here, although not without difficulties of interpretation, can from a New Testament perspective be understood. It parallels Daniel 2 and adds additional insight into the nature of the kingdom of Christ. The prophecy of Daniel 7 may be summarized as follows:

1. Between the time of Daniel and the coming of the Messiah, four great kingdoms will arise and have dominion (Babylon, Medo-Persia, Greece, and Rome).
2. During the reign of the fourth kingdom (the Roman Empire), God will pass judgment on the kingdoms of man.
3. This judgment will coincide with the resurrection and ascension of Christ, at which time all dominion will be given to Him and His kingdom will be established.
4. Those who are "in Christ" will reign with Christ in this kingdom.
5. The "not yet" aspect of the kingdom is hinted at in verse 12, where it is said that although the kingdoms of man have been judged, "an extension of life was granted to them for an appointed period of time." In other words, their judgment is declared, but they are given a stay of execution.

In Daniel 7, the chorus, which has been repeated so many times throughout the prophets, reaches a glorious crescendo. Daniel not only tells us that the Messiah will reign someday, but also tells us when His kingdom will be established. He tells us that the saints will share in Christ's reign, and that there will be no boundaries to Christ's dominion. It will extend over all the kingdoms, peoples, and nations of the earth.

Joel

> And it will come about after this that I will pour out My Spirit on all mankind; and your sons and daughters will prophesy, your old men will dream dreams, your young men will see visions. . . . And I will display wonders in the sky and on the earth, blood, fire, and columns of smoke. The sun will be turned into darkness, and the moon into blood, before the great and awesome day of the LORD comes. (Joel 2:28, 30–31)

The date and occasion of the book of Joel are difficult to ascertain with any precision, for the author is identified only as "Joel, the son of Pethuel" (1:1). Most commentators today believe that the book of Joel was written in the early postexilic period (c. 520–500), but there is no consensus.[19] Despite the difficulties of determining the historical context, one prophecy in Joel demands our attention.

In chapter 1, Joel describes the recent devastation of the land by locusts and drought. In 2:1–17, he turns his attention to the impending day of the Lord, and in 2:18–27 he calls upon the people to repent. Then, in a passage that is rich in eschatological importance, he prophesies of the universal outpouring of the Spirit.

Joel's prophecy is God's answer to the cry of Moses, "Would that all the LORD's people were prophets, that the LORD would put His Spirit upon them!" (Num. 11:29). In the Old Testament, God's pouring out of His Spirit to empower people for ministry was generally limited to certain men chosen for special tasks (e.g., Ex. 35:30–35). But Joel tells us that one day God will pour out His Spirit on all mankind (vv. 28–29). In the following verses, Joel ties the gift of the Spirit to the dawn of the messianic age and a judgment upon the nations (3:1–15).

When did this messianic age dawn? In the New Testament, we are told that Pentecost was the fulfillment of Joel's prophecy (Acts 2:14–21). The Holy Spirit was poured out upon the disciples, and they began to prophesy (Acts 2:4). Significantly, Peter does not say that only the "outpouring" portion of the prophecy was fulfilled. In addition, he quotes the remainder of the passage, which uses the language of cosmic upheaval to describe God's judgment.[20] The parallel between this passage in Joel and Daniel 7 is striking. Daniel tells us of a judgment of the nations that coincides in time with the resurrection and ascension of Christ. Joel tells us of a judgment of the nations that occurs in connection with the outpouring of the Spirit. Joel does not tie this judgment of the nations to the receiving of the kingdom by the Messiah as clearly as Daniel does, but he does tell us what the results of this judgment will be:

> And it will come about in that day that the mountains will drip with sweet wine, and the hills will flow with milk, and all the brooks of Judah will flow with water; and a spring will go out from the house of the LORD, to water the valley of Shittim. (Joel 3:18)

When we compare Daniel 7 with Joel 2–3, we are given a much fuller picture of the complex of events surrounding the dawn of the messianic kingdom. Daniel tells us that during the reign of the fourth kingdom (Rome), the Messiah will come, there will be a judgment of the nations in which their dominion will be taken away from them, and all dominion and authority will be given to Christ. Joel adds that the universal outpouring of the Spirit will be connected with this judgment and enthronement. The result will be the dawn of the messianic age.

Zechariah

> Rejoice greatly, O daughter of Zion! Shout in triumph, O daughter of Jerusalem! Behold, your king is coming to you; He is just and endowed with salvation, humble, and mounted on a donkey, even on a colt, the foal of a donkey. And I will cut off the chariot from Ephraim, and the horse from Jerusalem; and the bow of war will be cut off. And He will speak peace to the nations; and His dominion will be from sea to sea, and from the River to the ends of the earth. (Zech. 9:9–10)

Like Joel, little is known about the prophet Zechariah other than his name. He was a contemporary of Haggai, another postexilic prophet (see Ezra 5:1; 6:14). Zechariah prophesied from the second to the fourth years of the reign of Darius I (520–518). His message was primarily intended to encourage God's people about Jerusalem and to point them toward a greater future.

The book of Zechariah is divided into two basic sections. Chapters 1–8 focus primarily upon encouraging Zechariah's own generation, while chapters 9–14 focus upon the future aspects of the kingdom of God. In chapter 9, verses 9–10, we are given a prophecy of the coming of Zion's king. The prophecy reminds us immediately of the patriarchal blessing and promise given to Judah:

> The scepter shall not depart from Judah, nor the ruler's staff from between his feet, until Shiloh comes, and to him shall be the obedience of the peoples. He ties his foal to the vine, *and his donkey's colt to the choice vine*; he washes his garments

in wine, and his robes in the blood of grapes. (Gen. 49:10–11, emphasis added)

Zechariah's allusion to the blessing of Judah in Genesis has a purpose. One of the earliest messianic prophecies in the Old Testament is directly linked with one of the last, illustrating beautifully the unity and development of God's redemptive purpose.

In the New Testament, we are told that Zechariah's prophecy was fulfilled when Jesus entered Jerusalem on a donkey (Matt. 21:1–8). By doing so, the Messiah demonstrated the unique nature of his rule. It is achieved not by bloody warfare, but by peaceful means. In verse 10, the realm of the king is described as extending "from sea to sea, and from the River to the ends of the earth." In this prophecy, we are assured that the prayer of Psalm 72, that our King's dominion will extend over the entire earth, will be fulfilled by the same One who humbly entered Jerusalem on the back of a donkey.

Conclusion

The promises made to Abraham and David found provisional fulfillment under the old covenant, but were never fully realized because of the sin of Israel. Yet these very promises provided grounds for hope in a future fulfillment. This hope, which had been expressed in the prayers and psalms of Israel, became a glorious vision in the prophets. Many of their prophecies shed additional light on the fulfillment of those promises:

1. *Isaiah 2*. In fulfillment of the promise to Abraham, all nations will be blessed through the worship of the true God. The elimination of warfare suggests the extraordinary scope of this conversion.
2. *Isaiah 9*. A child will be born who will be called "Mighty God." His kingdom will increase until He rules over all the earth.
3. *Isaiah 11*. The reign of the Messiah will result in the worldwide restoration of the created order.

4. *Isaiah 65*. The restoration of the created order will occur in time and history.
5. *Isaiah 66*. There will be a worldwide conversion of all nations and tongues.
6. *Jeremiah 31*. The new covenant, which will be inaugurated by Christ at His first coming, will include the realization of all the covenant promises in the interadvental age.
7. *Ezekiel 47*. The Lord, who along with His people is the new temple, will send forth His Spirit in the messianic age like a gradually increasing river.
8. *Daniel 2*. The messianic kingdom, established during the Roman Empire, will overcome all opposition and grow into a kingdom that will fill the whole earth.
9. *Daniel 7*. At the ascension of the Son of Man, the nations will be judged and the Messiah and His people will be given a kingdom that will have no boundaries.
10. *Joel 2*. The inauguration of the messianic kingdom will involve the universal outpouring of the Holy Spirit and the judgment of the nations.
11. *Zechariah 9*. The One whose right it is to rule, who has been promised since the time of the patriarchs, will come to Jerusalem humbly and establish a kingdom that will extend throughout the whole earth.

Throughout the Old Testament, the covenantal themes are repeated, developed, and expanded. The promises made to Abraham and David and the covenant stipulations of the Mosaic Law are the framework within which the authors of the Old Testament view their past, their present, and their future. Despite their sin, despite their failure, and despite all appearances to the contrary, they all point to a day when One will come who will bring about the full realization of all the promises. He will restore creation to its original purposes. He will bless all the families of the earth and inherit a land without boundaries. He will fulfill the righteous demands of the law. He will establish a kingdom that will fill the earth.

PART FOUR

New Testament Considerations

CHAPTER EIGHT

The Gospels and Acts

And Jesus came up and spoke to them, saying, "All authority has been given to Me in heaven and on earth. Go therefore and make disciples of all the nations, baptizing them in the name of the Father and the Son and the Holy Spirit, teaching them to observe all that I commanded you; and lo, I am with you always, even to the end of the age."
—Matthew 28:18–20

After the death of Malachi, the voice of prophecy ceased in Israel for almost four hundred years, but the ancient covenant promises of God were not forgotten. When we open the pages of the New Testament, the first words we see are, "The book of the genealogy of Jesus Christ, the son of David, the son of Abraham" (Matt. 1:1). With this one simple pronouncement, Matthew declares that the centuries-old promises given to Abraham and David are to be fulfilled in their son, Jesus the Messiah.[1] The way in which the Gospels and the book of Acts interpret Jesus' fulfillment of these covenant promises will be examined in this chapter.[2]

Matthew

Our understanding of the book of Matthew will have enormous implications for our understanding of eschatology because in this gospel every effort is made to demonstrate that Jesus is the long-awaited one who will fulfill the ancient covenant promises. It is through Jesus that God will finally fulfill His promises to bless all the families of the earth (cf. Matt. 2:1–2; 4:25; 8:11; 28:19–20) and establish the messianic kingdom forever (cf. 2:2; 27:11; 28:18).

The Birth and Preparation of Jesus

In the first chapters of Matthew, we are told of the birth and preparation of Jesus. In these early chapters, there are two themes that are repeatedly emphasized:

1. *Jesus is the new Israel.* Almost every section of these early chapters draws a parallel between an event in Jesus' life and an event in the history of Old Testament Israel.
    a. The circumstances surrounding Jesus' birth parallel those surrounding Moses' birth (Matt. 2:16; cf. Ex. 1:15–22).
    b. His flight into Egypt and his return from Egypt remind the reader of the same events in Israel's history (Matt. 2:13–15, 19–21).
    c. In His period of trial and temptation in the wilderness, He relives Israel's time of testing in the wilderness (Matt. 4:1–11).
2. *Jesus is the Son of God.* Several extraordinary events pertaining to the birth and preparation of Jesus show that he is more than a man.
    a. He is conceived by the Holy Spirit and born of a virgin (Matt. 1:18, 20).
    b. He is said to fulfill the promise of a child who would be named Immanuel, meaning "God with us" (Matt. 1:23; cf. Isa. 7:14).
    c. At His baptism, the Father declares from heaven that Jesus is His beloved Son (Matt. 3:17).

The declaration of the Father from heaven at Jesus' baptism is particularly significant because it distinctly echoes Isaiah 42:1 (cf. also Ps. 2:7). As Holwerda notes, "God promises in Isaiah 42 that he will place his spirit on this servant to qualify him for his messianic work and declares that this servant is his elect one, called in righteousness to bring the salvation of the covenant to the peoples of the world."[3] It is also noteworthy that Isaiah 42 is one of the Servant songs of Isaiah.[4] Commentators have argued for centuries over whether these songs refer to an individual or to the corporate nation of Israel. In light of Matthew's understanding of Jesus it seems best to interpret them as referring both to Israel and to the one who represents and renews Israel.[5] Jesus is God's anointed servant, the true Israel who will fulfill the role originally assigned to ethnic Israel by being the mediator of God's covenant blessings to the world.

After Jesus' baptism, He continues to relive Israel's history when He is led into the wilderness to be tested. In the first temptation, Jesus is challenged to live apart from the direction of the Word of God. In the second temptation, His trust in the covenant promises is tested. In the third temptation, He is offered the world if He will worship God's enemy. Israel failed all of these tests in her history, but in this wilderness test, Jesus is faithful. He demonstrates that He loves God with all His heart and soul and strength (Deut. 6:5).

These two recurrent themes—Jesus as the new Israel of God and Jesus as the Son of God—prepare us to see the remainder of the gospel and the entire New Testament not simply as a collection of edifying stories, but as the true good news. The promised Messiah, who will bring to realization all of the ancient covenant promises, has finally come. And His name is Jesus.

Public Ministry in Galilee

Immediately after Satan was defeated in the wilderness, Jesus went to the regions of Zebulun and Naphtali (Matt. 4:13). Matthew sees this ministry in light of the prophecy of Isaiah 9, which connects the birth of Immanuel with the blessing of the Gentiles. By means of this reference, Matthew tells us that God has begun the work of fulfilling His promise to gather the Gentiles (cf. 4:19; 13:47; 16:18–19). The content of Jesus' preaching is described concisely: "Repent, for the kingdom of heaven is at hand" (4:17). Holwerda sums up the significance of this pronouncement:

> The kingdom of God is at hand! That exciting note of fulfillment is heard immediately after Satan's defeat. Centuries of patient waiting have come to an end, and the blessings promised long ago can now, finally, be poured out on God's people. Jesus' ministry inaugurates a kingdom, God's kingdom, a kingdom not made with human hands, a kingdom of peace and justice that will stand forever (Daniel 2).[6]

Fulfillment of the Old Testament promises began in Galilee and will continue to the ends of the earth (Matt. 28:18).

In chapters 5–7, Jesus delivers the well-known Sermon on the Mount. In 5:3–12, a section of the sermon commonly referred to as the Beatitudes, Jesus pronounces the covenant blessings of the messianic kingdom. In the verses that follow, He pronounces the law of the messianic kingdom that goes forth from Zion (cf. Isa. 2:1–4). In Matthew 5:17, Jesus makes the significant statement, "Do not think that I came to abolish the Law or the Prophets; I did not come to abolish, but to fulfill." What does the fulfillment of the Law and the Prophets entail? Again Holwerda offers an invaluable insight:

> Fulfillment of prophecies means simply that the reality promised in the prophetic word becomes an actual event in human history. What then is the fulfillment of the law? Obviously this fulfillment happens when the righteousness articulated in the law similarly becomes reality in human history. The law is an articulation, under the specific circumstances in which Israel lived, of the righteousness that will cover the face of the earth. Therefore, fulfillment of the law entails a realization in history of the righteousness articulated in the law. To bring that about was the intention and achievement of Jesus' mission.[7]

Jesus did not come to abolish the law of God, as many today emphatically declare. He could not abolish it because it is the expression of the righteous and holy will of God. Instead, He came to make the righteousness revealed in it a reality throughout the entire earth. This had always been a promised part of the mission of the Messiah (cf. Isa. 9:6–7; Jer. 31:33; Ezek. 37:24).

The Lord's Prayer. In the midst of the Sermon on the Mount, Jesus teaches His disciples how to pray. This model prayer, called the Lord's Prayer, contains a petition that is important for our study of eschatology. Jesus tells the disciples:

> After this manner therefore pray ye: Our Father which art in heaven, Hallowed be thy name. Thy kingdom come. Thy will be done in earth, as it is in heaven. Give us this day our daily

bread. And forgive us our debts, as we forgive our debtors. And lead us not into temptation, but deliver us from evil: For thine is the kingdom, and the power, and the glory, for ever. Amen. (Matt. 6:9–13 KJV)

The third petition of the Lord's Prayer, "Thy will be done, on earth as it is in heaven," is significant. By telling the disciples to pray in this manner, Jesus instructs them (and us) to pray that God's will will actually be carried out *on earth* as it is carried out in heaven. This point may seem rather obvious and pedantic, but its implications are far-reaching:

1. The presently existing earth is a legitimate sphere of God's redemptive work.
2. There is good reason to expect the redemption of this earth if Jesus commands us to pray that God's will will be carried out on earth to the extent that it is carried out in heaven.
3. It is pointless to pray that God's will will be done on earth as it is done in heaven, if true obedience to God's will is permanently impossible on earth.
4. Jesus' command to pray this prayer indicates that it is God's plan to bring it to pass.

After declaring to Israel the righteous law of the messianic kingdom, Jesus in chapters 8 and 9 demonstrates the power of the kingdom to reverse the effects of sin in man's body and the effects of the curse on nature. In Matthew 8:16–17, Jesus grounds the reversal of all other effects of sin upon His atoning death. In other words, sin has affected much more than the heart of man. It has affected his soul, his body, and his environment. Because of one sin, the whole creation has been brought under God's curse. And it is on the basis of one work of redemption that the effects of the curse are lifted. Christ's atonement lays the foundation for the work of restoring all of man and all of creation.

After demonstrating the power of the messianic kingdom over the effects of sin, Jesus commissions his disciples to go throughout the country. Their mission is to bring the good news of the arrival of God's kingdom to the Jews and to invite them to come to their king. Sadly, most of the Jews refuse the invitation.

In chapters 11–13, Jesus begins to declare judgment upon the unbelieving nation of Israel, and he begins to explain an unexpected aspect of the messianic kingdom. The Jews have expected the kingdom to arrive fully and catastrophically in a single momentous event, but in the kingdom parables of chapter 13, Jesus tells His disciples that the coming of the kingdom will not occur as the Jews have expected. Two of these parables are especially significant for our study.

The Kingdom Parables

> He [Jesus] presented another parable to them, saying, "The kingdom of heaven is like a mustard seed, which a man took and sowed in his field; and this is smaller than all other seeds; but when it is full grown, it is larger than the garden plants, and becomes a tree, so that the birds of the air come and nest in its branches."
>
> He spoke another parable to them, "The kingdom of heaven is like leaven, which a woman took, and hid in three pecks of meal, until it was all leavened." (Matt. 13:31–33)

The importance of these parables for discerning the present nature of the covenantal kingdom is evident. Each of them illustrates a slightly different aspect of the kingdom, and both combine to emphasize one overarching point.

1. *The Mustard Seed.* The main point of this parable is that despite unimpressive beginnings, the messianic kingdom will grow until it is huge.
2. *The Leaven.* This parable illustrates the extensive, pervasive growth and influence of the kingdom.

R. T. France summarizes the primary teaching of the kingdom parables, saying that both

> focus on the paradox of insignificant or hidden beginnings and a triumphant climax. . . . To them [the disciples], and to us today who may expect God to act dramatically and without delay, Jesus points out that the full growth . . . is assured from

the moment the seed is sown, however unpromising its appearance and whatever opposition it may meet in its development. The way of God is not that of ostentation but of ultimate success.[8]

In the following chapters (13:54–16:20), we read of the varying responses to Jesus' teaching and healing. He is rejected in His home town of Nazareth (13:53–58) and by the religious leaders of Israel, the scribes and the Pharisees (15:1–14). Jesus repudiates the teachings of these leaders in 16:1–12. Then, in the climactic episode of Jesus' public ministry, His disciples confess their faith (16:13–20). Jesus asks them, "Who do people say that the Son of Man is?" The disciples answer, "Some say John the Baptist; some, Elijah; and others, Jeremiah, or one of the prophets." Jesus then asks them the most important question, "But who do you say that I am?" Peter replies, "Thou art the Christ, the Son of the living God." As a result of Peter's confession, Jesus makes a promise that we must not overlook.

The Promise to the Church

> And Jesus answered and said to him, "Blessed are you, Simon Barjona, because flesh and blood did not reveal this to you, but My Father who is in heaven. And I also say to you that you are Peter, and upon this rock I will build My church; and the gates of Hades shall not overpower it." (Matt. 16:17–18)

What significance does this promise have for our study of eschatology? There are several important points to note about this passage:

1. The word "Hades" here, as elsewhere in the Gospels, means hell.[9]
2. The phrase "gates of hell" symbolically represents the forces of Satan sent forth to attack the church.
3. Christ here promises that His church will be victorious over the forces of Satan.

Christ's promise of victory to the church is nothing new. As we have seen, this is a common thread that runs throughout the Old Testament. What is not as clear in the Old Testament promises is the intimate connection between the church and the kingdom. Vos explains that Matthew 16:18–20 reveals a unity between the two:

> We notice, first, that the Church and the Kingdom of God do not appear here as separate institutions. The figure of which our Lord avails Himself for speaking of the Church and speaking of the Kingdom closely unites the two. On Peter . . . He promises to build up the Church in the near future. This is the structure in building [i.e., being built], vs. 18. In vs. 19, however, still using the same figure of building, He promises to Peter the keys of administration in this structure when completed. Undoubtedly then, the Church and the Kingdom are in principle one, and all . . . distinctions . . . break down before the simple logic of this unavoidable exegesis.[10]

This unity helps us to understand why these promises of victory, which in the Old Testament were made regarding the kingdom of God, are now given to His church. The church is intimately connected and identified with the kingdom which Christ inaugurates and which will grow from a stone into a mountain that fills the whole earth.

Private Ministry in Galilee and Ministry in Judea

Following Peter's confession, Jesus begins to teach His disciples about His mission (16:21–17:27). He tells them that He must go to Jerusalem, suffer, be killed, and be raised up on the third day (16:21). In 17:1–13, Christ is transfigured before Peter, James, and John, and God speaks from heaven to dramatically confirm the truth confessed by Peter (17:5).

Soon after that, Jesus begins the journey to Jerusalem (19:1–20:34). On the way, He continues to heal multitudes, and He continues to be challenged by the Pharisees. He also continues to teach His disciples by means of parables, most notably the parable of the workers (20:1–16), in which He demonstrates the extraordinary and unexpected nature of God's generosity and grace.

In chapter 21, Jesus enters Jerusalem on the back of a donkey in fulfillment of Jacob's blessing and Zechariah's prophecy (Gen. 49:10–11; Zech. 9:9–10). The King to whom the scepter belongs has finally arrived. Immediately His authority is challenged and rejected by the religious leaders, who pose question after question in attempts to trap Him. Finally, in chapter 23, Jesus declares that the covenant curses will be poured out on this nation that has obstinately rejected Him. In verses 32–36, Jesus declares that this recalcitrant generation will receive the stored-up wrath of God. As in the days of Jeremiah, their house is soon going to be left desolate (v. 38; cf. Jer. 22:5).

The Olivet Discourse. Following the pronouncement of impending judgment on this generation of Jews who are rejecting their Messiah, Jesus leaves the temple, and His disciples begin to point out the magnificent buildings. Jesus tells them, "Truly I say to you, not one stone here shall be left upon another, which will not be torn down" (24:2). After proceeding with Jesus to the Mount of Olives across the valley from Jerusalem, the disciples ask Him about His statement: "Tell us, when will these things be, and what will be the sign of Your coming, and of the end of the age?" (24:3). In the remainder of chapters 24 and 25, Jesus answers their question.

The interpretation of Jesus' Olivet discourse will have profound effects upon any study of eschatology. Many erroneous eschatological theories are based upon a fundamentally flawed approach to this portion of God's word. For these reasons, we must approach this text carefully, keeping in mind the immediate context of Matthew and the broader context of Scripture as a whole. What follows is a summary of the main points of the discourse.[11]

The key to understanding the entire discourse is found in verse 34, in which Jesus tells His disciples, "Truly I say to you, this generation will not pass away until all these things take place." Jesus declares that his prophecy will be fulfilled before the generation to whom He is speaking passes away. In other words, the events of which he speaks in this passage will be fulfilled by A.D. 70, one generation from the date He made the pronouncement. We know that the phrase "this generation" refers to the generation of Jews to whom Jesus was speaking for these reasons:

1. Every other time this phrase is used in Matthew (in 11:16; 12:41, 42, 45; 23:36), it clearly refers to the generation of Jews to whom Jesus was speaking.

2. In the immediately preceding context, the same phrase clearly refers to the generation of Jews to whom Jesus is speaking (23:36).

3. The phrase is used in Matthew 24 in a discourse that is a response to a specific question by the disciples regarding the time of the temple's destruction (24:1–3).

Clearly, then, Jesus expected His pronouncement of impending judgment to be fulfilled within forty years. Incredibly, in one of the most amazing demonstrations of the truth of our Lord's prophetic office, the nation of Israel was judged and the temple was destroyed within the time frame announced by Jesus. In A.D. 70, after a prolonged battle, Jerusalem was sacked by the Roman armies and every stone of the temple was thrown down.

But did the signs of which Jesus spoke actually occur prior to that? In order to answer this question, we must examine the signs themselves.

False Christs, Wars, and Rumors of Wars (24:4–6). There were a number of false messiahs between A.D. 30 and 70, according to both Scripture (see 1 John 2:18) and history. According to Josephus, the country was full of false messiahs.[12] During this same period of time, there were wars in Germany, Africa, Thrace, Gaul, Britain, and Armenia.

Famines, Pestilences, and Earthquakes (24:7). Scripture and history also record numerous famines during this forty-year period (see Acts 11:27–29; Rom. 15:25–28; 1 Cor. 16:1–5). Pestilence was widespread in both Jerusalem and Rome, according to the historians Josephus, Suetonius, and Tacitus. Earthquakes were recorded in Crete, Smyrna, Miletus, Chios, Samos, Laodicea, Hierapolis, Colossae, Campania, Rome, Judea, Pompeii, and many other locations.

Persecution, Apostasy, and Lawlessness (24:9–12). The testimony of Scripture bears abundant witness to the persecution (Acts 4:3; 5:40; 7:54–60; 8:1; 9:1; 12:1–2; 14:19), apostasy (Acts 20:29–30; 2 Cor. 11:13; Gal. 1:6; 2:4; 2 Tim. 1:15; Titus 1:10–16; 2 Peter 2:1–3; 1 John 2:18–19; 4:1; 2 John 7), and lawlessness (1 Cor. 5:1–2; 2 Tim. 3:8–9) of these years.

Gospel Witness to the Whole World (24:14). First, it must be noted that the word "world" in this verse translates the Greek word *oikoumene*, which often refers to the Roman Empire (cf. Luke 2:1; Acts 11:28; 24:5). As Kenneth Gentry points out, "The western hemisphere is not in view in . . . Matthew 24:14."[13] Second, the phrase "all the nations" in this context refers to all the nations of the Roman Empire. Third, this witness was primarily a witness to the Jews scattered throughout the Roman Empire that Jesus is the Messiah (cf. Acts 21:21; 24:5). The destruction of Jerusalem would prove the truth of this witness. Fourth, the prophecy is one of worldwide witness, not necessarily worldwide conversion. Fifth, the fulfillment of this gospel mission is recorded in Scripture itself. It began with Peter's sermon to Jews from across the Empire on Pentecost (Acts 2:5) and is spoken of by Paul as having been fulfilled (Rom. 10:18; Col. 1:6, 23).

The Abomination of Desolation and the Flight of Christians (24:15–20). A simple comparison with the parallel passage in Luke 21:20 reveals that the "abomination of desolation" is the destruction of Jerusalem by the Roman armies, who set up their ensigns and offered pagan sacrifices in the temple before tearing down every stone of this building. The flight of Christians from the city before the final siege occurred during an unexpected and temporary withdrawal of the Roman armies. History tells us that many of these Christians fled to a rock fortress in Pella, which is about sixty miles northeast of Jerusalem.

Great Tribulation (24:21–22). There are a number of reasons why this passage should also be interpreted as referring to the destruction of Jerusalem in A.D. 70. First, Jesus said that this great tribulation would occur within the lifetime of those to whom He was speaking (v. 34). Second, the final destruction of the temple had far greater covenantal significance than any other tribulation the Jews have ever suffered. Third, Matthew 23 indicates that this was the judgment of God that had been stored up and reserved for this wicked generation that rejected the Messiah (cf. Luke 19:41–44). Fourth, this verse cannot be interpreted absolutely literally, because there was at least one tribulation that entailed far greater destruction than that referred to in Matthew 24 on any interpretation—the Flood (Gen. 6–8), which destroyed all but one family on earth. Fifth, the language Jesus uses is common prophetic language referring to judgment (see Ex. 11:6; Ezek. 5:9; Dan. 9:12; 12:1; Joel 2:2). The "great tribulation" was the destruction of Jerusalem and the temple in A.D. 70.

False Reports of Christ's Coming (24:23–26). Because the disciples' original question contained some erroneous assumptions, Jesus tells them that when God's judgment upon this evil generation begins, He will not be coming back *visibly*. This will be a coming of Christ in judgment, not a visible coming (cf. Isa. 19:1).

The Judgment Coming of Christ (24:27–28). The fact that this coming in judgment was to occur in the first century is verified by the fact that Jesus tells the Sanhedrin that they will witness His coming (26:63–64; cf. 27:25). The mention of lightning seems to indicate both the direction from which the armies approached Jerusalem and the sudden nature of this destruction (cf. 2 Sam. 22:14–15; Ps. 18:9–15; Ezek. 21:1–10). The reference to corpses in verse 28 indicates the horrible devastation that the outpouring of the covenant curses will bring (cf. Deut. 28:26).

The Sun, Moon, and Stars (24:29). This is common prophetic language, which was used many times in the Old Testament to describe judgments upon nations that were fulfilled long ago (cf. Isa. 13:10; 34:4–5; Ezek. 32:7; Amos 8:9).

The Sign of the Son of Man (24:30). The Greek text of this verse does not state that the Son of Man will appear in the heavens. Rather, what appears is the *sign* of the Son of Man in heaven. In other words, the destruction of Jerusalem will be the sign that the Son of Man, who prophesied this destruction, is in heaven. The "tribes of the earth" who mourn are either the Jewish tribes in the "land" (*ge* in Greek) or the Jewish tribes scattered throughout the Empire. The "coming" of the Son of Man is His coming in judgment upon Jerusalem (see vv. 23–28), which is intimately connected with His ascension to the right hand of God (cf. Dan. 7:13–14).

The Gathering of the Elect (24:31). The word translated "angels" in this verse is the same word that means human "messengers" elsewhere (e.g., Matt. 11:10; Mark 1:2; Luke 7:24; 9:52), and there is no reason to assume that it cannot mean human messengers here. This prophecy was fulfilled on the Day of Pentecost when Christ sent His messengers to Jews and to Gentiles in all parts of the world with the goal of gathering His elect (cf. Acts 1:7–8; 28:28).

The Fig Tree (24:32–33). The parable of the fig tree does not refer to the restoration of the nation of Israel in 1948. In the parallel passage in Luke 21:29, Jesus refers to "the fig tree, and all the trees." The point that Jesus is making is that when the disciples see these things beginning to occur, they should know that His coming in judgment upon Jerusalem is near.

The Time Text (24:34–35). In these verses, Jesus assures His hearers that all of these things will take place within one generation. In verse 35, He guarantees the truthfulness of His pronouncement.[14]

Thus we see that the "great tribulation" spoken of by Jesus is not something in *our* future. It occurred when Jerusalem and the temple were destroyed in A.D. 70. The Olivet discourse has important implications for the millennial question. As we shall see, many of the most common objections to postmillennialism are based on futurist interpretations of this discourse. They argue that Matthew 24 points to worsening conditions and great apostasy before the coming of the Son of Man. But if these things have already occurred in connection with the coming of Christ in judgment on Jerusalem in A.D. 70, then they have no bearing on the repeated promises of victory for the gospel in this age.

The Death and Resurrection of Jesus

After delivering the Olivet discourse, Jesus begins to prepare Himself and the disciples for His impending death. In Matt. 26:6–13, Jesus is anointed for burial, and in verses 14–16 one of Jesus' disciples joins the plot to deliver Him over to the religious authorities. In 26:17–30, we read of the Last Supper and the declaration of the inauguration of the new covenant. After the Last Supper, Jesus is arrested by the authorities (26:47–56), brought up on false charges, and tried by the Jews (26:57–68).

In Matthew 27:1–26, Jesus is transferred to the Roman governor, tried, and sentenced to death by crucifixion. In all of this, He fulfills the prophecies of the Old Testament (see Ps. 22; Isa. 53). Jesus is crucified (27:32–44), dies on the cross (vv. 45–56), and is buried in a tomb (vv. 57–61). Then, after three days, He rises from the dead (28:1–10). At Galilee, the risen Lord gathers His disciples and gives them the commission that is to be the means of fulfilling the covenant promises to bless all the families of the earth.

The Great Commission

And Jesus came up and spoke to them, saying, "All authority has been given to Me in heaven and on earth. Go therefore and make disciples of all the nations, baptizing them in the name of the Father and the Son and the Holy Spirit, teaching them to observe all that I commanded you; and lo, I am with you always, even to the end of the age." (Matt 28:18–20)

In the Great Commission, we find a pronouncement of the instrumental means by which Christ will fulfill all of the great covenant promises of the Old Testament. The Son of Man is exalted to the right hand of God and is given all authority and dominion and a kingdom that will extend over the earth. All of His power and authority is put behind the command to disciple the nations, thereby bringing the covenant blessing to all families of the earth. Israel was given the responsibility of being the mediator of God's blessing to all nations in the Old Testament, but she failed. Christ has now been given this same responsibility, which He delegates to His people, the church.[15] With the power and authority of Christ the King behind the command, and with the outcome resting in His hands, ultimate failure is not possible.

Acts

The book of Acts was written by Luke the physician and companion of Paul sometime before the destruction of Jerusalem in A.D. 70. The book provides a history of the development and growth of the Christian church and the ongoing fulfillment of God's covenant promises in the decades following the death of Christ. It also provides the historical context for the epistles that follow in the New Testament. There are a number of significant passages in Acts which shed additional light on our study of eschatology.

A Visible Second Coming

And after He [Jesus] had said these things, He was lifted up while they were looking on, and a cloud received Him out of their sight. And as they were gazing intently into the sky while He was departing, behold, two men in white clothing stood beside them; and they also said, "Men of Galilee, why do you stand looking into the sky? This Jesus, who has been taken up from you into heaven, will come in just the same way as you have watched Him go into heaven" (Acts 1:9–11).

We noted in our discussion of the Olivet discourse that there are numerous references to a coming of Christ for judgment upon Jerusalem, which happened in A.D. 70. These passages are to be distinguished from those that refer to Christ's visible coming at the consummation of all things, such as Acts 1:9–11. There are several aspects of this passage that must be noted.

1. Jesus ascended into heaven visibly in a cloud of glory. The description of what happened when He was presented before the Father is found in Daniel 7:13–14. He was officially given an everlasting dominion, glory, and a kingdom, in order that all peoples, nations, and tongues would serve Him.
2. At some point in time, Jesus will return as visibly as He ascended. Christ came invisibly in judgment upon Jerusalem in A.D. 70, and He is invisibly present with us until the end of the age (Matt. 28:20). But He will someday return visibly when the work of the kingdom is completed.
3. The time frame for His return is hinted at in the preceding context. The disciples are given a commission to be Christ's witnesses "in Jerusalem, and in all Judea and Samaria, and even to the remotest part of the earth" (v. 8). The implication is that Christ's visible return will follow the completion of the mission to the remotest part of the earth.

Fulfillment of the Davidic Covenant

And so, because he [David] was a prophet, and knew that God had sworn to him with an oath to seat one of his descendants upon his throne, he looked ahead and spoke of the resurrection of the Christ, that He was neither abandoned to Hades, nor did His flesh suffer decay. This Jesus God raised up again, to which we are all witnesses. . . . For it was not David who ascended into heaven, but he himself says: "The Lord said to

my Lord, 'Sit at My right hand, until I make Thine enemies
a footstool for Thy feet.'" Therefore let all the house of Israel know for certain that God has made Him both Lord and
Christ—this Jesus whom you crucified. (Acts 2:30–36)

In his sermon on the Day of Pentecost, Peter declared that Jesus
had fulfilled the covenant promises made to David. He pointed to the
resurrection and ascension of Christ as the historical fulfillment of this
promise. The important point for our study is that the inauguration
of the messianic kingdom does not await the future return of Christ.
Jesus has already been seated at the right hand of God on the throne
of David, and, in fulfillment of Psalm 110, He will remain there until
all of His enemies are made a footstool for His feet.

Salvation to the End of the Earth

Paul and Barnabas spoke out boldly and said, ". . . we are turning to the Gentiles. For thus the Lord has commanded us, 'I
have placed You as a light for the Gentiles, that You should
bring salvation to the end of the earth.'" (Acts 13:46–47)

In Acts 13, Paul and Barnabas are sent out from Antioch to
spread the gospel. They arrive first on the island of Cyprus (vv. 4–12)
and then travel to Pisidian Antioch (vv. 13–52). While there, Paul
addresses the synagogue on the Sabbath (vv. 16–41), declaring that
Jesus is the Messiah. However, because of the strong Gentile interest
in the message, the Jews are provoked and begin reviling Paul and
Barnabas (vv. 44–46). Paul's response (vv. 46–47) provides some insight into the nature of the messianic kingdom.

Paul tells the Jews that he and Barnabas are now taking their message to the Gentiles. Then he quotes, as a command from the Lord,
a passage found in two of the Servant songs of Isaiah, "I have placed
You as a light for the Gentiles" (cf. Isa. 42:6; 49:6). As we have seen,
these Servant songs are ultimately fulfilled in Jesus, who is the true
Servant of God. God tells the Servant that He will be placed as a light
to the nations in order to accomplish a goal. The goal of the Servant
is to open blind eyes and bring salvation to the end of the earth (cf.
Acts 15:14–18).

Here in Acts, this Servant song is applied to the disciples of Jesus. Because of their covenantal union with Him, the body of Christ shares His mission and goal. As in the Great Commission, Christ delegates His authority and His task of bringing salvation to the end of the earth to His church. He will accomplish His purposes through the work of His body. The church, in union with the Messiah, has been placed as a light to the Gentiles for the purpose of bringing the covenant blessings of salvation to all the families of the earth.

Conclusion

The ancient covenant promises that were the foundation for redemptive history, the messianic Psalms, and the prophecies of the Old Testament find their fulfillment in Jesus Christ, the son of David and the son of Abraham. He is the promised Messiah, the One who will bring blessing to all families of the earth and whose kingdom will grow to fill the entire earth. We have learned in this overview of the Gospels and Acts:

1. Jesus is the Messiah, the son of David and the son of Abraham, who fulfills all of the Old Testament covenant promises.

2. His messianic kingdom has already been inaugurated, and He has already been seated at the right hand of God and given all authority in heaven and on earth.

3. The messianic kingdom, although barely visible at its beginning, will grow and overcome all Satanic opposition because God's purpose is that His will be done on earth as it is in heaven.

4. Christ came in judgment upon the first-century generation of Jews, in what He said would be "the great tribulation."

5. Although Israel failed to fulfill her calling, Jesus the Messiah will successfully accomplish it through His body, the church.

6. This calling is to be the mediator of the covenant blessings of salvation, which must be brought to all families of the earth.

7. After this mission has been successfully completed, Jesus will visibly return to earth.

In the Gospels, we meet Jesus the Messiah, born King of the Jews. He is the One who is restoring all things to their original purpose. He is fulfilling the Abrahamic covenant and bringing the blessings of salvation to all the families of the earth. He is fulfilling the Davidic covenant and has inaugurated the messianic kingdom, which will grow to fill the whole earth. He is fulfilling the new covenant, writing the law of God on the hearts of His people and giving them the Holy Spirit that they might obey. He is the covenantal head of His church, through whom He is accomplishing His purposes. In Jesus, all the promises of God will certainly be fulfilled.

CHAPTER NINE

The Epistles

Then comes the end, when He delivers up the kingdom to the God and Father,
when He has abolished all rule and all authority and power. For He must reign
until He has put all His enemies under His feet.
—1 Corinthians 15:24–25

In the New Testament epistles, we find the definitive apostolic witness to the risen Christ and His ongoing fulfillment of the covenant promises. These letters were occasional in nature, generally written to specific individuals or congregations in order to address specific issues that had arisen in the church. Yet each letter also contributes a unique perspective and insight into the person and work of Jesus the Messiah. Many of these epistles also contribute significantly to our understanding of the nature of the messianic kingdom.

Romans

The eschatological significance of Romans 9–11 and what, if anything, it teaches about the future of the Jews, is a hotly debated issue among conservative Christian commentators and theologians. What follows will not settle this debate, but two points must be made in order to correct several recurring misconceptions. First, the truth or falsity of postmillennialism does not rest upon a particular interpretation of this passage. As we have seen, postmillennialism rests upon themes that are woven throughout the Scriptures. Second, the interpretation of this passage has been too narrowly focused upon the words "all Israel" in 11:26. As we will see, this verse is simply the culmination of an argument that Paul has been developing for several chapters, and its interpretation depends upon what precedes it. In order to understand what Paul is teaching, we must begin by carefully examining the context.

The theme of Paul's letter to the church at Rome is the gospel of Christ (Rom. 1:16–17). The book contains the fullest discussion of the gospel and its implications in the New Testament.[1] Paul develops his theme logically and systematically, beginning with the declaration of the universal reign of sin over both Jew and Gentile (1:18–3:20). He continues with an explanation of justification by faith (3:21–4:25), using as an example the faith of Abraham (4:1–25).

In chapters 5–8, Paul discusses the life of those who have been justified by faith. It is characterized by peace with God (chap. 5), sanctification (chap. 6), freedom from the condemnation of the law (chap. 7), and the indwelling of the Holy Spirit (chap. 8). At the conclusion of chapter 8, Paul grounds the certainty of the Christian's hope on the purpose and love of God (8:28–39), saying finally, "For I am convinced that neither death, nor life, nor angels, nor principalities, nor things present, nor things to come, nor powers, nor height, nor depth, nor any other created thing, shall be able to separate us from the love of God, which is in Christ Jesus our Lord" (8:38–39).

An obvious question arises in light of all that Paul has said thus far. Throughout the Old Testament, God declares His purpose and love for Israel (e.g., Deut. 7:6–7; Jer. 31:3, 35–37), yet Israel has rejected the Messiah. As Cranfield points out, the implications are serious, because if God's purpose and love for Israel have failed, "then what sort of a basis for Christian hope is God's purpose" and "what reliance can be placed on Paul's conviction that nothing can separate us from God's love in Christ (v. 38f.)?"[2]

The purpose of chapters 9–11, therefore, is to demonstrate that, in spite of Israel's rejection of the gospel, God's promises have not failed. Paul has already alluded to this fact in 3:3–4, emphatically telling us that the unbelief of the Jews has not nullified the faithfulness of God. In chapters 9–11, he develops this theme in greater detail by giving a twofold answer to the questions that arise from his statements in chapters 1–8. In summary, his answers to the problem of Israel's unbelief are:

1. God's faithfulness is upheld because Israel's rejection is not *total*. The promises were never made to all of the *natural* descendants of Abraham, but instead to the *true* Israel, and even now there is a remnant of natural Israel being saved (9:6–13; 11:5, 7).
2. God's faithfulness is upheld because Israel's rejection is not *final*. The fulfillment of the promises will go beyond the mere preservation of a remnant. God's love for national Israel remains unchanged for the sake of the fathers (11:28), because the gifts and calling of God are irrevocable (11:29).[3]

Douglas Moo has provided an excellent outline of the overall structure of Paul's defense of these two answers in chapters 9–11:

9:1–5—Introduction of the issue Paul seeks to resolve: the Jews' failure to embrace the gospel (vv. 1–3) calls into question the value of the privileges and promises God has given them (vv. 4–5).

9:6–29—Defense of the proposition in v. 6a—"the word of God has not failed." Paul argues that God's word never promised salvation to all the biological descendants of Abraham (9:6b–13). Salvation is never a birthright, even for Jews, but always a gift of God's electing love (vv. 14–23), a gift he is free to bestow on Gentiles as well as Jews (vv. 24–29).

9:30–10:21—. . . Paul uses his understanding of the gospel to explain the surprising turn in salvation history, as Jews are cast aside while Gentiles stream into the kingdom.

11:1–10—. . . Paul summarizes the situation of Israel as he has outlined in the previous two sections and prepares for the next section by affirming the continuation of Israel's election.

11:11–32—. . . Paul argues that Israel's current hardened state is neither an end in itself nor is it permanent. God is using Israel's casting aside in a salvific process that reaches out to Gentiles and will include Israel once again.

11:33–36—Response to the teaching of Rom. 9–11 with extolling of God's transcendent plan and doxology.[4]

As we examine some of the details of Paul's argument, the context and structure of the passage must always be kept before us. In 9:1–5, Paul expresses his profound grief over Israel's rejection of their Messiah. To them belong the adoption, the glory, the covenants, the giving of the Law, the temple, the promises, and the fathers. But they have rejected Jesus Christ who fulfills all of these.

In light of Israel's rejection of their Messiah, Paul declares, "But it is not as though the word of God has failed" (v. 6a), and then explains why: "For they are not all Israel who are descended from Israel; neither are they all children because they are Abraham's descendants" (vv. 6b–7). Using the illustration of Jacob and Esau, Paul demonstrates that the covenant promises were never based upon mere physical descent from Abraham (vv. 7–13). Instead, God's mercy and grace are always given on the basis of His sovereign election (vv. 14–23), and He has always intended to bestow His mercy upon the Gentiles as well as the Jews (vv. 24–29).

In 9:30–33, Paul explains why only a remnant of Israel has been saved. The Jews pursued righteousness by works rather than by faith and stumbled over Christ, who is the "stumbling stone." In the first verse of chapter 10, however, Paul declares, "Brethren, my heart's desire and my prayer to God for them is for their salvation." He prays for the salvation, not of the remnant who are already saved, but for the rest of Israel who have remained hardened. In verses 2–4, Paul laments that these Jews have sought to establish a righteousness of their own rather than subject themselves to the righteousness of God. In verses 5–15, Paul declares that Christ is the fulfillment of redemptive history and that the gospel is for both Jews and Gentiles. Then, in the concluding verses of chapter 10, he begins to introduce an unexpected aspect of redemptive history, namely, that the Jews would largely reject their Messiah and be set aside while the covenant blessings go out to the Gentiles (vv. 16–21).

Paul begins chapter 11 with a significant and emphatic pronouncement. Having said that ethnic Israel has rejected her Messiah, he asks, "I say then, God has not rejected His people, has He? May it never be!" (11:1). Repeating what he has said in 9:6–13, 27, Paul explains that a remnant of the Jews has been saved, not on the basis of works, but on the basis of God's sovereign electing grace (vv. 2–6). The chosen remnant has obtained salvation, and the rest have been hardened (vv. 7–10). This alone would demonstrate that God is faithful and has not rejected His people Israel. However, Paul then begins to explain that the hardening of the greater part of Israel has a purpose and that it is not permanent.

Turning his attention back to the Jews who have rejected Christ, Paul asks and then answers a rhetorical question: "I say then, they did not stumble so as to fall, did they? May it never be!" (11:11a; cf. 9:32–33). For the remainder of the chapter, Paul deals with the majority of the natural descendants of Abraham who have stumbled over Christ. He explains the purpose for their rejection, and he points toward their future acceptance.

Several times in the remainder of this chapter, Paul explains the purpose and future of ethnic Israel in three stages. In verse 11, he explains that their transgression occurred in order that salvation might come to the Gentiles, and that the salvation of the Gentiles was intended by God to make ethnic Israel jealous. In verse 12, Paul outlines the three steps in the outworking of God's purpose: (1) Israel's transgression and failure, (2) riches for the Gentiles, (3) Israel's fullness, which entails more riches.

In verses 13–14, Paul explains to the Gentiles that he magnifies his ministry to them in order to make his countrymen jealous and pursue their salvation. Then in verse 15, he again explains God's purpose for their rejection of Christ: (1) their rejection leads to (2) the reconciliation of the world, which will lead to (3) their acceptance, which will be "life from the dead." In verses 16–24, Paul explains this development in redemptive history by using the analogy of an olive tree. The olive tree represents the covenant people of God. In verse 17, Paul tells us that the greater part of ethnic Israel, which has rejected the Messiah, consists of "branches" that have been broken off. Believing Gentiles are "wild olive branches" that have been grafted into the good olive tree (vv. 17–19). Paul warns the Gentiles not to boast about this new state of affairs because it has been done on the basis of God's grace (vv. 20–21). Then in verses 22–24, Paul uses the illustration of the olive tree to review the three stages again: (1) severity to those who have fallen (hardened

Israel), (2) God's kindness to you (Gentiles), and (3) natural branches grafted in again.

In verses 25–26, Paul refers to what he has been discussing since verse 11 as a "mystery." He then repeats the threefold process he has been setting forth throughout the chapter: (1) a partial hardening has happened to Israel, (2) until the fullness of the Gentiles comes in, (3) and thus all Israel will be saved. The word "thus" in verse 26, translated from the Greek *houtos*, indicates the manner in which "all Israel will be saved."[5] It refers to the historical process that Paul has outlined several times in verses 11–24. As Douglas Moo notes,

> God imposes a hardening on most of Israel while Gentiles come into the messianic salvation, with the Gentiles' salvation leading in turn to Israel's jealousy and her own salvation. But this means that *houtos*, while not having a temporal *meaning*, has a temporal *reference:* for the manner in which all Israel is saved involves a process that unfolds in definite stages.[6]

Paul, then, is saying that all Israel will be saved in the temporal manner that he has outlined throughout this chapter.

In verses 28–29, Paul explains that although ethnic Israelites are now enemies for the sake of the Gentiles, they remain beloved from the standpoint of God's choice. The reason is that the gifts and calling of God are irrevocable. The present calling of the Gentiles does not change the fact that ethnic Israel was originally called. In verses 30–32, Paul sums up the teaching of the entire chapter. The situation of the Gentiles and the Jews is paralleled. The Gentiles were once disobedient, but through the *transgression* of the Jews, the Gentiles have been shown mercy (v. 30). The Jews are now disobedient, and because of the *mercy* shown the Gentiles, now the Jews may be shown mercy as well (v. 31). Both Jew and Gentile have been shut up in disobedience, in order that both Jew and Gentile may be shown mercy (v. 32).

Because of the controversy surrounding its interpretation, we must look briefly at verse 26. Who is "all Israel" in verse 26? Three interpretations have been offered by conservative commentators: (1) the community of the elect, including both Jews and Gentiles, (2) the elect remnant within Israel throughout history, or (3) ethnic Israel. The first option was taught by a number of authors at the time of the Reformation, including John Calvin. As Charles Hodge explains, because this passage was used by various millennial sects as the basis for extravagant claims, many commentators attempted "to explain away its prophetic character almost entirely."[7] In attempting to curb one exegetical extreme, they went to another. The exegetical impossibility of this interpretation is demonstrated by several considerations:

1. *The immediate context.* One of the most basic rules of interpretation is that context determines the meaning of individual words. In verse 25, Paul writes, "A partial hardening has happened to Israel." The word "Israel" in verse 25 must refer to ethnic Israel, not the church. Verse 26 is a continuation of the same sentence and uses the same word "Israel." There is no indication in the immediate context that the word changes its meaning in the midst of the sentence.

2. *The proximate context.* Throughout 11:11–32, there is a constant differentiation between ethnic Israel and the Gentiles. Several times up to this point, Paul has taught that the greater part of ethnic Israel has stumbled in order that the Gentiles might receive salvation, which in turn will lead to the jealousy of ethnic Israel and their salvation. Paul is countering the arrogance of Gentile Christians who are assuming that ethnic Israel's stumbling is a complete fall (11:11).

3. *The covenant context.* As Paul indicates by his quotation of Isaiah 59:20–21 and 27:9, "the deliverance promised of old . . . included much more than the conversion of the comparatively few Jews who believed in Christ at the advent."[8] The covenant blessings are to be brought to all the nations and families of the earth, including ethnic Israel (cf. 11:28–29).

According to the second interpretation, "all Israel" in verse 26 refers only to the elect remnant within Israel throughout history. This option is more plausible than the first, but it also fails to do justice to the text. There are a number of reasons why this interpretation is not valid:

1. *The immediate context.* This interpretation has the same difficulties explaining verse 25 that the first interpretation has. There is simply no contextually rational explanation for a change in the meaning of the word "Israel" in the middle of this sentence. At the very least, "all Israel" in verse 26 must include the hardened Israel of verse 25.

2. *The proximate context.* The subject of 11:11–32 as a whole is the Jews who have stumbled. The antecedent of "they" in verse 11 is the hardened Israelites in verse 7, who are explicitly *distinguished* from the remnant. Furthermore, the word "some" in verse 17 indicates that the branches which were broken off are *only* the hardened Israelites, not the remnant who remained in the tree. At least thirty-one times in these verses, Paul refers specifically to hardened Israel. They, and not the remnant, are the subject of this passage.

3. *The time reference of 11:11–32.* The main point of this passage is that the hardening of ethnic Israel as a people is *temporary.* Their rejection is not permanent. It continues *until* the fullness of the Gentiles has come in. At that point, ethnic Israel will be restored (cf. vv. 12, 15, 24, 25).

We are left with the third interpretation, that "all Israel" who will be saved in verse 26 is the same "Israel" that is said to be partially hardened in verse 25. "All Israel" refers to the people as a whole, who have been hardened. But will "all Israel" be saved in the future? The evidence for this is as follows:

1. As we have already pointed out, the word translated "thus" in verse 26 has a temporal reference. It refers to the manner in which ethnic Israel will be saved, which includes the three historical stages that Paul has mentioned several times in this passage (vv. 12, 15, 22–24).

2. The acceptance of "all Israel" is spoken of in contrast to the situation as it existed in Paul's day and as it exists in ours, when Israel as a people remains "rejected."

3. The temporal reference is also found in the immediate context. In verse 25, Paul says that the hardening of Israel will continue *until* the fullness of the Gentiles comes in.

The common objection to the view that Romans 11:11–32 refers to a future massive restoration of the people of Israel as a whole to the covenant blessings of salvation is that it does not account for the multitudes of Jews who for two thousand years have died rejecting Christ. This objection, however, fails to take into account an important aspect of God's covenant dealings with man. Willem Van Gemeren explains:

> Prophets often ask one generation to participate by faith in a salvation that lies in the distant future. . . . The Old Testament views the covenant community as a historical unity. Every part of Israel participates in its past and future history.[9]

In other words, the promise that "all Israel will be saved" does not require that every individual Israelite throughout history be saved.

All of the promises, psalms, and prophets point forward to the covenant blessing of all the families of the earth. Jesus the Messiah has been anointed to accomplish this goal, and He is doing so through His church. According to the teaching of Paul, however, this salvation of all the families of the earth is being accomplished in an unexpected way. The people of Israel as a whole have stumbled, and only a remnant have believed. But through their transgression, salvation has come to the Gentiles. But this is not the end of the story. By bringing salvation to the Gentiles, God will stir the hearts of Israel and they will one day recognize their Messiah. And as their transgression has resulted in blessing for the world, their fullness will result in blessing beyond imagination. It is no wonder that Paul concludes these chapters with the exclamation:

> Oh, the depth of the riches both of the wisdom and knowledge of God! How unsearchable are His judgments and unfathomable His ways! For who has known the mind of the Lord, or who became His counselor? Or who has first given to Him that it might be paid back to him again? For from Him

and through Him and to Him are all things. To Him be the glory forever. Amen. (11:33–36)

1 Corinthians

Then comes the end, when He delivers up the kingdom to the God and Father, when He has abolished all rule and all authority and power. For he must reign until He has put all His enemies under His feet. (1 Cor. 15:24–25)

In Acts 2:29–36, we learned that Jesus was given the messianic kingdom when He was exalted to the right hand of God (cf. Dan. 7:13–14). In 1 Corinthians 15:25, Paul declares that the course of this kingdom will be exactly what was prophesied throughout the Old Testament (cf. Ps. 110; Isa. 9; Dan. 2, 7; Zech. 9). Christ the King is overcoming all opposition during the course of His present reign. The last enemy to be destroyed will be death, and this will be accomplished by our future resurrection from the dead at the second coming of Christ (1 Cor. 15:26, 51–56). Since death will be the *last* enemy of Christ to be put under His feet, and since this victory over death will occur on the Last Day, all of the rest of Christ's enemies must be put under His feet *before* the Last Day. In other words, the victory of Christ's kingdom must occur before His second coming, when He destroys death by raising His people from the grave.

Galatians

And the Scripture, foreseeing that God would justify the Gentiles by faith, preached the gospel beforehand to Abraham, saying, "All the nations shall be blessed in you." So then those who are of faith are blessed with Abraham the believer. . . . Christ redeemed us from the curse of the Law, having become a curse for us . . . in order that in Christ Jesus the blessing of Abraham might come to the Gentiles, so that we might receive the promise of the Spirit through faith. (Gal. 3:8–9, 13–14)

In Galatians 3, Paul reveals exactly how the Abrahamic promise of covenant blessing to all the families of the earth was to be received. Inheritance of the covenant promises was never to be based merely upon physical descent from Abraham. It was always intended to be received by faith. God gave Israel the privilege of being a kingdom of priests through which He would send the gospel of justification by faith to the families of the earth. Israel failed because she perverted her status as God's chosen people into a source of pride.

In order to accomplish God's purpose, Jesus died on the cross, bearing the covenant curses for His people. Because of Christ's atoning death and His resurrection from the dead, all the families of the earth may now receive by faith the promised covenant blessings. As Paul explains in verse 16, the promises were given to Abraham and his seed, and his true seed is Christ. Both Gentiles and Jews are able to receive the promises only through union with Him by faith. If we are in Christ, then we too are Abraham's seed and coheirs of the promises (v. 29). Justification by faith is the Abrahamic blessing intended for all the families of the earth.

Hebrews

The book of Hebrews contains the clearest revelation in the New Testament of Christ's absolute superiority over all things and His fulfillment of all the shadows of the old covenant. In Hebrews we find that Jesus Christ is the fulfillment of everything symbolized in the temple, the sacrifices, and the priesthood.[10] The first two chapters of Hebrews proclaim Christ's superiority over the prophets and the angels. In Hebrews 3:1–4:13, His superiority over Moses is demonstrated. Then, in the longest section of the book, 4:14–10:18, Christ's superiority over the Aaronic priesthood and sacrifices, and His fulfillment of all that they foreshadowed, is declared. In Hebrews 10:19–12:29, the greater responsibility required in light of this superior new covenant is emphasized. And finally, in chapter 13, the author concludes with some exhortations.

Because Hebrews focuses on these themes of fulfillment, it necessarily touches upon several eschatological issues which are important to our study. Before proceeding, however, we must take note of

two characteristics of the book that are crucial to a correct understanding of it. First, its original audience consisted of Jewish Christians who were being tempted to return to the shadows of the Old
Testament. Second, it was written before the destruction of the temple in A.D. 70.[11]

The New Covenant

Hebrews 8:1–10:18 expressly declares that the new covenant
promised by the prophets of the Old Testament is now being fulfilled
by Jesus the Messiah. In 4:13–7:28, the author of Hebrews has taken
great pains to show the superiority of Christ's high priesthood over
the Aaronic priesthood of the old covenant. He begins chapter 8 with
the statement, "Now the main point in what has been said is this: we
have such a high priest, who has taken His seat at the right hand of
the throne of the Majesty in the heavens" (v. 1). The remainder of
the chapter, building on this truth, declares Jesus to be the mediator
of a superior covenant, the new covenant spoken of by the prophet
Jeremiah (cf. 8:8–13).

In 9:1–10, the author continues his argument by explaining the
temporary nature of the Old Testament tabernacle and its ceremonies.
The tabernacle and its sacrifices were never intended by God to be
permanent. They were to continue until the "time of reformation"
(v. 10).[12] Hebrews 9:11–28 describes what happened when this time
of reformation arrived. Christ entered the heavenly tabernacle and
offered Himself in order to obtain eternal redemption and is now,
therefore, the mediator of the new and better covenant. The author
concludes, "Christ also, having been offered once to bear the sins of
many, shall appear a second time, not to bear sin, to those who eagerly await Him, for salvation" (v. 28). Philip E. Hughes explains the
parallel between the "appearances" of Christ mentioned in this verse
and the appearances of the high priest on the Day of Atonement:

> First the high priest appeared for the purpose of offering the
> atoning sacrifice on the altar which stood in the courtyard
> outside the sanctuary. Then he passed from sight as he en-
> tered the sanctuary with the blood of atonement, there to
> make intercession on behalf of the people. Thus Aaron bore
> the names of the sons of Israel upon his heart and in the sanc-

tuary brought them to continual remembrance before the Lord (Ex. 28:29). This done, he came out from the sanctuary and presented himself again to the people, who were assembled in eager expectation of the reappearance of their high priest. So also Christ, our unique High Priest of the order of Melchizedek, who appeared in the precincts of this world in order "to put away sin by the sacrifice of himself" (v. 26), and then passed from sight into the heavenly sanctuary, where he now appears "in the presence of God on our behalf" as our Intercessor and Advocate (v. 24; 7:25; 1 Jn. 2:1), "will appear a second time" to mankind when he comes forth from the true sanctuary to proclaim and to perform the completion of salvation for "those who are eagerly waiting for him" (v. 28). Thus will dawn the morning of the eternal day when those who love his appearing (2 Tim. 4:8) will see him as he is and, being at last fully conformed to his likeness, will be satisfied (1 Jn. 3:2; 2 Cor. 3:18).[13]

In chapter 10:1–18, the once-for-all nature of the sacrifice of Christ is further elaborated. It was impossible for the continual offering of the blood of bulls and goats to take away sin permanently (v. 4). Christ, on the other hand, was offered for sin once for all time (vv. 10, 12, 14). There is, therefore, no longer any offering for sin (v. 18). In verses 12–13, it is written that Christ, "having offered one sacrifice for sins for all time, sat down at the right hand of God, waiting from that time onward until His enemies be made a footstool for His feet" (cf. Ps. 110; 1 Cor. 15:25). In this we see the fulfillment of the original gospel promise in Genesis 3:15. It is by means of Christ's sacrifice, in which His heel was bruised, that He is crushing the head of Satan and putting all of His enemies beneath His feet.

The Heavenly Jerusalem

In Hebrews 11–13, there are a number of eschatologically significant passages concerning "the heavenly Jerusalem." In chapter 11, many of the faithful believers of the Old Testament are singled out for honor. The chapter begins with the well-known statement, "Now faith is the assurance of things hoped for, the conviction of things not seen" (v. 1). Then, in the following verses, we are told of the faith of

Abel, Enoch, Noah, and Abraham (vv. 4–12). Of Abraham, who was given the promise of land, we read that he lived by faith as an exile in the Promised Land because "he was looking for the city which has foundations, whose architect and builder is God" (v. 10). And in verses 13–16 we are told that all of these Old Testament believers "died in faith, without receiving the promises, but having seen them and having welcomed them from a distance, and having confessed that they were strangers and exiles on the earth," they desired a better country, a heavenly country, a city that God had prepared for them.

Hebrews then tells of the faith of Isaac and Jacob, Joseph and Moses, and Rahab the harlot (vv. 17–31). Then there is a magnificent testimony to some of what was accomplished by faith during Old Testament times (vv. 32–38). "And all these, having gained approval through their faith, did not receive what was promised, because God had provided something better for us, so that apart from us they should not be made perfect" (vv. 39–40). When the original Jewish audience of this book is kept in mind, the significance of what has been said thus far is apparent. These Old Testament saints were not concerned so much with the physical land of Palestine as they were with the spiritual reality that the land signified. P. W. L. Walker explains:

> The promise concerning the Land, whilst real and valid in its own terms, pointed typologically to something greater. Any subsequent focus on the Land would then be misplaced; for the faith commended by the author was one which looked beyond such things.[14]

The focus of the Old Testament promises was always upon Christ, and thus Jewish Christians who were being tempted to revert to a Judaism with a strong emphasis on the physical land are reminded that the true "promised land" is not the earthly land of Palestine, but the messianic kingdom of God.

This truth is reaffirmed throughout chapter 12 of Hebrews. In verses 1–4, the readers are urged to focus their eyes upon Christ as their example and run with endurance. They are reminded of the significance and necessity of God's discipline of His children (vv. 5–14).

They are warned not to follow the example of faithless Esau, who lost his inheritance (vv. 15–17). Then, in verses 18–24, we read:

> For you have not come to a mountain that may be touched and to a blazing fire, and to darkness and gloom and whirlwind. . . . But you have come to Mount Zion and to the city of the living God, the heavenly Jerusalem, and to myriads of angels, to the general assembly and church of the first-born who are enrolled in heaven, and to God, the Judge of all, and to the spirits of righteous men made perfect, and to Jesus, the mediator of a new covenant, and to the sprinkled blood, which speaks better than the blood of Abel.

This, and not merely a piece of land, is the magnificent inheritance that is ours in Christ. The faithful Old Testament saints did not receive this inheritance under the old covenant. They were not to be made perfect apart from us (cf. 11:39–40). But now, under the new covenant, we *have* come to Mount Zion. We *have* come to the heavenly Jerusalem. We *have* come to the church of the firstborn. We *have* come to God. And we *have* come to Jesus, the mediator of this glorious new covenant. And what does this passage have to say about those faithful Old Testament saints who did not receive the inheritance in their day because they were not to be made perfect apart from us? It says that we have come "to the spirits of righteous men made perfect" (12:23). That which the Old Testament believers looked for in faith has come, and they have now received what was promised.

In Hebrews 13, one further reference to the heavenly city is made. In the first verses of the chapter, the readers are exhorted to be godly (vv. 1–6). They are warned against being carried away by false teachings (vv. 7–11), and are told to bear the reproach of Jesus, who suffered outside the city (v. 12). Because of what Jesus did, they are encouraged to "go out to Him outside the camp, bearing His reproach" (v. 13). The reason is then given: "For here we do not have a lasting city, but we are seeking the city which is to come" (v. 14). Chapter 12 revealed that in one sense we have already come to that city. Chapter 13 reminds us that in another sense the fullness of the blessing is yet future, because we await the consummation. Unfortunately, this verse has often been used as the basis for unbalanced interpretations of the kingdom of God. As Walker observes,

> Wrenched from its context this verse can easily be interpreted in very general or even Platonic terms as teaching the "other-worldly" focus of Christian spirituality. In its context, however, and especially given the Jewish background of the readers, the resonance concerning Jerusalem cannot be avoided. Here is clearly a 'veiled reference to the city of Jerusalem.' The author was drawing them away from a religious interest in Jerusalem by alerting them to the impermanent (*ou menousan*) and transient nature of that city. As an object of religious hope it would disappoint them; not so "the city that is to come." This transient, earthly city was not to be part of their fundamental identity.[15]

This was a powerful statement to make to first-century Jewish Christians. They were being told that they would have to surrender the affection they had for the earthly city of Jerusalem and its temple. The picture given to them was clear:

> The Temple at the city's heart is defunct; the city itself through Jesus' death has been defiled; the earthly Jerusalem in comparison with the heavenly has been diminished. "Jerusalem has lost all redemptive significance because Christ has made the final sacrifice for sin outside the gates of Jerusalem. . . . Jerusalem has lost all eschatological significance, for there is no abiding city on earth."[16]

The book of Hebrews presents us with a magnificent picture of our Lord Jesus Christ, the Priest-King, who has become the mediator of the new covenant. As it describes the work of our Messiah, it presents several eschatological themes that are important for our study:

1. *The Importance of Faith*. Faith is defined in Hebrews as the "assurance of things hoped for" and "the conviction of things not seen" (11:1). Once God makes a promise, those

who have faith rest in that promise, regardless of circumstances that would appear to make the fulfillment of the promise impossible. Redemptive history has revealed again and again how God has waited until it appeared that there was no possible hope for His promises to be fulfilled before doing the "impossible." God has promised that He will bring blessing to all families of the earth, that the kingdom He has established will grow until it fills the whole earth, and that He will accomplish this through the preaching of the gospel of His Son. This being the case, nothing on earth, in heaven, or in hell will prevent this promise from being fulfilled.

2. *The Heavenly Jerusalem.* The book of Hebrews also reminds us that neither Palestine nor any other geographical location on earth is to be equated with the messianic kingdom. The true kingdom is a kingdom made without hands (cf. Dan. 2), and while it will *fill* the earth, it is not to be identified *with* the earth. This reminder provides a healthy corrective to dispensationalists who place so much attention on the earthly city of Jerusalem, a city that even the faithful Old Testament saints were looking beyond.

3. *The Already and the Not-Yet.* Hebrews also provides a healthy corrective to those postmillennialists who may be tempted to forget that, even though God's promises for history will be fulfilled before the consummation, there still *is* a consummation. Perfection will not be reached this side of eternity. This earth will not be free from the presence of death and sin until the second coming of our Lord.

Conclusion

The epistles of the New Testament are rich with insights into Christ's fulfillment of the Old Testament promises and prophecies. We have only been able to scratch the surface of a few of these great teachings. Each of the passages that we have focused upon presents an important contribution and reinforcement to that which has been promised and prophesied.

1. *Romans 9–11*. Israel as a whole rejected her Messiah and was therefore "broken off" the good olive tree. Her rejection was not total, however, because a remnant is even now being saved. But she did not stumble so as to fall. She was hardened so that mercy might come to the Gentiles. Her hardening will last until the fullness of the Gentiles has come in. The mercy shown to the Gentiles will lead to her jealousy, which in turn will lead to her acceptance and grafting back into the olive tree.
2. *1 Corinthians 15*. Jesus, who is now seated and reigning at the right hand of God, will do so *until* all enemies have been placed beneath His feet.
3. *Galatians 3*. Justification by faith is the Abrahamic blessing that God intends for all the families of the earth.
4. *Hebrews 8–10*. The promised new covenant, in which all the promises will be brought to fruition, is presently being fulfilled by Jesus the Messiah.
5. *Hebrews 11–13*. The Old Testament saints have now received that which they looked for in faith, namely, the heavenly city to which we have now all come.

The epistles of the New Testament testify that Jesus is the promised Messiah. All that the Old Testament promised is fulfilled in Him (2 Cor. 1:20). He is the promised seed who crushes the head of the serpent. He is the One through whom all the families of the earth will be blessed. He is the One who fulfills all righteousness. He is the One who now sits upon the throne of a kingdom made without hands, a kingdom that cannot be shaken, a kingdom that will grow until it becomes a mountain that fills the whole earth.

CHAPTER TEN

The Book of Revelation

Worthy art Thou to take the book, and to break its seals; for Thou wast slain,
and didst purchase for God with Thy blood men from every tribe and tongue
and people and nation. And Thou hast made them to be a kingdom and
priests to our God; and they will reign upon the earth.
—Revelation 5:9–10

The book of Revelation is the glorious capstone of Scripture, and when we approach this book, we must approach it as such. We cannot hope to comprehend what is revealed in the final book of the Bible if we do not have a grasp of what has been revealed in the preceding books of the Old and New Testaments.[1] All the themes and promises that we have traced throughout redemptive history come together in this last book in a magnificent vision of victory.

Methods of Interpretation

It is difficult and humbling to interpret the book of Revelation. Because of its symbolic language, the book has been interpreted in many different ways. However, there have been four main approaches to the book:

1. *The Idealist Approach.* This method of interpreting the book of Revelation sees it as a symbolic presentation of the cosmic conflict between good and evil. It does not see any ref-

erence to specific events or persons in the symbols of the book.

2. *The Historicist Approach.* This method of interpreting the book of Revelation understands it as a prophecy of church history from the First Advent until the Second. This view was popular during the Reformation, when the Antichrist was usually identified as the Roman Catholic Church.

3. *The Futurist Approach.* The futurist method of interpreting Revelation sees most of chapters 4–19 as precursors to the second coming of Christ. This view is generally endorsed by premillennial expositors.

4. *The Preterist Approach.* The preterist understanding of the book of Revelation teaches that a large portion of the book consists of a prophecy that was fulfilled in the first century. Specifically, it teaches that many if not most of the prophecies within the book pointed to the destruction of Jerusalem in A.D. 70.

For reasons that will become clearer as we discuss the text, the approach adopted in this study is essentially preterist. It should be noted, however, that postmillennialism does not depend upon any particular one of these methods of interpretation. Nor does it depend upon a particular interpretation of any one passage in Revelation. The preterist approach is adopted here simply because it does justice to the text. A full defense of preterism and a full critique of the other views would be well beyond the scope of this short chapter.[2] However, the main reasons why the other approaches are rejected may be briefly mentioned.

The idealist interpretation fails because it does not do justice to the numerous time references and descriptions in the text which almost certainly point to actual events to come. It does not do justice to the expectation of impending judgment expressed throughout the book. Although the idealist approach states a biblical truth, it is not so much an interpretation of Revelation as it is a restatement of one of its themes.

The historicist and futurist approaches are also guilty of ignoring the many time references in the book, but they have a more basic problem. Both methods of interpretation lack hermeneutical boundaries.

Historicist commentators down through the centuries have almost invariably identified the age in which they were living as the final age described in Revelation. The symbols of the book have then been identified with whatever important ecclesiastical and political events transpired between Christ's coming and their own day. Futurist commentators have been similarly arbitrary. They usually identify their own era as the time of the end and then attempt to find parallels between current events and the symbols within the book. Interpreters within each of these two schools of thought are forced with the passing of each generation to discard much of the speculation of their predecessors and reinterpret the symbolic language in a manner that will cover current events and bring it up to date. The lack of hermeneutical control inherent within these two approaches to the book of Revelation has resulted in wildly divergent opinions regarding virtually every sentence in the book.

Those who adopt an idealist, an historicist, or a futurist approach usually criticize the preterist interpretation on two main grounds. The first criticism is well expressed by dispensationalist John F. Walvoord, who writes, "The preterist view, in general, tends to destroy any future significance of the book, which becomes a literary curiosity with little prophetic meaning."[3] This sentiment is echoed by amillennialist W. J. Grier: "The Preterist interpretation would resolve Revelation into a handbook of the history of the Church under the Caesars."[4] In other words, unless the prophecies of Revelation deal largely with events in *our* future, they are essentially insignificant. The fallacy of this criterion becomes clear when we apply it to many of the books of the Old Testament. Are the inspired and inerrant books of Obadiah and Nahum, for example, any less significant because their prophecies of judgment upon Edom and Ninevah were fulfilled long ago? Is the book of Judges a mere "handbook of the history" of God's people under various foreign oppressors? Does the fact that a large number of Old Testament prophecies concerning Christ have been fulfilled render them any less meaningful or significant? The answer to each of these questions is obviously no.

A second criticism of the preteristic approach has to do with the date when the book was written. Many scholars believe that the relevant evidence supports a date sometime in the reign of the emperor Domitian. This would mean that Revelation was written sometime around 95. Such a date would effectively rule out a preterist inter-pretation that sees large portions of the book looking ahead to the destruction of Jerusalem in 70. As we will see, however, there is strong evidence for dating the composition of the book of Revelation dur-ing the reign of Nero, prior to 70.

The Date of the Book of Revelation

It is difficult to date any book of the Bible. Numerous pieces of evidence must be examined, both within the book itself and in the surrounding historical context. The dating of Revelation is no less complex, and it cannot be thoroughly examined within the scope of this book.[5] However, the basic argument for a date prior to the de-struction of Jerusalem should be presented before we survey the book itself.

The External Evidence

External evidence refers to evidence not found within a book itself. In the case of the book of Revelation, the external evidence is usually regarded by proponents of a late date as decisive. By far the most important evidence is a statement made by Irenaeus (130–202) in his book *Against Heresies*, which was written about 180–90. The statement reads:

> We will not, however, incur the risk of pronouncing positively as to the name of Antichrist; for if it were necessary that his name should be distinctly revealed in this present time, it would have been announced by him who beheld the apoca-lyptic vision. For that was seen no very long time since, but almost in our day, towards the end of Domitian's reign.[6]

There are several reasons why this statement is inconclusive at best. For the sake of brevity, we shall mention only two:

1. The translation of the Greek word *heorathe*, "that was seen," is not certain. It is possible that Irenaeus is referring to the

vision itself, but the broader context and the word itself leave open the possibility that he is referring to the apostle John.[7]

2. Even if Irenaeus is referring to the vision that John saw, a number of other historical errors in his writings should keep us from placing too much weight upon his statement. It is a matter of record, for example, that Irenaeus believed that Jesus' ministry lasted approximately fifteen years and that he lived to be almost fifty (*Against Heresies*, 2.22.5).

There is other external evidence in addition to that supplied by Irenaeus, but it generally falls into one of three categories. First, much of it simply repeats the position of Irenaeus, and thus cannot be regarded as independent testimony. Second, there is a large amount of testimony that is unclear and therefore inconclusive. Third, there is external evidence that supports a pre-70 date.[8]

The most that can be said of the external evidence for the date of the book of Revelation is that it is inconclusive. The primary external witnesses for a late date either are vague or merely repeat uncritically the opinions of earlier writers. The remaining witnesses are divided, some pointing to a later date and others pointing to an early date. In order to determine the date of the composition of Revelation, it is necessary to examine the evidence found within the book itself.

The Internal Evidence

The internal evidence, found within the book itself, for the dating of Revelation is much clearer than the external evidence, and it points decisively to an early date. Kenneth Gentry offers seven lines of evidence,[9] which we will summarize below.

1. *The Theme of Revelation.* The theme of the entire book, the exaltation of Christ, is stated in 1:4–8. A central element of this exaltation is found in 1:7, "Behold, He is coming with the clouds, and every eye will see Him, even those who pierced Him; and all the tribes of the earth will mourn over Him. Even so. Amen." This theme is repeated throughout the book (2:5, 16, 25; 3:3, 11; 16:15; 22:7, 12, 20). The language of coming for judgment is used elsewhere in the Old

Testament (Pss. 18:7–15; 104:3; Isa. 19:1; Nah. 1:2–8) and in the New Testament (Matt. 24:4–34; Mark 13:5–30; Luke 21:8–36) to refer to contemporary judgments, and, as we will see, it refers here to a contemporary judgment. This coming for judgment is directed at "those who pierced" Christ and "the tribes of the earth."[10] This is the coming for judgment that Jesus said would come upon the generation of Jews to whom he spoke (Matt. 24:34; Mark 13:30; Luke 21:32).

2. *The Nearness of the Coming.* John writes a number of times in Revelation that his prophecy will be fulfilled very soon: see 1:1, 3, 19; 2:16; 3:10–11; 22:6–7, 10, 12, 20. Nothing in these verses indicates that the coming of Christ referred to in 1:7 is to occur thousands of years later. Everything in them points to an impending "coming." There was only one event that occurred within a generation of the ascension of Christ that carried so much redemptive and covenantal significance that it could be called a "coming of Christ," and that was the utter destruction of Jerusalem and the temple in A.D. 70 by the armies of Rome.

3. *The Sixth King.* Revelation 17:9–10 comes close to indicating the date when the book was written. It tells of "seven kings": "five have fallen, one is, the other has not yet come; and when he comes, he must remain a little while." These kings are associated with "seven mountains" (v. 9), which surely refers to Rome, the city built on seven hills. The "kings" would therefore be the line of Roman emperors. If we begin with Julius Caeser (as many contemporaries of John did), we have the following list:

1. Julius Caeser (49–44 B.C.)
2. Augustus (27 B.C.–A.D. 14)
3. Tiberius (14–37)
4. Gaius (37–41).
5. Claudius (41–54)
6. Nero (54–68)
7. Galba (68–69)
8. Otho (69)
9. Vitellius (69)
10. Vespasian (69–79)

The sixth king, the one who "is" when John is writing, would then be Nero. He was preceded by five kings who "have fallen," and was followed by a king who reigned only a very short time. By no calculation can the sixth king possibly refer to the emperor Domitian.

4. *The Existence of the Temple.* Revelation 11:1–2 describes John measuring the temple. While this language could conceivably refer to a symbolic temple, the statement that this temple will be tread upon by the nations for forty-two months seems to indicate that the Jewish temple is in view and that it had not yet been destroyed at the time of writing.

5. *The Symbolic Descriptions of Nero.* There seems to be a reference to Nero in Revelation 13:18, which speaks of a man whose number is 666. A strong case can be made that this number is a symbolic designation of Nero. While all of the evidence for and against this theory cannot be explained here, suffice it to say that the ancient Hebrew spelling of Nero Caesar has the numerical value of 666.[11]

6. *The Strong Presence of Jewish Christianity.* The book of Revelation gives evidence that it was written during a time when there remained a strong Jewish and even Judaizing element in the church (2:9; 3:9; 7:4–8; 14:1; 21:12). The Jewish influence and threat dwindled rapidly after A.D. 70, and was hardly a factor in the late first century.

7. *The Impending Jewish War.* There are a number of passages in the book that seem to point to the catastrophe that was about to befall Jerusalem. Several references to time, for example, fit the actual course of events in the Jewish War:

   a. *Revelation 9:1–12.* John sees a vision in which all those without the seal of God are tormented for five months. Significantly, the actual siege of Jerusalem by Titus lasted five months.[12]

   b. *Revelation 11:2.* The temple is given to the nations for forty-two months. Similarly, the time between the declaration of war by Rome until the fall of Jerusalem was almost exactly forty-two months.

   c. *Revelation 13:5–7.* In John's vision of the beast, he is told that the beast makes war with the saints for forty-two months. Nero's persecution of Christians began late in 64 and lasted until his death in June 68, a period again of almost exactly forty-two months.

When all of the evidence is examined and weighed carefully, it points to an early date. We conclude, therefore, that the book of Revelation was written sometime during the Neronic persecution (64–68).

The Interpretation of Revelation

Once the early date of Revelation has been established, a number of the seemingly inexplicable passages of the book become much clearer. We have already mentioned the parallels between several passages and first-century people, places, and events. At this point, we will briefly survey the main sections of the book in order to grasp its central message.[13]

Things Which Must Shortly Take Place

The first five chapters of Revelation prepare the reader for the impending judgment, which is revealed in the longest section of the book. The author, the historical circumstances, the original audience, and the One who reveals this vision are all introduced in these chapters.

Chapter 1. A number of times in chapter 1, the nearness of the events prophesied is emphasized. The judgments "must shortly take place" (1:1); they are "near" (1:3). The theme of the book is revealed in 1:4–8. Jesus Christ is now the exalted ruler of the kings of the earth, the One who has redeemed us from our sins, and He is coming in judgment very soon.

Chapters 2–3. In these two chapters, we find preliminary letters to seven churches in Asia Minor: Ephesus, Smyrna, Pergamum, Thyatira, Sardis, Philadelphia, and Laodicea. These were seven real churches facing real tribulation and persecution (cf. 1:9), and John was to show them what "must shortly take place" (1:1).[14] Within these letters are additional indications that the judgments revealed in the remainder of the book are near at hand. In the letter to the church at Philadelphia, for example, Christ says:

Because you have kept the word of My perseverance, I also
will keep you from the hour of testing, that hour which is *about
to come* upon the whole world, to test those who dwell upon
the earth. I am coming *quickly;* hold fast what you have, in
order that no one take your crown. (3:10–11, emphasis added)

This passage poses a difficulty for nonpreterist exegetes. Why
would Christ promise to keep a first-century church from an hour of
testing, if that hour of testing was not to occur for many centuries?[15]

Chapter 4. In chapter 4, the seven churches are assured that the
sovereign God of creation is in control despite the seemingly chaotic
persecution they were experiencing. God is shown sitting on His
throne, surrounded by angelic creatures and twenty-four elders who
worship Him continually. Various interpretations have been offered
to explain the twenty-four elders seated on thrones around the throne
of God, but it seems best to understand them to be symbolic of the
church. The reasons for this are:

1. Elsewhere in the New Testament, the church is spoken of
   as having been seated with Christ in the heavenly places
   (Eph. 2:6; cf. Rev. 1:6; 3:21).
2. The term *elder* is nowhere in Scripture applied to any be-
   ings other than men, and it is consistently used to describe
   leaders in the church (Ex. 12:21; 24:9–11; 1 Tim. 3:1–7;
   Titus 1:4–9).
3. The number of the elders indicates their priestly nature.
   There are twenty-four divisions of priests mentioned in 1
   Chronicles 24 and twenty-four divisions of worship leaders
   mentioned in 1 Chronicles 25. Since John has already declared Christians to be "priests" to God (1:6), the identification of the twenty-four elders becomes clearer.

It appears, then, that John is simply giving his readers a more vivid
picture of the truth he stated in 1:6, namely, that Christians are a kingdom of priests who reign with Christ.

Chapter 5. Chapter 5 continues the heavenly vision with a description of Christ as the victorious judge. In verse 1, John sees a vision

of God holding a scroll that has writing on both the front and the back and that is sealed with seven seals. An Old Testament parallel sheds light on the identity of this scroll. Just as the old covenant was written on both the front and the back of the stone tablets (Ex. 32:15), so also the new covenant inaugurated by Christ is written on both the front and the back. In verses 2–4, no one is found worthy to open the book, and John begins to weep. The angel then tells John to stop weeping because the Lion from the tribe of Judah has overcome and will open the book (vv. 5–6). This indicates the fulfillment of one of the first messianic prophecies in Scripture, Genesis 49:8–12. It also points to Christ as the promised son of David who now reigns as king (cf. 2 Sam. 7:18–29).

The Judgment of Israel

In Revelation 6–19, the impending coming of Christ for judgment upon Israel is prophetically described in a series of visions in which John sees the seven seals of the scroll broken one at a time. In chapter 6, six of the seals are broken. Then, after an interlude (chapter 7), the seventh seal is broken (8:1), initiating the seven trumpets that bring further judgment.

Chapter 6. In chapter 6, John describes his vision of the breaking of the first six seals by the Lamb of God. There is a close parallel between the judgments described in Revelation 6 and the events described as leading up to the destruction of Jerusalem in the Olivet discourse:[16]

1. War (6:1–2; cf. Matt. 24:6; Mark 13:7; Luke 21:9)
2. International strife (6:3–4; cf. Matt. 24:7; Mark 13:8; Luke 21:10)
3. Famine (6:5–6; cf. Matt. 24:7; Mark 13:8; Luke 21:11)
4. Pestilence (6:7–8; cf. Luke 21:11)
5. Persecution (6:9–11; cf. Matt. 24:9–11; Mark 13:9–13; Luke 21:12–19)
6. Earthquake, cosmic upheaval (6:12–17; cf. Matt. 24:15–31; Mark 13:14–27; Luke 21:20–27)

John is clearly speaking of the very events prophesied by Christ in the Olivet discourse, events which were to fall upon the generation of Jews who rejected and crucified their Messiah.

The breaking of each of the first four seals releases a horseman who brings judgment with him (cf. Zech. 6:1–7; Hab. 3:3–15). On the white horse is a crowned rider with a bow who goes forth conquering and to conquer (6:1–2; cf. Ps. 45:3–5). The rider is none other than Christ Himself. This is apparent when we compare the description of the rider here with descriptions of Christ elsewhere in the book. He is riding a white horse (cf. 19:11–16); He is crowned (cf. 14:14); He is conquering (cf. 2:7, 11, 17, 26; 3:5, 12, 21). The vision is one of Christ coming in judgment.

The breaking of the second seal releases a rider on a red horse, who takes peace from the land. This points to the outbreak of the Jewish War. The third horseman brings famine, one of the covenant curses for disobedience (cf. Deut. 28:15–34). Josephus records the horrible famine that occurred during the Jewish War, a famine which drove many of the Jews to the brink of insanity and some of them over it (*Wars*, 5.10.2). The fourth horseman is Death and is followed closely by Hades (6:7–8). This horseman is given authority to kill one-fourth of the population with sword, famine, pestilence, and wild beasts (cf. Ezek. 14:21). Here again we see the pouring out of God's covenant curses (Lev. 26; Deut. 28).

When the fifth seal is broken (6:9–11), John is given a vision of an altar in heaven under which he sees the souls of the martyrs. The martyrs are each given white robes and promised that vindication will soon be theirs. During this period of tribulation in the first century, many Christians were martyred for their faith. The churches are given assurance here that the blood of these saints has not been shed in vain. As the sixth seal is broken (6:12–17), a vision of judgment upon the nation of Israel is given in the familiar prophetic language of cosmic upheaval (cf. Isa. 13:10–14; 34:4–5; Ezek. 32:7; Amos 8:9).

Chapter 7. Revelation 7 provides an interlude in the scenes of judgment. It describes the sealing of 144,000 people from the tribes of Israel (7:1–8). These are probably Jewish converts to Christianity who are given an opportunity to escape the impending judgment. This opportunity was prophesied by Christ (see Luke 21:20–22) and was fulfilled when the Roman general Vespasian was temporarily distracted by events back in Rome. Nero had died, and as a result civil war had erupted. This brief interlude allowed the Christians in Judea to escape, and many of them fled from Jerusalem.

Chapter 8. In chapter 8, the seventh seal of the book is broken and the sounding of seven trumpets begins. Like the seals, each trumpet initiates judgment. The judgments of the first four trumpets reflect the judgments poured out upon Egypt in Exodus 7–11. The first trumpet brings forth "hail and fire, mixed with blood," which results in the burning up of one-third of the earth, trees, and grass. It is a matter of record that the Roman army, in its advance on Jerusalem, left the land a desolate waste.

The second trumpet parallels the first plague on Egypt, in which the Nile was turned to blood (Ex. 7:17–21). In Revelation 8, this is caused by "something like a great mountain being thrown into the sea." It is likely that this refers to the casting down of Israel. Similar language is used in the Old Testament to refer to the judgment of Babylon centuries before Christ (Jer. 51:25, 42). Jesus may have used this same language to refer to the judgment of Israel when, immediately after cursing the fig tree, a symbol of Israel (Matt. 21:18–20), He told His disciples, "Truly I say to you, if you have faith, and do not doubt, you shall not only do what was done to the fig tree, but even if you say to this mountain, 'Be taken up and cast into the sea,' it shall happen" (Matt. 21:21). Since Jesus was in Jerusalem when He said this, it is possible that "this mountain" refers to the mountain upon which Jerusalem stands.

The third trumpet causes a great star to fall from heaven, burning like a torch. It falls upon the waters, causing them to become bitter. The language of this judgment also parallels Old Testament language used by God to describe His judgment upon Israel for her apostasy (cf. Deut. 29:18; Jer. 9:15; 23:15; Lam. 3:15, 19). The fourth trumpet describes a vision of cosmic upheaval, which is used many times to picture God's judgment upon a nation (cf. Isa. 13:10–14; 34:4–5; Ezek. 32:7; Amos 8:9). Chapter 8 concludes with a vision of an eagle announcing the coming blast of the last three trumpets.

Chapter 9. In chapter 9, the judgments of the fifth and sixth trumpets are revealed. When the fifth trumpet sounds, a five-month demonic torment of those without the seal of God on their foreheads begins (9:1–12). As mentioned above, this seems to be a vision of the final siege of Jerusalem, which lasted five months. At the sounding of the sixth trumpet, four angels, who are bound at the great river Euphrates, are released in order to kill one-third of the people. Since the Euphrates was the direction from which the historic invasions of Israel by Assyria, Babylon, and Persia had come, it would seem to be a symbolic picture of another invading army, this time the army of Rome. Chapter 9 concludes by declaring that even in the midst of these judgments, the people did not repent of their wickedness (vv. 20–21).

Chapter 10. At this point, John sees a vision of a "strong angel" descending from heaven and standing with his right foot on the sea and his left foot on the land. He declares that "there shall be delay no longer" (v. 6). Israel's judgment has come in response to the cries of the martyrs (Rev. 6:10). With the destruction of the temple, the mystery will be finished (cf. Eph. 3:4–6). Finally, John is told to eat the book that the angel holds in his hand (10:9–10). Like the scroll of judgment that Ezekiel was told to "eat" (Ezek. 2:8–3:3, 14), the book of judgment is sweet in John's mouth but bitter in his stomach.

Chapter 11. In Revelation 11:1–2, John is instructed to measure the temple and is then told that the outer court will be given to the nations, who will trample it down for forty-two months. This apparently refers to the time from the declaration of war by Rome until the fall of Jerusalem, which was almost exactly forty-two months. In verses 3–13, John is told that God will give authority to two witnesses, who will prophesy against Jerusalem during these forty-two months. The vision has a number of similarities to Zechariah 4:1–14, but the identity of the two witnesses is not revealed in Revelation. The judgment of Milton Terry, that they are two individuals, appears to be the most straightforward way of reading the text.[17] These two Christian prophets remain in Jerusalem as legal witnesses against Israel (cf. Deut. 17:6). Their prophetic ministry is described in terms that are similar to that of Jeremiah, to whom God said, "Behold, I am making My words in your mouth fire and this people wood, and it will consume them" (Rev. 11:5; cf. Jer. 5:14). Their prophetic ministry is also described in terms that are reminiscent of

Moses and Elijah (Rev. 11:6). In due course they are killed, but after three days they are raised from the dead, and like Elijah they are taken into heaven (Rev. 11:7–12; cf. 2 Kings 2:1–11). Then the seventh trumpet is sounded, and the heavenly chorus declares the fulfillment of Daniel 2, singing, "The kingdom of the world has become the kingdom of our Lord, and of His Christ; and He will reign forever and ever" (11:15).

Chapter 12. In chapter 12, John sees a great sign in heaven. The chapter is filled with symbolic language, but most of it either is explained or is understandable when parallel passages are examined. The woman clothed with the sun and crowned with a crown of twelve stars represents the church under the old covenant (cf. Gal. 4:26, 31). The great dragon who is cast out of heaven is identified as Satan (Rev. 12:9). The son who is born, who will rule all nations with a rod of iron, is undoubtedly Christ. The main point of the chapter is that Satan has been thrown down from his former place of power and Christ has been given all authority (12:10).

Chapter 13. In chapter 13, John sees a vision of the persecution of the church by the beast. The reference to the beast is both generic (Rome) and specific (Nero). The beast, like Satan (cf. 12:3), has seven heads and ten horns (13:2). The ten horns are the governors of the ten imperial provinces (cf. 17:12), while the seven heads are the line of the Caesars (cf. 17:9–11). The beast persecutes Christians because they refuse to join the emperor cult and worship Caesar (13:4–10). The second beast that John sees arises from within the land (13:11–17). He is identified in 16:13 and 19:20 as the false prophet (cf. Matt. 24:5, 11). This beast represents, generically, the Jewish leaders who enforced submission to Rome and persecuted Christians and specifically, perhaps, Gessius Florus, the Roman procurator over Israel. The last verse of chapter 13 provides a veiled identification of the specific man referred to as the first beast: his number is 666. We have already noted that the Hebrew spelling of Nero Caesar has the numerical value of 666.

Chapter 14. Chapter 14 is a vision of the fall of Jerusalem, referred to here as "Babylon the great" (14:8). As we will see in chapters 17–18, the evidence that "Babylon" is a symbolic description of Jerusalem is compelling. At this point, we merely note that this "great city" has already been identified as Jerusalem in 11:8, where she is referred to as Sodom and Egypt. In chapter 14, she is also called Babylon.

Chapters 15–16. In these two chapters, John sees "seven bowls of the wrath of God" poured out upon the land. The vials are poured forth in rapid succession, paralleling and intensifying the judgments described in the breaking of the seven seals. The way was prepared for "the kings from the east" (16:12); Josephus tells us that the Roman armies surrounding Jerusalem were reinforced by troops from the east (*Wars*, 3.4.2; 5.1.6). He also records that with the city surrounded by so large an army, Jerusalem divided into three internally warring factions (*Wars*, 5.1.1; cf. Rev. 16:19).

Chapters 17–18. These two chapters describe the judgment of Jerusalem, the harlot bride. The identification of the harlot with Jerusalem is supported by several pieces of evidence. First, the language of harlotry is commonly used in the Old Testament to refer to apostate Israel (cf. Isa. 1:21; Jer. 2:20–24, 30–33; 3:1–3; Ezek. 16, 23; Hos. 9:1). Second, she is sitting upon the scarlet beast, indicating her apostasy with the Roman Empire (cf. John 19:15). Israel certainly cooperated with Rome in crucifying her Messiah. Third, she is clothed in purple and scarlet, still passing herself off as the true bride (cf. 2:9; 3:9). Josephus notes that the temple veil was embroidered with scarlet and purple (*Wars*, 5.5.4). Fourth, she is drunk with the blood of the saints (cf. Matt. 23:29–37; Acts 7:51–52).

The angel explains the mystery of this vision to John in 17:8–18. We have already noted that the succession of kings in verse 10 points to Nero as the reigning emperor. The chaos involved in the Roman civil war will not be the end of the beast. Later emperors will also manifest the anti-Christian evil of Nero (v. 11). The persecuting beast will not, however, be victorious. Christ will judge this persecutor as He is judging Israel (vv. 12–14). Verse 16 points once again to the destruction of Jerusalem by the Gentiles. In connection with this verse, it should be noted that the nations surrounding Israel massacred thousands of Jews as the Jewish War began. There were huge massacres in Caesarea, Syria, Scythopolis, Ascalon, Ptolemais, Tyre, Alexandria, and elsewhere (Josephus, *Wars*, 2.8). The nations truly did "hate the harlot" (17:16).

Chapter 18 records the final pronouncement of judgment upon Jerusalem by an angel who cries out, "Fallen, fallen is Babylon the great!" (v. 2). As she had in the Old Testament, Jerusalem declares to herself, "I sit as a queen and I am not a widow" (v. 7; cf. Isa. 47:8–15). But her judgment will surely come because she has filled up the cup of God's wrath.

Chapter 19. Revelation 19:1–6 is a glorious vision of rejoicing in heaven over the judgment of God upon Jerusalem. In verses 7–9, John reveals that even as the harlot is being judged, the bride of Christ is preparing herself for the wedding feast. With the destruction of the old temple comes the establishment of the new temple (cf. 1 Cor. 3:16; 2 Cor. 6:16; Eph. 2:21). The destruction of Jerusalem and the temple was the final redemptive act in the entire complex of events which inaugurated the present age. Jesus was born as the King (Matt. 2:2); He was identified as the King at His baptism and transfiguration (Matt. 3:17; 17:5; cf. Ps. 2); He was demonstrated to be the Davidic King by virtue of His resurrection (Acts 2:30–31); He was officially crowned at His ascension (Dan. 7:13–14); finally, the destruction of Jerusalem was the definitive sign that He was the promised messianic King, whose kingdom will grow until it fills the earth (Matt. 24:30).

Revelation 19:11–21 is a vision of the King of kings going to war against His enemies. This is a vivid description of the fulfillment of Psalm 110. Now that Christ has been seated at the right hand of God as the King of kings, His reign will include His triumph over all His enemies (cf. 1 Cor. 15:25–26). The scene described in these verses of Revelation parallels that of Daniel 7. In Daniel's prophecy, the coronation of Christ as King is connected with His judging of the nations, specifically the "little horn" of the fourth kingdom. The fourth kingdom in Daniel is Rome, and the parallels between the "little horn" and the "beast" of Revelation are too numerous to be ignored. We conclude, therefore, that this coming of Christ for judgment upon the nations and the beast is the same one described by Daniel as occurring in connection with His ascension.

The King and His Bride

Revelation 20. We turn now to the chapter of Revelation that has been at the center of the millennial question. Revelation 20 is the only chapter in the Bible in which we find a direct and explicit mention of the "thousand years," often called "the Millennium," and therefore this chapter has been the focus of much debate. Before we survey the chapter, it should be noted again that postmillennialism (and amillennialism), in contrast to premillennialism, does not teach that this single passage, in this highly symbolic book, should be the cornerstone of one's system of eschatology. As we have attempted to demonstrate, the basic themes of postmillennial eschatology rest upon promises and prophecies found throughout the Old and New Testaments. Revelation 20 does not overturn the basic eschatological structure that is clearly evident in the rest of Scripture. In fact, when properly understood, it adds further support to it.

Revelation 20 describes a vision of the Millennium (vv. 1–10) and the Great White Throne judgment (vv. 11–15). John tells us three things that characterize the Millennium. First, at its inception and for most of its duration, Satan is bound. Second, Christ is reigning with all Christians. Third, at its conclusion, Satan is briefly released to lead a rebellion and is then cast into the lake of fire. From our study of the Scriptures, we should recognize that the Millennium is the present age between the two advents of Christ.

The New Testament resounds with the truth that Satan was decisively defeated and restrained at Christ's first advent (Matt. 12:29; Luke 10:18; John 12:31; 1 John 3:8). Hebrews 2:14 is abundantly clear on this point: "Since then the children share in flesh and blood, He Himself likewise also partook of the same, that through death He might render powerless him who had the power of death, that is, the devil." This binding of Satan does not entail the cessation of his activity (cf. 1 Peter 5:8), but it does mean that he is no longer able to prevent the spread of the gospel to the nations (Rev. 20:3). Scripture also declares that Christ was given His kingdom at His first advent (Daniel 2, 7; Matt. 2:2; Acts 2:30–31; 17:7; Col. 1:13; Rev. 1:5), and that Christians now reign with Him (Rom. 5:17; Eph. 2:6; Rev. 1:6). Revelation 20 also tells us that at the end of this millennial age, Satan will be released and will lead a rebellion against Christ. This is a reminder for those whose vision for this present age tends toward utopianism. Satan, sin, and death will not be completely destroyed until the final consummation at the second coming of Christ.

In Revelation 20:4–6, John describes those whom he sees reigning with Christ during the Millennium. First he tells us that he saw "thrones, and they sat upon them." He does not tell us here who "they" are, but in the book of Revelation, he has only used this term with reference to the twenty-four elders. In our discussion of chapter 4, it was shown that these elders are a symbolic representation of the church. John also tells us that he saw the Christian martyrs reigning with Christ (20:4). The churches to whom he is writing are encouraged by this message that the Christian brothers and sisters who have been martyred are also reigning with Christ until the last day.

Another indication that those of whom John is here speaking refer to the entire community of the redeemed, both living and dead, is his reference to their partaking of the first resurrection (20:5–6). The first resurrection is the resurrection of Christ (1 Cor. 15:20–23), and only those who are in Christ partake of this resurrection. Our participation in this first resurrection is spoken of in the past tense in terms of our regeneration, or spiritual resurrection (Eph. 2:5–6; Col. 2:12), and in the future tense in terms of our bodily resurrection (Rom. 6:5; 1 Cor. 15:23, 52–56; 1 Thess. 4:16). In other words, all who have been raised spiritually will be raised bodily. John also tells us that the second death, the lake of fire, has no power over those who have a part in the first resurrection (20:6, 14).

In verse 5, John tells us that "the rest of the dead did not come to life until the thousand years were completed." This "second resurrection" specifically describes the raising of the dead who are not in Christ to be judged at the Great White Throne. This final judgment is described in detail in 20:11–15. John elsewhere refers to this resurrection as "a resurrection of judgment" (John 5:28–29). The bodies of all men, believers and unbelievers, will be raised at this last hour, but there is a distinct difference in the nature of their resurrections. Unbelievers never partake in any sense of the resurrection of Christ. They remain in a state of spiritual death until they are raised to face the second death. The bodily resurrection of believers, on the other hand, is referred to as "a resurrection of life" (John 5:28–29).

Revelation 20:7–11 reveals that at the end of the millennial age (the present age), Satan will be released and will deceive the nations one last time. At this point, God will execute His final judgment upon Satan by casting him into the lake of fire. Then, following the destruction of Satan, all men will be raised to be judged before the Great White Throne of God. Those who are not in Christ will be thrown into the lake of fire. Those who are in Christ and have partaken of His resurrection will be saved. Then death, the last enemy, will finally be destroyed (20:14; cf. 1 Cor. 15:26), and God will be all in all.

Revelation 21–22. Revelation 21 introduces the vision of a new heaven and a new earth and the new Jerusalem. This fulfills Isaiah 65:17–25 and numerous other Old Testament prophecies. As we explained in our discussion of Isaiah's prophecy, the new heaven and new earth is not wholly future. This kind of language is used to describe aspects of Christ's present work of salvation (cf. 2 Cor. 5:17; Gal. 6:15). But neither is it wholly present. The whole creation will not be completely set free from corruption until the Second Coming (cf. Rom. 8:19–23). It is the progressive aspect of the redemption of creation. Sin affected more than the souls of men; it affected all of creation. In Revelation 21–22, we see that the redemptive work of Christ is as worldwide in scope as were the effects of God's curse. The original purpose of God for creation will finally be accomplished.

Revelation 21:2–22:5 describes the new Jerusalem coming down from heaven. In this vision, we see the original covenant purposes of God fulfilled. The descriptions of the New Jerusalem in these chapters indicate that it is a symbolic representation of the people of God, the church of the Old and New Testaments. The city is called the bride of the Lamb, a designation of the church (21:2, 9; cf. John 3:29; Rom. 7:4; 2 Cor. 11:2; Eph. 5:25–33; Rev. 19:7–8). Upon the twelve gates of the city are written the names of the twelve tribes of Israel (21:12), and upon the foundation stones are written the names of the twelve apostles (21:14). This magnificently symbolizes the unity of Old Testament and New Testament believers in the one church of God.

In this new Jerusalem, the covenant promise that God will dwell with men, and that He will be their God and they will be His people, is being fulfilled (21:3). In this new Jerusalem, God's promise to bless all the families and nations of the earth is being fulfilled

(21:22–26). In this new Jerusalem, Ezekiel's prophecy of a temple from which flows an ever-deepening river is being fulfilled (22:1–2). All of the covenant promises of God are now being progressively fulfilled by the work of Christ through His body, the church. At a future point in time, this work will be complete. All of Christ's enemies will have been put beneath His feet. He will come again to consummate His kingdom. By raising His people bodily from the grave, He will destroy the last enemy, death. God's plan will be completed, and He will be glorified.

Conclusion

The book of Revelation is a wonderful, but often misunderstood prophecy. Our brief overview of it has revealed a number of important eschatological themes:

1. *The Theme of Revelation*. The primary message of Revelation is that Jesus the Messiah is now the exalted ruler of the kings of the earth. He has redeemed us from our sins, and he is conquering all of His enemies.
2. *The Subject and Time Frame of the Prophecy*. The largest part of the book of Revelation is a prophecy of the destruction of Jerusalem and the temple, which took place in A.D. 70.
3. *The Millennium*. The Millennium of Revelation 20 is the entire present age, between Christ's first and second advents, during which Satan is bound and the church is sharing in the victorious reign of Christ.
4. *The Fulfillment of the Covenant Promises*. With the inauguration of the messianic kingdom at the first advent of Christ, God began fulfilling all of the covenant promises through Jesus and the church in order to progressively accomplish His original plan for a creation and creatures without sin, who submit to Him and worship Him forever.

Our survey of the covenant promises and prophecies of Scripture has revealed a clear and consistent scriptural foundation for postmillennialism. God's original purposes and plans for His creation are now being accomplished. Through His Son, Jesus the Messiah, God is bringing blessing to all the families of the earth and is subduing every enemy. Jesus was given His messianic kingdom at His first advent, and during His present reign He is gradually putting all of His enemies beneath His feet. He has commissioned His people to be the instrument by which He will accomplish His purposes. Through their faithful preaching of the gospel, "all the ends of the earth will remember and turn to the LORD, and all the families of the nations will worship before Thee" (Ps. 22:27).

PART FIVE

Theological Considerations

CHAPTER ELEVEN

Reformed Theology and Eschatology

The postmillennial outlook is not so much a matter of chronology as it is of
Christology—a focus on the grandeur and the power of the ascended Lord and the
greatness of his power that is available to the church in its mission.
—John Jefferson Davis[1]

When studying any doctrine of Scripture, it is wise to move from the known to the unknown. This is especially true when we study a doctrine as controversial as biblical eschatology. We must seek to discover what the doctrines upon which there is a measure of agreement imply or demand of our eschatology. In other words, our eschatology must be consistent with our doctrines of God, Scripture, Christ, man, salvation, and the church. The purpose of this and the following chapters is to demonstrate that postmillennialism is the system of eschatology that is most consistent with the generally agreed upon doctrines of Reformed theology.

Theology Proper

There is nothing more foundational to Christianity than its insistence that it alone is the truth of God revealed by God to bring glory to God. Our understanding of who God is and what He is doing affects everything else we believe. What implications does the orthodox Christian doctrine of God have for eschatology?

The Trinity. All Christians confess that "In the unity of the Godhead there be three persons, of one substance, power, and eternity: God the Father, God the Son, and God the Holy Ghost" (Westminster Confession of Faith, 2.3). Within the Godhead, there is not only a unity of being, but also a unity of will and purpose.[2] The Father has solemnly purposed and promised to bless all families of the earth and to establish His Son's kingdom over all the earth (Gen. 12:1–3; Ps. 110; Isa. 9:6–7; Dan. 2:31–35, 44). The Son has come to accomplish this purpose and is fulfilling it (Matt. 28:18–20). And finally, the Holy Spirit has been given to empower all of God's people to fulfill these goals (Acts 1:8). Postmillennialism affirms that anything promised by the Father, fulfilled by the Son, and empowered by the Spirit cannot fail to come to pass.

The Attributes and Decrees of God. The attributes of God are those characteristics or perfections which He has revealed about Himself in Scripture. The Westminster Larger Catechism lists several of them:

> God is a Spirit, in and of himself infinite in being, glory, blessedness, and perfection; all-sufficient, eternal, unchangeable, incomprehensible, every where present, almighty, knowing all things, most wise, most holy, most just, most merciful and gracious, long-suffering, and abundant in goodness and truth. (Q. 7)

Several of the attributes of God have significant ramifications for eschatology. We shall focus here upon only one of these, the gracious disposition of God toward man.

Scripture teaches us that because of sin, man fell and became radically corrupt and defiled in every part of his being (Rom. 3:10–18). He is dead in sin, hates God, and is inclined to all manner of evil and wickedness (Ps. 51:5; Rom. 1:30; 5:12; 8:7–8; Eph. 2:1–3; 4:17–19; Col. 2:13). Scripture also teaches us that God is holy and righteous (Isa. 6:3; Rev. 4:8), that He hates sin (Deut. 12:31; Ps. 5:5–6), and that His punishment for sinners is eternal and fearsome (Matt. 13:41–42; Rev. 14:11).

Yet what does Scripture reveal about the general disposition of God toward man? Repeatedly we are told that God is gracious and merciful (Ps. 145:8; James 5:11), and that He does not take pleasure in the death of the wicked (Ezek. 18:23, 32). This gracious disposition of God toward man and the fact that He does not take pleasure in the death of the wicked raise some significant eschatological questions.

The Westminster Confession of Faith teaches that "God from all eternity, did, by the most wise and holy counsel of His own will, freely, and unchangeably ordain whatsoever comes to pass" (3.1). God did not decree anything because He foresaw that it would happen in the future. He decreed everything that comes to pass for His own glory and for His own good pleasure (Eph. 1:3–14). So, does God's decretive will contradict His generally gracious disposition toward man? Every orthodox eschatological system except postmillennialism teaches that the vast majority of mankind will be lost and eternally punished in hell.[3] But if God does not take pleasure in the death of men, we are forced to ask why He would foreordain that the vast majority of them will perish eternally.

If the popular eschatological positions are true, God does not take pleasure in sending men to hell, but He has foreordained that most of them will go there anyway, while only a small fraction are saved. This is not impossible, nor would it be unjust, since all men deserve hell. But we must ask if it is consistent with the long-term vision of Scripture. According to postmillennialism, God does not take pleasure in sending men to hell, but for reasons known only to Him, it was necessary that some suffer eternal punishment while the majority are foreordained to salvation and eternal life. Christians may be the minority now, but there are scriptural and theological reasons for believing that this will not always be the case.[4]

Bibliology

One of the fundamental doctrines of Reformed theology has always been its high doctrine of Scripture. According to the Westminster Larger Catechism, "The holy scriptures of the Old and New Testament are the word of God, the only rule of faith and obedience" (Q. 3). Scripture is the inspired, infallible, and inerrant word of the living God. The implications of this for our study of eschatology are important. Too often, the promises of God found in Scripture are either rejected or radically reinterpreted in order to conform to a "realistic" view of the world. When eschatology is the doctrine under consideration, the world around us tends to become the determiner of what is possible and impossible, and newspapers rather than Scripture become our rule of faith.

A consistently Reformed approach to eschatology should disavow any final rule for faith other than the word of God found in Scripture itself. However improbable or impossible they may appear to us, the promises of God are sure and will certainly be fulfilled. At the time when Jesus was born, the promise to Abraham was almost two thousand years old, yet Simeon did not lose faith in the word of God, however unrealistic it may have seemed to others. He believed God, and He saw the One who was born to fulfill the promise (Luke 2:25–32). Postmillennialism rests firmly upon the promises of almighty God in Scripture. Current world events, even if they appear to deny the possibility of the postmillennial hope, are not a cause for alarm. Quite often in the history of redemption, God has waited to accomplish His purposes until "current events" rendered their fulfillment impossible by human standards. Postmillennialists believe that He is going to do it again.

Christology

Central to all Reformed theology is the doctrine of the person and work of Jesus the Messiah. As Thomas Watson explains,

> Jesus Christ is the sum and quintessence of the gospel; the wonder of angels; the joy and triumph of saints. The name of Christ is sweet, it is as music in the ear, honey in the mouth, and a cordial at the heart.[5]

All of our theology revolves around Christ, especially His crucifixion, resurrection, and exaltation. All of the promises and all of the prophecies of the Old Testament find their fulfillment in and through Jesus of Nazareth. We will focus here on two aspects of Christ's person and work.

Seated at the Right Hand of God the Father Almighty. One of the truths explicitly set forth in the ecumenical creeds of the early church and embraced by Reformed Christians is that after Christ ascended into heaven, He was seated at the right hand of God. The significance of this is stated throughout the Bible (e.g., Ps. 110; Acts 2:30–36; 1 Cor. 15:25; Eph. 1:19–23). It means that Christ is King *now*. He has already been given all authority in heaven and on earth (Matt 28:18; cf. Dan. 7:13–14). Discussing the ascension of Christ to the right hand of the Father, Charles Hodge explains:

> Having been committed to Him for a special purpose, this universal dominion as Mediator will be relinquished when that purpose is accomplished. He will reign until all his enemies are put under his feet. And when the last enemy is subdued He will deliver up this kingdom unto the Father, and reign forever as King over the redeemed.[6]

The inauguration of the kingdom does not await the second coming of Christ. The coronation of Jesus is a fact that has already been accomplished.

The eschatological significance of the present mediatorial reign of Christ becomes apparent when we seek to discover the ultimate course of this present age. According to some systems of theology, especially dispensationalism, each redemptive era or "dispensation" ends in utter failure.[7] The problem with this notion is its application to the present age. Jesus Christ has been given all authority over everything. In other words, the outcome of this present age is His responsibility. Are we to believe that Christ will fail to carry out His mission to bring the world into submission during His present reign? Postmillennialism denies that this can or will be the case. Regardless of how many times men have failed to carry out their God-given responsibilities, our Lord Jesus Christ cannot fail.

Already, Now, and Not Yet. Many evangelical theologians regard the kingdom of God as an "already and not yet" kingdom.[8] That is, the kingdom has "already" been inaugurated, but it has "not yet" been consummated. However, we must not forget the period of time between the inauguration and the consummation. As we have seen, that whole period of time is often described in Scripture as a time during which the kingdom is growing (cf. Dan. 2:34–35, 44; Matt. 13:31–33) and as a time during which Christ is putting all of His enemies under His feet (cf. 1 Cor. 15:25). Thus, the development of the kingdom of God is *progressive*.

Postmillennialism agrees that the kingdom has already been inaugurated in connection with the first advent of Christ. It also agrees that the kingdom will not be consummated until the second advent of Christ. However, it also insists that we not forget the implication of these facts: the kingdom is *now* progressing as Christ reigns. Thus, the messianic kingdom is already, now, and not yet realized.

Pneumatology

Pneumatology, or the doctrine of the Holy Spirit, is not often associated with eschatology.[9] However, there is at least one important point of connection. Under the old covenant, the Holy Spirit was given to empower only a few individuals for specific ministries.[10] But today, in the new covenant age, the Holy Spirit empowers all of God's people for ministry. This work of the Holy Spirit is intimately connected with the work of Christ in fulfilling all of the old covenant promises. Sinclair Ferguson explains the significance of the promise of the Spirit like this:

> There are two aspects to this promise. The gift of the Spirit is a central element in the new covenant promise that God had given to his people (*cf.* Ezk. 36:27), and the inner essence of the promise given to Abraham (*cf.* Gal. 3:14). But another aspect emerges, for the gift of the Spirit was promised *to Christ* in order to fulfil the messianic promises: 'so will he sprinkle many nations, and kings will shut their mouths because of him . . . I will give him a portion among the great, and he will divide the spoils with the strong' (Is. 52:15; 53:12). It is through the gift of the Spirit to Christ and the bestowal of the Spirit by Christ that the Father's promise to his Son in Psalm 2:8 is fulfilled: 'Ask of me, and I will make the nations your inheritance . . .' The fulfilment of the Great

Commission takes place in the power of the Spirit. The hidden reality revealed publicly by Pentecost is that the ascended Christ had now asked the Father to fulfil his promise, had received the Spirit for his people, and had now poured him out on the church so that the messianic age begun in the resurrection of Christ might catch up in its flow those who are united to him by participation in the one Spirit. Thus, in Abraham's seed all the nations of the earth would now be blessed (Gn. 12:3; Gal. 3:13–14).[11]

The implications of this outpouring and empowering by the Holy Spirit for eschatology are enormous.

The Father has promised to establish a kingdom that will grow to fill the whole earth and to bless all the families and nations of the earth. Jesus Christ has been seated at the right hand of the Father as the King of kings and has been given all authority in heaven and on earth to fulfill these promises and to put all of His enemies under His feet. Finally, the Holy Spirit has been poured out upon all of God's people in order to empower them to fulfill the Great Commission. With God the Father, God the Son, and God the Holy Spirit working toward the fulfillment of these goals, how can we expect anything less than the triumph in this present age of Christ the King?

Soteriology

One of the fundamental causes of the Protestant Reformation was a dispute over the basic doctrines of salvation.[12] To this day, soteriology remains a central focus in the work of Reformed theologians. Some of its implications for eschatology must, therefore, be examined.

The Humiliation of Christ. Reformed theology has tended to distinguish between two aspects of Christ's state of humiliation. The first is His laying aside of the majesty that belonged to Him as the supreme ruler of the universe and taking human nature upon himself. The second aspect of Christ's humiliation involves His suffering and death on the cross.[13]

There are two implications of Christ's humiliation that are significant for eschatology. The first is expressed by W. G. T. Shedd:

> It is utterly improbable that such a stupendous miracle as the incarnation, humiliation, passion, and crucifixion of one of the Persons of the Godhead, should yield a small and insignificant result; that this amazing mystery of mysteries, 'which the angels desire to look into,' and which involves such an immense personal sacrifice on the part of the Supreme Being, should have a lame and impotent conclusion. On a priori grounds, therefore, we have reason to conclude that the Gospel of the Cross will be successful, and the Christian religion a triumph on the earth and among the race of creatures for whom it was intended. But this can hardly be the case, if only a small fraction of the human family are saved. The presumption, consequently, is that the great majority of mankind, not the small minority of it, will be the subjects of redeeming grace.[14]

When we stop to consider for a moment exactly what was involved in the work of redemption itself, the difficulty mentioned by Shedd becomes unavoidable. After the Fall, God would have been perfectly just to send our first parents to eternal punishment, but He did not do this. Instead, He initiated a plan of salvation that would span thousands of years, involve billions of people, and, most importantly, would involve the death of His only begotten Son on a cross.

For the sake of saving men, the Son of God laid aside His supreme majesty and took the form of a bond servant (Phil. 2:7). He condescended to undergo all manner of testing and temptation (Heb. 4:15). He willingly endured suffering at the hands of wicked men. He was slapped and scourged and mocked and spat upon. He was condemned to death on a cross between common thieves. On the cross, not only did he endure a physically torturous death, but the wrath of His Father was poured out upon Him as He was made a curse for the sake of sinful men. He who knew no sin, the Second Person of the Trinity Himself, was made sin on our behalf (2 Cor. 5:21). The agony of this was so extreme that He cried out, "My God, My God, why hast Thou forsaken Me?" (Mark 15:34). The Son of God suffered death as the penalty for our sin, and then he was buried in a tomb. Now, did the Son of God undergo all of this humiliation and suffering in order to save only a small percentage of men? Our survey of Scripture has indicated that he did not.

A second significant implication of Christ's humiliation has to do with its visibility. Some would argue that the victory which is so often connected with the exaltation of Christ occurs primarily, if not exclusively, in the invisible spiritual realm. It does not matter, they argue, what happens on the earth, because the earth is not the stage of Christ's exaltation. There are a number of serious problems with this theory. At this point, we will emphasize only one.

Postmillennialism does not deny that victory has been, is being, and will be won by Christ in the heavenly, spiritual realm. However, it does deny that the victory of Christ will be any less visible in history and on earth than His humiliation. His suffering, death, and burial were visible and were witnessed by both men and angels, and His vindication will likewise be witnessed in history by both men and angels.

Individual and Cosmic Salvation. A second aspect of Reformed soteriology that is important for our study is the parallel between individual redemption and cosmic redemption. While there are obvious differences between the two, there are also numerous parallels. Sinclair Ferguson notes this parallel:

> In the New Testament, . . . glorification is seen to begin already in the present order, in believers. Through the Spirit they are already being changed from glory to glory, as they gaze on/reflect the face of the Lord (2 Cor. 3:17–18). But the consummation of this glorification awaits the eschaton and the Spirit's ministry in the resurrection. Here, too, the pattern of his working is: as in Christ, so in believers and, by implication, in the universe.[15]

This parallel pattern is seen most clearly when the "already, now, and not yet" character of individual salvation is compared to the "already, now, and not yet" character of the kingdom. The work of redemption is applied to individuals definitively (in justification), progressively (in sanctification), and completely (in glorification). In the same way, the work of redemption is applied universally to the kingdom definitively (in its inauguration), progressively (in its expansion), and completely (in its consummation).

The significant aspect of this parallelism for our study is the progressive stage of redemption. The progressive element of individual salvation is strongly affirmed in Reformed theology. The Westminster Confession of Faith, for example, declares that "although the remaining corruption, for a time, may much prevail; yet, through the continual supply of strength from the sanctifying Spirit of Christ, the regenerate part doth *overcome*; and so, the saints *grow* in grace, perfecting holiness in the fear of God" (14.3).[16] Reformed theology teaches that believers are already justified. They have been declared righteous. It also teaches that final perfection and freedom from the presence of sin will not occur until we are glorified. But this does not deny the progressive growth in holiness that is demanded by God. No Reformed theologian would affirm that the growth of holiness in an individual is or will be paralleled by a growth in sinfulness.

But when the discussion turns to the nature of cosmic redemption and the establishment of the messianic kingdom, precisely the opposite is often argued. The inauguration is affirmed and the consummation is affirmed, but the necessity of cosmic "progressive sanctification" is denied. For example, amillennialist Anthony Hoekema explains that "Satan's kingdom, if we may call it that, will continue to exist and grow as long as God's kingdom grows, until Christ comes again."[17] In other words, when cosmic redemption is in view, the "regenerate part doth *not* overcome."

Postmillennialism maintains consistency between the application of redemption on an individual scale and the application of redemption on a cosmic scale. In both cases, God has already accomplished a definitive work. In both cases, this work will be perfected and consummated on the Last Day. And, in both cases, there is a progressive growth in holiness as the remaining corruption is overcome through the supernatural power of the Holy Spirit.

Conclusion

The thesis of this book is that the postmillennial system of eschatology is not only the eschatological system that is most consistent with a covenantal approach to Scripture and with the relevant texts of Scripture, but that it is also the system of eschatology that is most consistent with Reformed theology. We have discussed several aspects of the relationship between postmillennialism and Reformed theology in this chapter. In the following chapter we will examine the shortcomings and inconsistencies of both premillennialism and amillennialism.

CHAPTER TWELVE

The Inadequacy of Premillennialism and Amillennialism

The most serious error in much of the current "prophetic" teaching of today is the claim that the future of Christendom is to be read not in terms of Revival and Victory, but of growing impotence and apostasy.
—Oswald T. Allis [1]

Postmillennialism has not always been a minority view in the church. Between the seventeenth and the late nineteenth centuries, it was widely held by conservative Protestants. In the twentieth century, however, it has been overshadowed by other millennial positions. Premillennialism is the most widely held position among conservative evangelicals as a whole in the late twentieth century. And among Reformed theologians today, amillennialism is the predominant view.

In the preceding chapters, we have examined the promises and prophecies of Scripture from Genesis to Revelation. We have discovered the glorious outworking of God's covenant promises in and through His Son, Jesus the Messiah. Implicitly, the preceding chapters have been a critique of the prevailing eschatological systems. In this chapter, however, we will explicitly critique both premillennialism and amillennialism as eschatological systems.

The Inadequacy of Premillennialism

The fundamental problem with all forms of premillennialism is its understanding of the time of the millennial kingdom.[2] There are two main forms of premillennialism in the evangelical church today, dispensationalism and historic premillennialism. There are important differences between these two eschatological systems, but we will focus on what they hold in common.[3]

According to both forms of premillennialism, the "thousand years" described in Revelation 20 are a literal, thousand-year period of time that will begin at the second coming of Christ. At that time, Satan will be bound, all believers will be resurrected, and the thousand-year messianic reign of Christ with His people will begin. At the end of the Millennium, Satan will be released, there will be a widespread rebellion that will be immediately crushed by God, all unbelievers will be raised from the grave, and the final judgment will begin. As widespread and popular as this view is, there are a number of serious problems with it.

The Fundamental Hermeneutical Flaw. First, it must be noted that premillennialism violates one of the most basic principles of sound biblical hermeneutics. Rather than interpreting an admittedly difficult text in light of clearer passages of Scripture, premillennialism interprets the clearer texts of Scripture in light of the less clear text. The symbolic passage in Revelation 20 is made the touchstone for end-time chronology, despite the many passages throughout the rest of Scripture which indicate that Jesus was given the messianic kingdom at His first advent.

Excessive Reliance on a Single Text. The basic hermeneutical problem of premillennialism points to a closely related difficulty. The fact that so many other Scriptures are interpreted to fit in with a particular understanding of Revelation 20 indicates that far too much weight is being placed on a single text.[4] Unlike amillennialism and postmillennialism, premillennialism relies almost entirely on a single passage of Scripture. And not only does it rest on one text of Scripture, it rests on an interpretation of this one text that requires several assumptions to be granted:

1. The premillennial interpretation of Revelation 20 requires that the book as a whole be interpreted futuristically. As we have already mentioned, there has been a great deal of dis-

agreement among Christians as to how to interpret Revelation. Four basic methods have been suggested: futurism, preterism, idealism, and historicism. The truth or falsity of amillennialism or postmillennialism does not depend upon which of these approaches is adopted. Premillennialism, on the other hand, requires the futuristic approach.

2. Premillennialism also requires that Revelation 19:11–16 be a vision of the Second Coming. This is a highly disputed interpretation, but it is absolutely necessary for premillennialism.

3. Premillennialism also requires the assumption that the visions in Revelation 19 and 20 describe events in chronological order. But even if it were granted that Revelation 19 is a vision of the Second Coming, this would not require that the millennium of Revelation 20 follow chronologically. All that is explicitly said in the text is that John saw the visions in a particular order, not that they would be fulfilled in a particular order. Elsewhere in the book of Revelation it is clear that the visions of John sometimes do not follow in historical succession. If they all did, then the birth of Christ (chap. 12) follows the sounding of the seventh trumpet of judgment (chap. 11).

If any one of these underlying assumptions is false, then the premillennial interpretation of Revelation 20 is false. And if this particular interpretation of Revelation 20 falls, then premillennialism falls because it has no other possible scriptural basis.

The Completeness of Christ's Church at His Coming. Another problem faced by premillennialism is the fact that Scripture repeatedly asserts that all who are to be saved will be saved *before* the Second Coming. If this is the case, then obviously no one can be saved after the Second Coming, during the time that premillennialism understands to be the kingdom age.[5] Paul teaches that all believers will be resurrected at Christ's second coming (1 Cor. 15:23). He teaches that all believers will be presented as a spotless bride to Christ at that time (Eph. 5:25–27; cf. 1 Thess. 3:13). Nowhere is there the slightest indication that the offer of salvation will extend beyond the Second Coming.

Christ's Kingdom Has Already Been Inaugurated. Premillennialism is also contradicted by the continual testimony throughout the Old and New Testaments that the messianic kingdom has already been inaugurated in connection with the events of Christ's first advent. In the sermon recorded in Acts 2, Peter declares that Christ fulfilled the covenant promise made to David and has been seated at the right hand of God as King (Acts 2:29–36). This was in fulfillment of many Old Testament prophecies and promises (cf. 2 Sam. 7:1–13; Pss. 2:7–9; 110:1–4; Isa. 9:6–7; Dan. 2:31–35, 44; 7:13–14). Jesus Himself affirms this truth when He declares that He *has been given* all authority in heaven and on earth (Matt. 28:18). Paul declares several times in his epistles that Christ is now reigning as the messianic King (e.g., 1 Cor. 15:24–25; Col. 1:13). The apostle John refers to Christ as presently "the ruler of the kings of the earth" (Rev. 1:5). If Christ already has all authority in heaven and on earth, what more authority could He possibly receive at His second coming?

Contradiction to the End-Time Chronology of the New Testament. Premillennialism ultimately fails because its interpretation of Revelation 20 contradicts the basic chronology of the Second Coming that is set forth in the rest of the New Testament. We may briefly outline this chronology as follows:

1. Paul teaches that *the end* immediately follows the resurrection of Christ's people at His second coming (1 Cor. 15:22–24).
2. Jesus teaches that this resurrection will occur on the Last Day (John 6:40). There is complete agreement, then, between Jesus and Paul. Both teach that the resurrection of believers will occur on the Last Day, that is, at the end.
3. Jesus teaches that the resurrection of the wicked will occur at the same time as the resurrection of His people (John 5:28–29). He tells us that an "hour" is coming, a point in time, when "all" will rise. If the resurrection of the righteous and the resurrection of the wicked occur at the same "hour," then they cannot be separated by a thousand-year interval.
4. Paul teaches that the bodily resurrection of believers at the second coming of Christ marks the defeat and destruction of the last enemy—death (1 Cor. 15:26, 54–55).

5. John teaches us that the destruction of death takes place at the Great White Throne judgment, which all commentators understand to take place at the end of the Millennium (Rev. 20:11–14). Since the destruction of death is said to occur at the Second Coming by Paul and at the Great White Throne judgment by John, these two events cannot be separated by a thousand-year interval. Death is only destroyed once.

6. Finally, Paul teaches that on the Last Day, Christ gives the kingdom over to the Father (1 Cor. 15:24). The Last Day is not the day when Christ receives the kingdom; it is the day when the kingdom is consummated. The messianic kingdom, therefore, is prior to the Second Coming.

We must conclude that there is no scriptural warrant for believing that there will be a thousand-year reign of Christ following His second coming. This view is based on a flawed hermeneutical principle. It rests almost entirely upon one highly disputed passage of Scripture. It requires that the "hour" in which all men are raised from their graves be stretched over a period of a thousand years. It requires that death be destroyed twice, once before the Millennium and once afterward. And it conflicts with the simple end-time chronology presented throughout the rest of the New Testament. Premillennialism in any form must, therefore, be rejected.

The Inadequacy of Amillennialism

Amillennialism and postmillennialism are in general agreement regarding the time of the Millennium.[6] Both teach that Christ's second coming consummates the messianic kingdom. Amillennialism interprets Revelation 20 as a description of the heavenly reign of Christ with the saints throughout the entire present age, an age which is characterized by the parallel growth of good and evil. The present "millennial" age will be followed by the second coming of Christ, the general resurrection, the judgment, and the new heavens and new earth. According to amillennial eschatology, there is insufficient scriptural warrant for believing that righteousness will prevail on earth prior to the second coming of Christ. Instead, the Second Coming will be preceded by increased lawlessness and apostasy. The fundamental disagreement between amillennialism and postmillennialism, then, pertains not to the time of the messianic kingdom, but to the *nature* of this period of time.

In Heaven and on Earth. Amillennialism often teaches that Christ's messianic kingdom has little to do with the present created order. The kingdom is often limited to the hearts of the regenerate, heaven, or the eternal state.[7] This virtually denies that the messianic kingdom has anything to do with this present earth. In contrast to this tendency, Scripture makes it abundantly clear that this earth, although not the source of the kingdom, is a part of the kingdom. Christ's messianic authority and reign extend over *all* of heaven and earth (Matt. 28:18), and He is in the process of subduing all of His enemies, whether in heaven or on earth (1 Cor. 15:25). In addition, it must be remembered that Christ has now been given authority over all of the kingdoms and nations on earth (cf. Dan. 2; Rev. 1:5). Every nation on this earth is presently under the dominion of Christ. He is the ruler of the nations. He has been given the nations as His inheritance. Amillennialism fails to deal with these scriptural truths satisfactorily.

The Growth of the Kingdom. Amillennialism also fails to deal adequately with the many passages of Scripture that tell us about the progressive growth of the messianic kingdom. In the Old Testament, this present kingdom is described as a stone that grows to fill the whole earth (Dan. 2:34–35, 44) and as a stream of water that steadily increases in depth until it becomes a mighty river (Ezek. 47). In the New Testament, the progressive growth of the kingdom is described in the parables of the mustard seed and the leaven (Matt. 13:31–33) and in terms of the ongoing subjugation of Christ's enemies (1 Cor. 15:25). Amillennialism cannot do justice to these and other texts that describe the gradual growth of the messianic kingdom and the subjugation of all other kingdoms. It substitutes the idea of the parallel growth of Satan's kingdom alongside Christ's kingdom.

The Parallel Growth of the Two Kingdoms. Amillennialists sometimes attempt to reconcile their position with Scripture by asserting that while Christ's kingdom does grow spiritually, its growth is paralleled by the growth of Satan's kingdom. According to amillennialist Anthony Hoekema, "Satan's kingdom, if we may call it that, will continue to exist and grow as long as God's kingdom grows, until Christ comes again."[8] In response to this, we must first say that we agree that Satan's activity will continue and that there will continue to be conflict until Christ returns. But it does not follow that Satan's kingdom will *grow* until Christ comes again. This notion is implausible for several reasons:

1. Satan is presently bound, which renders growth difficult at best (Rev. 20:1–3).
2. Satan's "kingdom" is presently being plundered by Christ (Mark 3:27).
3. Christ's kingdom grows until it fills the whole earth, and it crushes all opposing kingdoms to dust (Dan. 2).
4. The parallel growth of these two kingdoms would mean that at the very point in history when Christ will have put all but the last of His enemies under His feet, Satan's kingdom will be at the apex of its power.
5. Another matter that amillennialists have not adequately considered is the course of Satan's kingdom *prior* to the cross. Was it growing, declining, or holding steady? If, as amillennialism asserts, it is growing during the present age, then what effect did the life, death, resurrection, and ascension of Christ have on Satan's kingdom? If it was growing before the Cross and it is still growing after the Cross, then the life and death of Christ had virtually no effect on the growth of Satan's kingdom. If it was declining or holding steady until the first coming of Christ and then began growing, then Christ's life, death, resurrection, and ascension jump-started the kingdom of Satan. Amillennialism would force us to believe that the work of Christ had either no effect or a positive effect on the growth of Satan's kingdom.
6. Finally, we must ask amillennialists why the growth of Satan's kingdom should have both historically visible and spiritual effects, while the growth of Christ's kingdom should have almost only spiritual effects.

As Christ's kingdom is extended throughout the earth, there will be conflict and suffering. But the extensive growth of Christ's kingdom results in the decline of Satan's kingdom, not its rise.

Unnecessary Agnosticism. Amillennialists often say that, while they would like to believe that the postmillennial hope is true, there is simply no scriptural warrant for believing it to be so.[9] The purpose of a large section of this book has been to demonstrate that there is scriptural warrant for such a hope.[10] The entire Bible from Genesis to Revelation gives us sufficient warrant for such faith. All of the covenant promises and all of the prophecies of Scripture point to a world-wide blessing of all the families of the earth and to the universal extension of Christ's kingdom on this earth.

The Wilderness Motif. A misunderstanding of the millennial kingdom has led to the suggestion that the wilderness wandering of Israel in the Old Testament is the controlling motif for the church during this period of time. As explained by amillennialist Richard B. Gaffin, "Until Christ returns the church remains a wilderness congregation."[11] There are several difficulties with utilizing the wilderness wandering of Israel as the controlling metaphor for the New Testament church.

1. First, both the Old Testament and the book of Hebrews tell us that the wilderness wandering was the judgment of God upon a faithless people (Num. 13–14; Heb. 3:7–19). The notion that the controlling motif of the present age is the wilderness wandering implies that the church is essentially under the judgment of God.
2. The Old Testament believers were "strangers and exiles on the earth" who looked beyond the promises of the land toward the true messianic kingdom which the land signified (Heb. 11:13). And, as we saw in our survey of Hebrews, those saints are now partakers with us in the messianic kingdom.
3. There are a number of metaphors used in the New Testament to describe the present age. As we have repeatedly demonstrated, Christ has already been seated upon the throne in fulfillment of the Davidic covenant (cf. Acts

2:30–36). In this we find a parallel to the era of the united kingdom in the Old Testament. Also, Christ goes forth into the earth which He has inherited to put all enemies under His feet (1 Cor. 15:25), much like the conquest under Joshua.[12] Thus, we cannot simply take one period of Israel's history and declare it to be the controlling metaphor of the present age.

If the church is presently experiencing a "wilderness wandering," it may be for the same reasons that Israel had to wander in the wilderness. Israel was forced to wander in the wilderness as a judgment for failing to trust God to fulfill His promise to go forth before Israel and conquer the Promised Land. She saw too many "giants in the land" and doubted God's promise.

God has now given Christ the entire earth as His inheritance, and He has promised that all of Christ's enemies will be placed beneath His feet, that all the families of the earth will be blessed, and that Christ's kingdom will grow until it fills the earth. He has promised to accomplish all of this through the church's faithful preaching of the gospel. The question for us today is simple. Will we be like the majority of Israel and continue to look in fear at the giants in the land and urge our fellow Christians to be "realistic," or will we be like Joshua and Caleb and faithfully follow our King, trusting Him to fulfill every one of His promises to the fullest degree?

Scriptural Grounds for Pessimism? Amillennialists (and premillennialists) point to a large number of passages which they believe to teach a gradual worsening of conditions on earth prior to the Second Coming. They include Matthew 24, 2 Thessalonians 2, and Revelation 6–19. However, the vast majority of them refer specifically to first-century conditions at the time of Christ's coming in judgment upon Jerusalem.[13] Amillennialists, of course, object to a preterist interpretation of these texts. Anthony Hoekema, for example, argues that a preterist interpretation of them is "not justified."[14] However, as we have seen in our discussion of a number of these passages, the alternative futurist interpretations normally require that exegetical violence be done to the text.[15]

Suffering and the Church. Another problem with amillennial eschatology is that it has sometimes overreacted to abuses with abuses of its own. Amillennialist Richard B. Gaffin, for example, objects to postmillennialism because, he believes, it misunderstands the basic identity of the church: "Over the interadvental period in its entirety, from beginning to end, a fundamental aspect of the church's existence is (to be) 'suffering with Christ'; *nothing, the New Testament teaches, is more basic to its identity than that.*"[16] As proof of this claim, he cites three passages: 2 Corinthians 4:7ff., Philippians 3:10, and Romans 8:17ff.[17] In response, the following must be noted.

1. Second Corinthians 4:7ff. is, strictly speaking, an autobiographical passage. Paul is defending his personal authority as an apostle. Nowhere do we find any indication that these verses are paradigmatic for the church over the entire course of her history.
2. In Philippians 3:10, all that Paul is saying is that all believers, regardless of how bad their circumstances may be, may come to know the sustaining power of Christ and His resurrection. The suffering he speaks of is dying to sin. This struggle will remain until the Second Coming.
3. Romans 8:17 does not contradict postmillennialism. It is found in the concluding chapter of a section that deals with the struggle of Christians with sin. Postmillennialism does not argue that indwelling sin will be eradicated before the Second Coming.
4. Finally, it is wrong to say that "nothing" is more basic to the identity of the church than suffering. Nothing is more basic to the identity of the institutional church than the preaching of the gospel, the correct administration of the sacraments, and the worship of God in Spirit and in truth (Westminster Confession of Faith, 25.4). Nothing is more basic to the identity of the individual Christian than faith, hope, obedience, and love, the fruit of the Spirit (cf. 1 Cor. 13:4–13; Gal. 5:22–24; 1 John 2:3; 3:10, 24; 4:7–21; 5:1–3).

Until the Second Coming, sin will remain a part of earthly existence. And as long as there is sin, there will be suffering and pain.

But suffering by persecution is not a *sine qua non* of the church. If it is, there are few if any true churches in North America today.

Amillennialism does not do justice to the many texts, examined earlier in this book, which point to the progressive growth of the kingdom of Christ during the present age. Nor does it adequately deal with the progressive subjugation of all of Christ's enemies during this same period of time. It does not sufficiently explain the authority that Christ has been given on earth as well as in heaven, and, as a result, it has wrongly placed the fulfillment of promises meant for this age in the eternal state. Amillennialism, therefore, must also be rejected.

Conclusion

In this chapter we have briefly examined some of the main problems and difficulties with both premillennialism and amillennialism. The fundamental problem of premillennialism is its conception of the *time* of the messianic kingdom, and the fundamental problem of amillennialism is its conception of the *nature* of the messianic kingdom. Postmillennialism is the system of eschatology that is most consistent with the entire teaching of Scripture. In the following chapter, we shall present a summary of postmillennialism in order to draw together the various strands we have studied so far.

CHAPTER THIRTEEN

The Answer of Postmillennialism

We find that Christ's work of redemption truly has as its object the people of the entire world and that His Kingdom is to become universal.
—Loraine Boettner[1]

We have examined the teaching of Scripture from Genesis to Revelation and found that the postmillennial hope has abundant support in it. We have also examined some of the basic doctrines of orthodox Reformed theology and found that postmillennialism is consistent with these doctrines. We have discovered that both premillennialism and amillennialism are scripturally inadequate systems of eschatology. The purpose of this chapter, then, is to provide an overview of the teaching of postmillennialism.

What Postmillennialism Is Not

A great deal of confusion surrounds the true nature and teaching of postmillennialism, especially on the part of some of its dispensationalist opponents. It is necessary, therefore, to clarify what postmillennialism is not, before proceeding to explain what it is.

Postmillennialism Is Not Liberalism

A false accusation that dispensationalists commonly make against postmillennialism is that it is virtually indistinguishable from theological liberalism. John F. Walvoord, for example, claims that "postmillennialism lends itself to liberalism with only minor adjustments."[2]

Fellow dispensationalist J. Dwight Pentecost echoes this claim.[3] However, there are a number of reasons why such accusations are false:

1. Postmillennialism existed long before theological liberalism arose in the late nineteenth century.
2. Biblical postmillennialism affirms the doctrines (such as inerrancy, the virgin birth, the resurrection, etc.) which modern liberalism denies. Many of the staunchest opponents of liberalism, such as Charles Hodge and B. B. Warfield, were postmillennialists.
3. The argument reduces to absurdity. If the mere fact that some liberal theologians believe in a humanistic type of postmillennialism means that postmillennialism is liberal, then the fact that many cults are premillennial would mean that premillennialism is cultic.

The accusation that postmillennialism is inherently liberal is one that is unworthy of Christian scholarship.[4]

Postmillennialism Is Not the Social Gospel

Another dispensationalist, Charles C. Ryrie, attempts to tie postmillennialism to the social gospel. In his explanation of postmillennialism, he says that the "social gospel . . . has been an outgrowth of this system since the idea of a world free from evil is envisioned as a result of man's efforts."[5] There are a number of reasons why this statement is false.

1. Postmillennialism does not teach that any of its hopes will be achieved merely as a "result of man's efforts." Rather, it teaches that the spread of the kingdom and of the gospel will be accomplished through the supernatural work of the Holy Spirit.
2. Late nineteenth-century advocates of the social gospel believed that man was essentially good, that he was theoretically perfectible, that sin was curable, and that the kingdom of God could be ushered in by the united efforts of mankind. Postmillennialism rejects all of these teachings.

3. The fact that postmillennialism believes that the growth of the messianic kingdom will affect more than the souls of men does not mean that it is identical to the social gospel. Postmillennialism does not deny the spiritual needs of man simply because it is also concerned with his physical needs (cf. James 1:27; 2:15–16).

The identification of postmillennialism with the social gospel movement is as groundless as the identification of it with theological liberalism.

Postmillennialism Is Not Universalism

Another misunderstanding of postmillennialism is the belief that it somehow entails universalism, or the salvation of every human being. Amillennialist Floyd Hamilton objects to postmillennialism because the "belief that all will become righteous would seem to contradict the plain teaching of election, that some are saved and others lost."[6] Similarly, amillennialist W. J. Grier tells us that "the Bible does not hold forth the prospect of a converted world before the Lord comes; are not the wheat and the tares to grow together till the harvest at the end of the world?"[7] These are both fine objections to universalism, but neither has any bearing on biblical postmillennialism, since postmillennialism agrees that not all men are to be saved. Postmillennialism would disagree with amillennialism not over the presence of tares in the field, but over the number of tares compared to the number of wheat plants.

Postmillennialism Is Not Perfectionism

Amillennialist Geerhardus Vos states another misconception regarding postmillennialism when he asserts that this system of eschatology teaches that "this world can be in course of time brought to a point of ideal perfection, so as to need no further crisis."[8] As a matter of fact, however, postmillennialism does not teach that perfection can be achieved prior to the consummation. Postmillennialism teaches that there will be tares until the end. There will be sin and death and suffering until the end. The progressive growth of the messianic kingdom no more entails perfectionism than does the doctrine of the progressive sanctification of the believer.

Postmillennialism Is Not Nationalism

Some recent critics of postmillennialism have wrongly claimed that this system of theology has an "obsession with the fate of America and the preservation of the American way of life."[9] The same author continues: "Christians must avoid a civil religion that confuses the kingdom of God with the American way of life, and we must be willing to recognize that the church can—and will—survive the fall of this country, should God bring it about."[10] While there have doubtless been those who have elevated America to an undue place of prominence in the covenantal work of God, postmillennialism as such does not support or demand such thinking. Postmillennialism is primarily concerned with the growth of the messianic kingdom of Christ. It no more demands the continuation and restoration of America than it does of any other earthly nation. All nations, including America, are under the authority of Jesus the Messiah. And all nations, including America, will be brought to recognition of this fact even if that requires the judgment of God.

What Postmillennialism Is

We will now summarize the fundamental teachings of postmillennial eschatology. On the basis of the covenant promises and prophecies found throughout the Scriptures, postmillennialism holds to the eschatological convictions discussed below.

The Kingdom of Christ Has Been Inaugurated

Fundamental to postmillennial eschatology is the doctrine that the messianic kingdom has been inaugurated, and that Christ has been given this kingdom in connection with the events of the First Advent. Because Satan has been bound and the saints are now reigning with Christ, postmillennialism identifies the "thousand years" of Revelation 20 with the entire period between the two advents of Christ. There is no need for the church to "bring in the kingdom" because the kingdom already exists.

Postmillennialists believe that there is abundant scriptural support for the belief that the First Advent witnessed the inauguration of the kingdom and the coronation of Christ. The prophecies of the

Old Testament connect the beginning of the kingdom to the First Advent (cf. Daniel 2:44; 7:13–14; Zech. 9:9–10). The New Testament repeatedly confirms that these prophecies were fulfilled in connection with the first advent of Christ (cf. Matt. 2:2; 28:18–20; Luke 1:32–33; Acts 2:29–36; 17:7; 1 Cor. 15:23–25; Col. 1:13; Rev. 1:5).

Jesus the Messiah has been seated at the right hand of God and has been given universal authority over all of heaven and earth. He has been given dominion, glory, and a kingdom which will not be destroyed. He is now the ruler of the nations of the earth. The inauguration of the messianic kingdom and the coronation of Christ do not await His second coming.

The Kingdom Is Redemptive

According to postmillennialism, the messianic kingdom is fundamentally redemptive. Its primary purpose is to redeem and restore mankind and creation (cf. Isa. 11, 65, 66). As the messianic King, Christ is to fulfill the Abrahamic promise and bring blessing to all the families and nations of the earth (Ezek. 37:24–28).

The messianic kingdom of Christ is not political or violent in nature (cf. Heb. 11–13). This kingdom is furthered by spiritual regeneration rather than violent revolution. As Paul so clearly states,

> For though we walk in the flesh, we do not war according to the flesh, for the weapons of our warfare are not of the flesh, but divinely powerful for the destruction of fortresses. We are destroying speculations and every lofty thing raised up against the knowledge of God, and we are taking every thought captive to the obedience of Christ. (2 Cor. 10:3–5)

The source of Christ's authority is not earthly or political (cf. John 18:36). His authority is from God (cf. Dan. 2:34, 44).

The Growth of the Kingdom Is Progressive

An essential doctrine of postmillennialism is that prior to the Second Coming, the messianic kingdom will grow until it has filled the whole earth. Postmillennialism denies that this growth will be paralleled by the growth of Satan's kingdom. Instead, Christ's kingdom will overcome all opposing kingdoms and bring all nations into submission to Him.

The progressive growth of Christ's messianic kingdom is abundantly taught by both the Old and New Testaments. According to the prophet Isaiah, there will be no end to the increase of Christ's government (Isa. 9:7). The prophet Daniel compares the progressive growth of the messianic kingdom to a stone that grows and crushes all opposing kingdoms until it fills the whole earth (Dan. 2:34–35, 44).

In the New Testament, we learn that although the messianic kingdom has a visibly insignificant beginning, it will grow and overcome all Satanic opposition. Its growth will be both intensive (Matt. 13:33) and extensive (Matt. 13:31–32). During his present reign, Christ is putting all His enemies under His feet (1 Cor. 15:25). As his kingdom grows, all opposing and rebellious kingdoms decline. The kingdoms of the enemy will not grow in strength as they are being crushed by the kingdom of Christ.

The subjugation of the enemies of Christ, either through conversion or judgment, does not require the second coming of Christ to be accomplished. It has been definitively accomplished already. It is being progressively realized throughout this present age, and once this process has been completed, the kingdom will be consummated at the Second Coming.

The Kingdom Grows Supernaturally

Postmillennialism teaches that the kingdom grows entirely supernaturally. Only the Holy Spirit can accomplish the regeneration necessary for the spread of the kingdom, and only Christ can supernaturally judge those who resist His work. The efforts of man to further God's kingdom apart from His power are utterly futile.

The preaching of the gospel is God's ordained means of spreading the kingdom. When the church remains faithful to her calling to preach the word, administer the sacraments, and worship God in Spirit and in truth, the kingdom grows. When individual Christians fulfill their calling in every area of life and bring glory to God, the kingdom grows. When the church begins to believe that it can bring about lasting change through political means, the growth of the kingdom is drastically slowed. Politics and legislation cannot take the place of regeneration.

This is not to say that national governments are outside the boundaries of the messianic kingdom, for they are not. Christ is their ruler, and they should acknowledge that in their actions and in their legislation. But while the church and the state are both under the messianic authority of Christ, they have different spheres of authority and different responsibilities. The church is neither the state nor a political party. It has a message for states and political parties, but if these fail to perform their God-given responsibilities, the church is not authorized to step in and exercise those duties. Postmillennialism renounces all political or earthly attempts to further the messianic kingdom and relies solely upon the supernatural work of God.

This Growth Will Lead to Worldwide Conversion

Many passages of Scripture point to conversion on an unprecedented, worldwide scale before the second coming of Christ. The primary promise of the Abrahamic covenant was worldwide in scope, declaring that through the seed of Abraham "all the families of the earth" would be blessed. This theme continues in the Psalms, where we are told that "all the ends of the earth will remember and turn to the LORD, and all the families of the nations will worship before Thee" (Ps. 22:27–28), and that "all the earth will worship Thee, and will sing praises to Thee" (Ps. 66:4).

The Abrahamic promise is repeated throughout the Prophets, where we learn that "all the nations" will go up to the house of the Lord (Isa. 2:2), and that there will be a worldwide conversion of the nations (Isa. 66:18–19). Jesus indicates that He is the One who will fulfill this promise, when He commands His disciples, "Go therefore and make disciples of all the nations" (Matt. 28:19).

In the book of Romans, we learn how this promise will be fulfilled (see Rom. 9–11). We learn that the salvation of all the families of the earth is to occur in an unexpected way. Only a remnant of Jews have believed in their Messiah; the rest have stumbled in disbelief. But through their transgression, salvation has come to the Gentiles. But by bringing salvation to the Gentiles, God will cause the Jews to become jealous and come to their Messiah. And as their transgression resulted in blessing for the world, so their salvation will result in even greater blessing (Rom. 11:15).

Postmillennialism teaches that the growth of the kingdom will reach a point where the majority of men and nations have willingly submitted to Jesus the Messiah. It does not teach that every individual who has ever lived on earth will be saved, nor does it teach that there will be a time prior to the Second Coming when every living individual will be converted. But it does believe that there is sufficient scriptural warrant to say that at some point in history there will be worldwide conversion on an unprecedented scale.

The Kingdom Will Be Perfectly Consummated Only at the Second Coming

Postmillennialism teaches that the present millennial age will end at the second coming of Christ. At that time, all of the dead will be raised from their graves (1 Thess. 4:16; cf. Rev. 20:13). Immediately following the resurrection of the dead, all living believers will be changed and caught up in the air to meet the Lord (1 Thess. 4:17; cf. 1 Cor. 15:51–52). When all have been gathered before the Great White Throne of God, the final judgment will proceed (Rev. 20:11–12). All who are Christ's will be saved, and all who do not belong to Christ will be thrown into the lake of fire (Rev. 20:15). Only at this point will there finally be no more sin, no more suffering, and no more death.

Conclusion

In this chapter we have summarized the main doctrines of postmillennial eschatology. We have argued that postmillennialism is not liberalism, the social gospel, universalism, perfectionism, or nationalism. It is an eschatology of Christ, an eschatology of His kingdom, and an eschatology of His victory.

PART SIX

Objections to Postmillennialism

CHAPTER FOURTEEN

Theological and Practical Objections

Christians are apt to feel discouraged when they reflect on the extensive prevalence of error compared with the limited success of the true religion, and despondingly to inquire, 'By whom shall Jacob arise? For he is small.' But if they can only have faith in the mediatorial dominion, they may dismiss their fears, and confidently rely in, not merely the preservation, but the triumphant success and universal establishment of the church.
—*William Symington*[1]

Thus far in the course of our study, we have primarily examined the positive evidence for postmillennialism, and in so doing we have necessarily dealt with a few objections raised by its opponents. It is now time to deal systematically with the most serious objections that have been raised. Because we have dealt briefly with some of them, there will be a certain amount of repetition. But most of the objections dealt with in these final chapters have not yet been examined in detail. In this chapter, we shall examine some of the most common theological and practical objections to postmillennialism. In the next chapter, we shall consider the biblical texts that are most often offered as evidence against postmillennial eschatology.

Theological Objections

How can we expect righteousness to prevail prior to the final eradication of sin? This objection to postmillennialism is important because it addresses a fundamental tenet of Christian orthodoxy, namely, the inherent sinfulness of man. As explained in the West-minster Confession of Faith, because of sin our first parents "fell from their original righteousness and communion with God, and so became dead in sin, and wholly defiled in all the parts and faculties of soul and body" (6.2). This sin was imputed to all of Adam and Eve's pos-terity, with the result that all people are now "conceived in sin and are born children of wrath, unfit for any saving good, inclined to evil, dead in their sins, and slaves to sin; without the grace of the regen-erating Holy Spirit they are neither willing nor able to return to God, to reform their distorted nature, or even to dispose themselves to such reform" (Canons of Dort, 3rd-4th points, art. 3).

The doctrines of original sin and total depravity are fundamental to a correct understanding of the gospel, and any doctrine that under-mines these basic Christian beliefs must be rejected. But does biblical postmillennialism deny either of these doctrines? The answer is no. In fact, many of the staunchest supporters of these doctrines have been post-millennialists. A large number of the Puritans who composed the West-minster Confession of Faith were postmillennialists, and yet they wrote one of Christendom's strongest statements of the sinfulness of man. There are a number of reasons why postmillennialism is entirely con-sistent with the biblical doctrines of original sin and total depravity:

1. It is no more of a problem to believe that God can sover-eignly save multitudes of totally depraved sinners than it is to believe that He can sovereignly save one totally depraved sinner.

2. Grace is more powerful than sin. The Canons of Dort say that what "neither the light of nature nor the law can do, God accomplishes by the power of the Holy Spirit, through the Word or the ministry of reconciliation" (3rd-4th points, art. 6).

3. Christ's redemptive work, which was intended to overcome sin, is an accomplished fact. In the present age, this finished work is being applied by the Holy Spirit across the face of the earth.

4. Postmillennialists do not believe that perfection will be at-tained before the Second Coming. But just as we expect in-dividual redemption to result in the progressive growth of

righteousness, so we expect cosmic redemption to result in the progressive growth of righteousness.

This objection would be valid only if postmillennialism taught the inherent goodness of man or the inherent power of man to effect righteousness. Since postmillennialists believe in the inherent power of God, this objection fails.

The messianic kingdom is inaugurated at the Second Advent, not the First. This objection is often raised by dispensationalists against the postmillennial belief in the present existence of the millennial kingdom. They argue that Christ is not presently fulfilling the Davidic covenant because His reign at the right hand of the Father is not a literal fulfillment of the promise, and the New Testament does not view that present reign as the fulfillment of the Davidic covenant. Both of these propositions are crucial in the debate between premillennialism and postmillennialism.

The first claim involves a basic dispensationalist misunderstanding of hermeneutics. The problem is that dispensationalists, when interpreting prophecy, rarely take into consideration the broader context of Scripture. But Christians simply cannot ignore the New Testament when interpreting the Old. Joseph Braswell explains:

> Literalism cannot be given a criteriological status as the way we are to interpret texts. We must rather pay attention to the way the NT treats OT texts, learning our paradigms of interpretation from canonical examples of New-Covenantal interpretation. We must read the OT bearing in mind that what God promised to the patriarchs God has fulfilled in his raising up Jesus (Ac. 13:32b–33a) and that all the promises of God are affirmed as fulfilled in Christ (2 Cor. 1:20). We must look at the time inaugurated by the coming of Christ as the last days and time of eschatological fulfillment—the antitypical substance of which the Old Covenant was but the typological shadow.[2]

Dispensationalism has failed to understand this basic requirement for Christian hermeneutics, and all manner of curious interpretation has followed. This problem can be avoided, however, if we remember the canonical context. Braswell continues:

> We will understand, for example, that Isaiah 2:2–4 does not refer to fleshly Israel's future glory in a coming millennial age (a judeocentric reading), but to the result of Pentecost. We will not look to *another* New Covenant (to be made in the future with fleshly Israel and Judah) as the fulfillment of Jeremiah's prophecy, but will take literally what Hebrews tells us, even as we will accept at face value what Peter said at Pentecost regarding the prophecy of Joel 2. We will understand OT eschatological expectation as that which the NT gospel announces as fulfilled. We will not allow an abstract (self-contained, stand-alone) OT theology—an Old-Covenantal theology—to determine the shape of NT theology and Biblical theology as a whole, but we will use NT theology as a key to interpreting the OT and read the OT as a part of a whole Biblical theology that is the canonical theology of the New Covenant, seeking to understand how the end was declared from the beginning and how the NT develops OT themes.[3]

The point of all this is that the proper method of interpreting Scripture must be the method employed by Scripture itself. Since the New Testament does not interpret Old Testament prophecy in the same manner as dispensationalism demands, postmillennialists see no reason to conform to its hermeneutical standard.

The second part of this argument is stated by dispensationalist John F. Walvoord: "A search of the New Testament reveals that *there is not one reference connecting the present session of Christ with the Davidic throne.*"[4] However, this assertion is simply not true. In Peter's sermon on the Day of Pentecost, he explicitly points to Christ's resurrection and exaltation to the right hand of God as the fulfillment of the promise made to David (Acts 2:29–36; cf. Dan. 7:13–14).

Is victory only in the church's future, or is it in the past and present as well? This objection is stated by Richard B. Gaffin, who argues that emphasis "on the golden era as being entirely future leaves the unmistakable impression that the church's present (and past) is something other than golden and that so far in its history the church has been less than victorious."[5] This objection focuses on the postmillennial belief that there will be a future time when righteousness will prevail upon the earth to a much larger degree than it does now.

But if this objection were consistently applied, it would also deny the progressive sanctification of individual Christians. Personal, progressive sanctification, as Charles Hodge explains, "consists in two things: first, the removing more and more the principles of evil still infecting our nature, and destroying their power; and secondly, the growth of the principle of spiritual life until it controls the thoughts, feelings, and acts, and brings the soul into conformity to the image of Christ."[6]

Scripture teaches us that sanctification has a definitive aspect. In 1 Corinthians 6:11, Paul says, "But you were washed, but you were sanctified, but you were justified in the name of the Lord Jesus Christ, and in the Spirit of our God" (cf. Acts 20:32). Scripture also often indicates that sanctification is not perfect in this life (see Prov. 20:9; James 3:2; 1 John 1:8). But neither of these truths negates the progressive aspect of sanctification. Even though Paul declares that victory has been won (cf. Rom. 6:11, 18), he still urges believers to strive for victory (cf. Phil. 3:13–14). Elsewhere he teaches us that believers who are beholding as in a mirror the glory of the Lord "are being transformed into the same image from glory to glory, just as from the Lord, the Spirit" (2 Cor. 3:18).

Anticipation of future victory over sin in the progressive sanctification of the believer does not deny the definitive victory already won, nor does it deny ongoing present victory. Neither does the postmillennial anticipation of the future victory of the messianic kingdom deny Christ's past definitive victory or His present progressive victory. Thus, this objection to postmillennialism fails.

Practical Objections

Historical decline disproves postmillennialism. A commonly heard objection to postmillennialism is the claim that the world is progressively getting worse. George Eldon Ladd, for example, writes:

In New Testament times, civilization enjoyed the great Pax Romana—two centuries when the Mediterranean world was at peace. This has never been repeated. Our lifetime has seen two worldwide wars and an unending series of lesser wars—in Korea, Vietnam, the Near East, Ireland, Lebanon. We have witnessed the rise of Nazism with its slaughter of six million Jews, the rise and fall of fascism, the rise and stabilization of Communist governments. The world today is literally an armed camp.[7]

There are three reasons why this objection fails to invalidate the postmillennial thesis of this book:

1. Postmillennial hope is founded on the infallible Word of God, not on historical conditions. Neither improving historical conditions nor declining historical conditions should be our rule of faith.
2. The fact that the messianic kingdom has not yet filled the whole earth does not prove that it never will. If it did prove this, then the fact that the Second Coming has not yet occurred would prove that it never will occur.
3. Although it does not affect the truth or falsity of postmillennialism, the assertion that historical conditions or conditions in the church have declined since the first century is debatable.[8] Most of the readers of this book, for example, own a Bible and are not facing death or imprisonment for being a Christian.

The world is not the standard for any Christian doctrine, including eschatology. If God has promised to accomplish something, He will accomplish it, regardless of whether or not world conditions appear to be favorable to such fulfillment.

Recent world developments disprove postmillennialism. This related objection is frequently mentioned by dispensational authors. John F. Walvoord, for example, explains that a major problem with postmillennialism is its "failure to fit [the] facts of current history."[9] J. Dwight Pentecost concurs: "World War II brought about the demise of this system."[10]

Again we must emphasize that the facts of Scripture, not the so-called facts of history, should determine our eschatology. Even though many postmillennialists of the early twentieth century may have changed their views on something other than scriptural grounds, this does not mean that they should have. Perhaps many postmillennialists have been as guilty as others in basing their eschatology on current events or the state of the world. But for any Christian to do so undermines the principle of *sola Scriptura*. The Scriptures of the Old and New Testaments, not newspapers, are our doctrinal authority.

Postmillennialism entangles church and state. Some have argued that postmillennialism, by insisting that the kingdoms of this world have been given to Christ, violates the separation of church and state and endangers democracy.[11] Like the preceding objections, this one fails because of serious flaws:

1. It rests upon a mistaken presupposition. The doctrinal standard of the church is not the U.S. Constitution; it is the Bible.[12]
2. The postmillennial assertion that Christ is presently the ruler of all the nations of the earth does not alter the fact that civil governments and churches have different spheres of authority. They are both under the authority of Jesus the Messiah, but they do not have the same responsibilities and duties.

At his first advent, Jesus was given authority over all the nations and kings of the earth, whether they presently acknowledge his authority or not. Christ also has all authority over the church. Both the church and the state are responsible to fulfill their God-given duties, but neither the church nor the state has the authority under any circumstances to assume the tasks given to the other. The church never has the right to wield the sword, and the state never has the right to administer the sacraments.

Postmillennialism undermines watchfulness. A final practical objection to postmillennial eschatology is raised by amillennialist Richard B. Gaffin, who warns that "postmillennialism deprives the

church of the imminent expectation of Christ's return and so under-
mines the quality of watchfulness that is incumbent on the church."[13]
This is true, according to Gaffin, because the New Testament teaches
that "Christ *could* have returned at virtually any time since the ministry of the apostles."[14]

Before responding to this objection itself, it is interesting to note
that it has been raised by a Reformed amillennialist. The use of this
argument by a Reformed theologian is ironic because, as Oswald T.
Allis points out in his classic critique of dispensationalism, the doctrine of the imminent return of the Lord is one of "the great funda-
mentals of Dispensationalism."[15] It is not a historically Reformed
doctrine.[16] John Murray, for example, argues that "the insistence that
the advent is imminent is . . . without warrant, and its falsity should
have been demonstrated by events."[17] The Reformed amillennialist
Morton H. Smith points out the same fact:

> The question of whether or not the coming of the Lord is
> imminent is one of interest. The *pretribulation premillenari-*
> *ans hold that it is*, and that to all intents and purposes, as far
> as we can see, all the precursory signs have been fulfilled for
> the first stage of the Lord's [second] coming. . . . *All of the other*
> *views* tend to have certain elements of negative dating, which
> would take away from the idea of the immediate imminence
> of his return.[18]

Allis points out that the doctrine of an imminent return of Christ
first began to be emphasized in the 1820s and was adopted by the
Brethren movement, the forerunner of modern dispensationalism.[19]

The fact that the doctrine of imminence is a distinctive doctrine
of dispensationalism does not in itself prove that it is false. We mention Gaffin's use of it only to demonstrate how influential dispensational thinking has become. In response to the objection itself, we
must note that it faces several problems:[20]

1. Biblical watchfulness and preparedness do not demand the
   doctrine of imminence. As Morton Smith explains, "The
   Bible clearly teaches that we should be prepared for his return at any time, and that he will come unexpectedly, as a

thief in the night, but this does not necessarily say that it has been imminent for every age of the church's life."[21]

2. The Greek word translated "watch" in passages such as Matthew 24:42 and 25:13 is *gregoreo*, which literally means "keep awake." This implies that we should be actively and obediently serving Christ, watching ourselves and not the sky (cf. Acts 1:11).

3. The other texts that are used as proof of the doctrine of Christ's imminent return (e.g., Rev. 1:1, 3; 22:6, 7, 10, 12, 20) do not support this doctrine.

   a. The words used in these verses mean "soon" or "near." They do not allow for an interval of thousands of years. They indicate that the event referred to was impending at the time of writing.

   b. They must therefore refer to Christ's first-century coming in judgment on Jerusalem, not to his personal return at the end of the age.

   c. Passages that refer to Christ's second coming (e.g. Acts 1:11; 1 Thess. 4:15–17) do not include time references such as "soon" or "near." Nothing is said regarding the nearness of the Second Coming.

4. As Allis points out, the objection falsely implies that "men cannot expect and watch for the coming of Christ and be stimulated and safeguarded by the thought of it unless they can believe that it may take place 'at any moment.' "[22] He explains, "A mother may live in the constant, ever present hope and expectation of seeing her absent boy, even when she knows that he is on the other side of the globe."[23]

5. If the doctrine of imminence is true and the early church believed it, but did not realize that the concept would include at least two thousand intervening years, how could the doctrine possibly be an encouragement for the church today, when we know that it has already included two thousand years? In other words, if "imminence" can include an interval of two thousand years, then it can include an interval of four thousand or ten thousand more years. And in that case, it ceases to be an encouragement to the kind of watchfulness demanded by dispensationalism.

This objection fails because Scripture simply does not teach the dispensational doctrine of the "imminent" return of Christ. What it teaches us is always to be prepared for His coming by continuing to serve Him. We do not know how many generations remain before Christ comes again, but we do know that every remaining generation needs to hear the gospel.

Conclusion

We have examined some of the most common theological and practical objections to postmillennialism, and we have found them wanting. These objections involve either a misunderstanding of what postmillennialism teaches, a misunderstanding of what the ultimate standard for eschatology should be, or a biblically unsound premise. Thus, the common objections do not falsify or weaken biblical postmillennialism.

CHAPTER FIFTEEN

Biblical Objections

It is the constant teaching of Scripture that Christ must reign until He shall have put all His enemies under His feet—by which assuredly spiritual, not physical, conquest is intimated; that it is inherent in the very idea of the salvation of Christ, who came as Saviour of the world, in order to save the world, that nothing less than the world shall be saved by Him; and that redemption as a remedy for sin cannot be supposed to reach its final issue until the injury inflicted by sin on the creation of God is repaired, and mankind as such is brought to the destiny originally designed for it by its creator.

—Benjamin B. Warfield[1]

We have examined some of the major theological and practical objections to postmillennialism and found that they do not succeed in disproving this system of eschatology. Postmillennialism is theologically consistent with orthodox Christianity in general and with Reformed theology in particular. We will now consider some of the specific biblical texts that are often said to be contrary to postmillennialism.

Isaiah 10:20–23

Now it will come about in that day that the remnant of Israel, and those of the house of Jacob who have escaped, will never again rely on the one who struck them, but will truly rely on the LORD, the Holy One of Israel. A remnant will return, the remnant of Jacob, to the mighty God. For though your people, O Israel, may be like the sand of the sea, only a remnant within them will return; a destruction is determined, overflowing with righteousness. For a complete destruction, one that is decreed, the Lord GOD of hosts will execute in the midst of the whole land.

According to opponents of postmillennialism, this text and others like it in the Old Testament demonstrate that only a small remnant of Jews will be saved. These texts contradict postmillennialism, it is claimed, because it predicts a large-scale conversion of the Jews to Christ. However, postmillennialism is not inconsistent with these passages for these reasons:

1. Postmillennial eschatology, as we noted in our discussion of Romans 11, does not require a large-scale conversion of Jews, or of any other ethnic group, to Christ. The ultimate salvation of a large majority of mankind does not require the salvation of a large majority of every ethnic group.
2. Most postmillennialists do believe in a future conversion of the Jews, but that view is not contradicted by these passages. The remnant passages nowhere state or imply that they are describing permanent conditions. Postmillennialists understand that even to this day it is only a remnant of Jews who are being saved, but most also believe that this will not always be the case.
3. If the remnant passages provide the controlling paradigm for our understanding of the entire present age, then there is a fundamental contradiction in the prophets themselves. As we have seen, the language of their eschatological visions is cosmic in scope, incorporating "all nations" and "all families" and promising a glorious kingdom that fills and subdues the earth. A vision of Satan's kingdom growing to fill the earth while a small number of believers are saved from his power is nowhere to be found in the prophets.

The remnant passages, when properly interpreted, are perfectly consistent with the overwhelming testimony of Scripture, which points to worldwide conversion and the prevalence of righteousness prior to Christ's return.

Matthew 7:13–14

> Enter by the narrow gate; for the gate is wide, and the way is broad that leads to destruction, and many are those who enter by it. For the gate is small, and the way is narrow that leads to life, and few are those who find it.

This text, along with Matthew 22:14 and Luke 13:23–24, is often used to prove that the ultimate number of those saved will be comparatively small. It is claimed that postmillennialism directly contradicts the clear teaching of Jesus at this point. We would make several points in response to this objection:

1. The narrowness of the gate refers specifically to the exclusivity of Jesus. This is a truth that is mentioned several times in the New Testament (cf. John 14:6; Acts 4:12).
2. As Warfield points out, Christ's purpose in this chapter is ethical, rather than prophetic: "Spoken out of the immediate circumstances of the time to the immediate needs of those about Him, His words supply valid motives to action to all who find themselves with similar needs in like circumstances."[2] Jesus is urging these Jews (and us) to place their faith in Him as the Messiah.
3. In the passage, Jesus is dealing with the state of affairs as it *then* existed. There were very few Jews who believed in Him at that time. Over the course of His ministry, this did not significantly change. The majority of Jews became more and more hardened in their rejection of Jesus until they finally crucified their Messiah. This passage simply does not address the question of how many people will *ultimately* accept or reject Christ.
4. Nothing in the passage indicates that it is describing a permanent state of affairs. As Warfield again notes, there is no reason to think "that the circumstances intimated or implied are necessarily constant and must remain forever unchanged."[3] In other words, the passage is descriptive, not prescriptive.
5. The contexts of the two related passages, Matthew 22:14 and Luke 13:23–24, indicate that they, too, deal specifically with the rejection of Christ at that time by all but a remnant of Jews.

The use of these passages to refute postmillennialism fails because they must be taken out of their historical context and made normative for the entire present age in order to contradict postmillennialism. But nothing in the passages themselves demands such an application, and, as we have seen, many other passages of Scripture prohibit it.

Matthew 13:24–30

> He presented another parable to them, saying, "The kingdom of heaven may be compared to a man who sowed good seed in his field. But while men were sleeping, his enemy came and sowed tares also among the wheat, and went away. But when the wheat sprang up and bore grain, then the tares became evident also. And the slaves of the landowner came and said to him, "Sir, did you not sow good seed in your field? How then does it have tares?" And he said to them, "An enemy has done this!" And the slaves said to him, "Do you want us, then, to go and gather them up?" But he said, "No; lest while you are gathering up the tares, you may root up the wheat with them. Allow both to grow together until the harvest; and in the time of the harvest I will say to the reapers, 'First gather up the tares and bind them in bundles to burn them up; but gather the wheat into my barn.' "

The parable of the wheat and the tares is also used as an objection to postmillennialism, since it teaches that some men are saved and others are lost.[4] While on the surface this may appear to be a plausible objection, it is not for a number of important reasons:

1. The objection implies that postmillennialism teaches universalism. But, as we have already stated, postmillennialism is not universalism. The fact that all men will not be saved is abundantly clear in Scripture.
2. Postmillennialism affirms the central point of the parable—that unrighteousness and unrighteous men will exist until the Second Coming. Jesus is informing His disciples that the

worldwide spread of the kingdom, which He describes in the following parables (Matt. 13:31–33), will not result in total perfection in this present age.

3. The parable is actually more favorable to a postmillennial interpretation. At the end of the age, the Son returns to a field of *wheat*, not a field of tares.

All that the parable of the wheat and the tares demands is that our eschatology recognize that evil will remain until the end. It does not demand that evil be dominant until the end. Since postmillennialism is neither universalistic nor perfectionistic, this objection fails to address anything relevant to the discussion.

Matthew 24:4–34

Jesus' Olivet discourse is one of the passages most frequently used against postmillennialism. Amillennialist Anthony Hoekema, for example, treats this passage as a primary argument against postmillennialism.[5] Premillennialist Millard J. Erickson agrees:

> Perhaps more damaging to postmillennialism is its apparent neglect of Scripture passages (e.g., Matt. 24:9–14) that portray spiritual and moral conditions as worsening in the end times. It appears that postmillennialism has based its doctrine on very carefully selected Scripture passages.[6]

We have already examined the text of the Olivet discourse in some detail.[7] However, due to the weight placed upon this passage in the millennial debate, we must briefly reiterate some of the reasons why it does not in any way contradict postmillennialism:

1. In Matthew 24:34, Jesus emphatically declares that this prophecy will be fulfilled before the generation of people to whom he is speaking passes away. His words do not allow for the fulfillment of this prophecy thousands of years later.
2. The worsening conditions, including the "great tribulation," described in the Olivet discourse were conditions

that led up to and included the coming of Christ in judgment upon Jerusalem in A.D. 70.

3. Those interpretations of the Olivet discourse which see its fulfillment as either partially or totally future are forced to ignore its context in Matthew, ignore the similar language of judgment in the Prophets, and distort the words of Christ in 24:34. Jesus said that "all" (not some) of the signs mentioned in verses 4–33 would take place before that generation (not some future generation) passed away.

4. The preterist interpretation of this passage is confirmed by the fact that all of these signs were in fact fulfilled within forty years, or one generation, of the time Jesus spoke this prophecy. This prophecy was fulfilled in detail in the events leading up to and including the destruction of Jerusalem and the temple.

The Olivet discourse does not prove that conditions in Christ's messianic kingdom will worsen before His return, because it is a prophecy that has already been fulfilled. It refers to the worsening conditions that led up to the destruction of Jerusalem, not to conditions in our future.

Luke 18:7–8

> Now shall not God bring about justice for His elect, who cry to Him day and night, and will He delay long over them? I tell you that He will bring about justice for them speedily. However, when the Son of Man comes, will He find faith on the earth?

It is sometimes argued that this passage teaches the scarcity of faith on earth at the second coming of Christ and therefore that it contradicts postmillennialism. There are several reasons to believe that it teaches no such thing:

1. Luke 18:1 indicates that the purpose of this parable is to teach the disciples "to pray and not to lose heart." In other words, the purpose of the passage is ethical, not necessarily eschatological.

2. The Greek text does not require either a negative or a positive answer to Christ's question. The answer is not implied in the Greek construction.

3. Which "coming" Christ is referring to here is open to serious debate. There are several indications that He is speaking of His impending coming in judgment, not His second coming:

   a. In the preceding chapter (Luke 17:20–37), he speaks of the coming destruction of Jerusalem in A.D. 70.

   b. In 18:7, Christ assures His listeners that God will not delay long in bringing about justice for His elect. It could reasonably be argued that two thousand years is a long delay.

   c. In verse 8, Christ assures us that God will bring about justice speedily. Again, this would seem to indicate a fulfillment within a short amount of time.

Since this passage probably does not refer to the Second Coming, and since it does not demand a negative answer in any case, it can hardly be considered to stand in opposition to postmillennialism.

2 Thessalonians 2:3–4

> Let no one in any way deceive you, for it [the day of the Lord] will not come unless the apostasy comes first, and the man of lawlessness is revealed, the son of destruction, who opposes and exalts himself above every so-called god or object of worship, so that he takes his seat in the temple of God, displaying himself as being God.

According to amillennialist Anthony Hoekema, this is the one "specific New Testament passage which points unambiguously to a final apostasy which will occur just before the Parousia."[8] As a matter of fact, however, the eschatology of this passage is anything but unambiguous. Because this passage cannot be properly explained apart from a detailed consideration of the final chapters of 1 Thessalonians, we have devoted a lengthy appendix to a full discussion of all of these chapters. At this point, we shall merely note the following facts:

1. As Hoekema admits, this apostasy is linked with, and will accompany, the appearance of the man of lawlessness.[9]
2. Whoever or whatever the man of lawlessness is, Paul explicitly refers to him as being restrained "now" (2:6), referring to the time when Paul was writing the letter (c. 51–52). In other words, the man of lawlessness was alive at the time Paul wrote 2 Thessalonians. Therefore, if his appearance is linked with the apostasy, both must have occurred sometime in the first century.

2 Thessalonians 2 tells of a time of apostasy which would occur within several years of the time when Paul wrote this letter. It does not foretell a time of apostasy immediately preceding the second coming of Christ.

2 Timothy 3:1–5, 13

> But realize this, that in the last days difficult times will come. For men will be lovers of self, lovers of money, boastful, arrogant, revilers, disobedient to parents, ungrateful, unholy, unloving, irreconcilable, malicious gossips, without self-control, brutal, haters of good, treacherous, reckless, conceited, lovers of pleasure rather than lovers of God; holding to a form of godliness, although they have denied its power; and avoid such men as these. . . . But evil men and impostors will proceed from bad to worse, deceiving and being deceived.

This text, it is often argued, contradicts postmillennialism because it points to rising apostasy in the last days before the Second Coming. Like many of the objections considered in this chapter, this one arises because of a failure to observe the context. There are several contextual observations that refute this objection to postmillennialism:

1. The context indicates that Paul is writing to Timothy about conditions that Timothy himself will have to deal with in his own time (see, e.g., 3:10, 14).
2. The meaning of the phrase "last days" must be determined from the context. It and similar phrases are often used to refer to the last days of the Jewish age (e.g., Heb. 1:2; 1 Pet. 1:20; 1 John 2:18). In other words, it must not be automatically assumed that the "last days" immediately precede the Second Coming.
3. The passage itself teaches that these evil men "will not make further progress" (v. 9).

Nothing in this passage is a relevant objection to postmillennialism when it is read in its context. It speaks to a pastoral situation that Timothy was dealing with in his own day. It is not a prophecy of conditions at the end of the world.

Revelation 20

One of the most common objections to postmillennialism is the claim that it does not do justice to Revelation 20.[10] Millard Erickson, for example, argues that there "is some artificiality in the postmillennialists' treatment of the two resurrections and the millennium in Revelation 20."[11] Postmillennialism teaches that this passage speaks of a spiritual resurrection and a physical resurrection. The objection is that such an interpretation introduces a distinction where none exists. It is argued that since the same Greek verb for "come to life" is used to describe the two resurrections (vv. 4, 5), it is arbitrary to find a qualitative difference between them. We have already discussed the postmillennial interpretation of Revelation 20 in detail, but several comments are in order:

1. The reason why postmillennialists do not interpret this passage as teaching two physical resurrections separated by a thousand years is that the rest of Scripture teaches that there will be only *one* physical resurrection and that it will occur at a single point in time (cf. John 5:28–29).

2. The same author who wrote the book of Revelation else-where speaks of two different types of resurrection, one spir-itual and one physical, in a single passage (John 5:24–29). In John 5:24–25, John refers to the spiritual resurrection (re-generation) of believers, while in verses 28–29 he speaks of the physical resurrection of both believers and unbelievers. There is, therefore, no *a priori* reason to assume that he can-not be doing the same thing in Revelation 20.

3. Paul identifies the first resurrection as Christ's resurrection (1 Cor. 15:20–23), and only those who are in Christ par-take of it. Scripture speaks of believers' participation in this first resurrection in the past tense, in terms of regeneration (cf. Eph. 2:5–6; Col. 2:12). Scripture also speaks of believ-ers' participation in this first resurrection in the future tense, in terms of the bodily resurrection (cf. Rom. 6:5; 1 Cor. 15:23, 52–56; 1 Thess. 4:16).

4. Unbelievers, "the rest of the dead" (Rev. 20:5), never par-take of the resurrection of Christ, the first resurrection. They remain in a state of spiritual death until they are raised to face the second death (Rev. 20:5, 13–14).

In light of the clear teaching of the rest of Scripture, a disputed, symbolic passage such as Revelation 20 should not be used to support the belief in two physical resurrections separated by a thousand years. In light of the rest of the Bible, this passage does not contradict post-millennialism.

Conclusion

Most of the objections to postmillennialism that are based on spe-cific biblical texts either misunderstand postmillennialism or mis-takenly assume that the text refers to the Second Coming. Other ob-jections involve highly debatable interpretations of particular texts. In the course of our study, we have observed that the covenant prom-ises and prophecies revealed throughout Scripture give us a clear and consistent scriptural foundation for postmillennialism. The objections raised against it do not undermine this biblical testimony.

Conclusion

Instead of obliterating the distinction between the Kingdom and the world, or on the other hand withdrawing from the world into a sort of modernized intellectual monasticism, let us go forth joyfully, enthusiastically to make the world subject to God.
—*J. Gresham Machen[1]*

In the Westminster Larger Catechism, we read the following exposition of the second petition of the Lord's Prayer:

> In the second petition, (which is, *Thy kingdom come,*) acknowledging ourselves and all mankind to be by nature under the dominion of sin and Satan, we pray, that the kingdom of sin and Satan may be destroyed, the gospel propagated throughout the world, the Jews called, the fulness of the Gentiles brought in; the church furnished with all gospel-officers and ordinances, purged from corruption, countenanced and maintained by the civil magistrate: that the ordinances of Christ may be purely dispensed, and made effectual to the converting of those that are yet in their sins, and the confirming, comforting, and building up of those that are already converted: that Christ would rule in our hearts here, and hasten the time of his second coming, and our reigning with him for ever: and that he would be pleased so to exercise the kingdom of his power in all the world, as may best conduce to these ends. (Q. 191)

One of the purposes of this book has been to demonstrate that this prayer is not futile because God Himself has solemnly promised to accomplish that for which we are here told to pray. From the earliest chapters of Genesis to the final chapters of Revelation, we read of the unfolding of God's worldwide covenantal work of redeeming man and creation. This work is ultimately accomplished by the promised Messiah, Jesus of Nazareth.

Our eschatology must exalt Jesus, if it is to be consistent with the Bible. All of the covenant promises and prophecies of Scripture find their fulfillment in and through Christ. It is Christ who humbled Himself and took on the form of a servant for the sake of our redemption. It is Christ who suffered and died on the cross to atone for our sins. It is Christ who was raised from the grave on the third day and appeared to over five hundred witnesses. It is Christ who ascended into heaven, sat down at the right hand of God, and was given dominion, glory, and a kingdom that will grow until it fills the whole earth. It is Christ who will reign from that throne until He puts all His enemies under His feet and brings blessing to all the nations of the earth. It is Christ alone who is the way of salvation for all men.

As mediator of the new covenant, Jesus Christ has poured out the Holy Spirit upon His church for the purpose of empowering her to fulfill the goal of bringing the gospel to the entire world. Christ has promised the church that the very gates of hell will not be able to stop the accomplishment of this goal. The will of God shall be done on earth as it is in heaven.

As the church enters the third millennium since the birth of Christ, she has no reason to despair that God's promises will not be kept. She has no reason to conclude that Christ will become increasingly irrelevant in a pagan culture. Instead, the church of our age, like the saints of the Old Testament, must have faith—the *assurance* of things hoped for, the *conviction* of things not seen. She must place her faith not in what she can see, but in the infallible word of her Savior.

Two thousand years ago, Jesus Christ gave a handful of believers the mission of taking the gospel to the world, and through this small group of men, He turned the world upside down. Today the church numbers in the millions, and the spiritual resources available to her are no less than they were then. The church must begin again to pray fervently that the kingdom of sin and Satan may be destroyed, the gospel propagated throughout the world, the Jews called, and the fullness of the Gentiles brought in. God has promised to accomplish this, and His word will not fail.

Soli Deo Gloria

The Seventy Weeks

Seventy weeks have been decreed for your people and your holy city, to finish the transgression, to make an end of sin, to make atonement for iniquity, to bring in everlasting righteousness, to seal up vision and prophecy, and to anoint the most holy place. So you are to know and discern that from the issuing of a decree to restore and rebuild Jerusalem until Messiah the Prince there will be seven weeks and sixty-two weeks. . . . Then after the sixty-two weeks the Messiah will be cut off and have nothing, and the people of the prince who is to come will destroy the city and the sanctuary. And its end will come with a flood; even to the end there will be war; desolations are determined. And he will make a firm covenant with the many for one week, but in the middle of the week he will put a stop to sacrifice and grain offering; and on the wing of abominations will come one who makes desolate, even until a complete destruction, one that is decreed, is poured out on the one who makes desolate. (Dan. 9:24–27)

The prophecy of the seventy weeks in Daniel 9 must be discussed briefly because of its foundational importance to the dispensational system of eschatology. While the prophecy does not have any significant bearing on the debate between amillennialists and postmillennialists, the dispensational interpretation has become a virtual truism for most modern evangelicals. For this reason alone, the prophecy deserves our attention. The dispensational interpretation of this vision may be summarized as follows:[1]

1. Verse 24 is a presentation of the whole prophecy.
2. The six purposes of God in verse 24 are ultimately fulfilled only at the second coming of Christ.
3. The decree to restore and rebuild Jerusalem (v. 25) was issued in 445 B.C. by Artaxerxes (Neh. 2:1–8).
4. The seven sevens and sixty-two sevens, when understood as 483 years of 360 days each, terminate shortly before the death of Christ.
5. Between the end of the sixty-ninth week and the beginning of the seventieth week, there is an indefinite time gap, during which the prophetic clock is stopped for Israel and the church age transpires.
6. The entire seventieth week is future and will begin when a political leader makes a "covenant" with the people of Israel.
7. At the beginning of the seventieth week, the rapture of all believers will occur.
8. In the middle of this seventieth week, the political leader will stop the sacrifices in a rebuilt temple, and a period of great tribulation will commence in Israel.
9. The seventieth week ends with the second coming of Christ.

Traditionally, the church has interpreted this passage in Daniel as a prophecy of the first advent of Christ and the destruction of Jerusalem by the Roman armies. The dispensational "gap" interpretation first emerged in the nineteenth century in order to provide support for this new eschatology. In order to demonstrate the truth of the traditional interpretation and prove the inadequacy of the dispensational interpretation, several observations must be made:

1. The seventy sevens of verse 24 are 490 years. These seventy sevens are divided into three periods of time: seven weeks (49 years), sixty-two weeks (434 years), and one week (7 years). These time periods were specified so that Daniel might "know and discern" the length of time involved, just as he had discerned the length of time in Jeremiah's prophecy (9:2). Such discernment is impossible if an indefinite gap exists between the sixty-ninth and seventieth week—especially when that

gap, as dispensationalism insists, is already over four times longer than the entire seventy-week period itself.

2. It is possible that the decree of Artaxerxes in Nehemiah 2 is the decree mentioned by Daniel in verse 25. Regardless of whether it is this decree or another of the suggested options, the point of this statement is that a specific amount of time will pass between the decree and the coming of the Messiah.

3. The six things to be accomplished during the 490 years (v. 24) were all fulfilled in the first century.

   a. *Finish the transgression.* Israel's sinful rebellion against God climaxed with her rejection and crucifixion of the Messiah (Matt. 21:33–45; Acts 7:51–52).

   b. *Make an end of sin (seal up sins).* Israel's sins were reserved for punishment until the generation that rejected the Messiah (Matt. 23:29–36).

   c. *Make atonement for iniquity.* This was fulfilled in Christ's atoning death (Heb. 2:17; 9:12–14, 26; 1 John 4:10).

   d. *Bring in everlasting righteousness.* This has been accomplished through the redemptive work of Jesus (Rom. 3:21–22).

   e. *Seal up vision and prophecy.* The eyes and ears of the Jews were "sealed" from understanding the prophecies of God (cf. Isa. 6:9–10; 29:10–11; Matt. 13:11–16; John 12:37–41).

   f. *Anoint the most holy.* This was fulfilled by Christ (a name which literally means "the Anointed One") in several ways (cf. Luke 4:18–19; Heb. 1:9; 9:22–28).

4. After the seven weeks and the sixty-two weeks, which would imply a time during the seventieth week, the Messiah is "cut off." That is, he suffers the death penalty.

5. At an (unspecified) point following the cutting off of the Messiah, the city and sanctuary are destroyed. The destruction of Jerusalem (vv. 26–27) in A.D. 70 was a consequence of the rejection and crucifixion of Christ. It is not said by Daniel to occur within the seventieth week.

6. The one who confirms a covenant in verse 27 is the Messiah in verse 26. That the antecedent of "he" is not the "prince" of verse 26 is confirmed in several ways:

a. The word "prince" is not even the subject of the sentence in verse 26. The main subject is the Messiah.

b. The "end" in verse 26 is the "end of destruction," not "his" end.

c. The Messiah is the focus of the entire passage.

7. The Messiah did fulfill or confirm the stipulations of the old covenant, and Christ's covenantal work was directed toward the many (faithful Jews) for almost exactly seven years, or one week. The three and one-half years of Christ's own ministry were focused primarily on the Jews (Matt. 10:5; 15:24), and for approximately three and one-half years after His death and resurrection, the ministry of His apostles was focused almost exclusively on the Jews (Acts 1:8; 2:14; Rom. 1:16; 2:10).

8. Christ did put an end to sacrifices by His once-for-all sacrifice on the cross (Heb. 8–10; esp. 10:8, 9, 12).

9. The text of Daniel, while providing a clear statement of the events which mark the end of the sixty-ninth week and the middle of the seventieth week, says nothing about an event marking the end of the seventieth week. It is not necessary therefore to find such an event either in Scripture or in history.

The prophecy of Daniel 7 provides us with a specific time frame in which to expect the coming of the Messiah and the inauguration of the kingdom. In Daniel 9, we find the coming of the Messiah predicted to the exact year and are told what must come to pass in order for the kingdom promises to be fulfilled. The coming Messiah will be "cut off." He will be executed. But in His death, He will make an atonement for iniquity and bring in everlasting righteousness. All of this was fulfilled at the first advent of Christ.[2]

1 and 2 Thessalonians

Like the Olivet discourse, the eschatological passages of 1 and 2 Thessalonians are a source of controversy.[1] In these chapters, Paul offers some of the most detailed eschatological comments to be found in his letters. Because they are so difficult to understand, we must proceed with caution and humility.

1 Thessalonians

Caught Up in the Clouds

In 1 Thessalonians 4:13–18, Paul addresses a question that the Thessalonians have about their Christian brothers who have died (v. 13). He wants to assure them that there is no need for worry, and in verse 14 he gives them the reason. As certainly as Jesus died and rose again, He will bring with Him those Christians who have died. They are absent from the body, but present with the Lord (cf. 2 Cor. 5:8). In verse 15, he states that at the coming of the Lord, those believers who have died will actually precede those who are alive. In verses 16–17, he explains that the Lord will descend from heaven with a shout, and that the bodies of those Christians who have already died will be resurrected first. Following this, those who are alive will be caught up together with them to meet the Lord in the air (cf. 1 Cor. 15:51–55). We will all then be with the Lord forever. That this chapter refers to the second coming of Christ is virtually undisputed.[2]

The Day of the Lord

If we did not have 2 Thessalonians, the interpretation of 1 Thessalonians 5 would probably not raise many questions. But, as we will argue in the following paragraphs, 2 Thessalonians 2 poses serious problems for the popular evangelical interpretations of this chapter. In chapter 4, Paul speaks of the resurrection at Christ's second coming; in chapter 5, it is commonly argued, he speaks of the timing of this event.[3] However, there are good reasons to believe that Paul may not be speaking of the same event in the two chapters.

Paul begins chapter 5 by saying, "Now as to the times and the epochs, brethren, you have no need of anything to be written to you." Essentially, he is telling the church that they already know the answer to the question that has apparently been asked of him. However, for their sake he tells them again that "the day of the Lord will come just like a thief in the night" (v. 2). In the remaining verses, he contrasts the readiness of believers with the unreadiness of unbelievers. On the day of the Lord, destruction will come upon unbelievers suddenly like birth pangs, and they will not escape (v. 3). But the day will not overtake Christians like a thief because they are sons of light (vv. 4–6), who do not sleep and get drunk, but are alert and sober (vv. 7–8). In verses 9–11, Paul summarizes the teaching of chapters 4–5 by reminding these Christians that they are not destined for wrath, as are those who persecute them (5:2–8; cf. 1:10; 2:16), but for obtaining salvation and resurrection through Jesus Christ (cf. 4:13–18).

The difficulty with assuming that chapter 5 refers to the same event as chapter 4 is not immediately apparent when one examines only 1 Thessalonians. The difficulty will become clear when we examine 2 Thessalonians. At this point, we shall merely summarize the problem:

1. First Thessalonians 4 refers to our bodily resurrection at the second coming of Christ.
2. First Thessalonians 5 refers to the day of the Lord.
3. Second Thessalonians 2 also refers to the day of the Lord, and it does so in terms of first-century fulfillment (specifically A.D. 70).

This leaves us with several options:

1. All of the chapters refer to the second coming of Christ. This is the most popular option, and is found in all dispensational

works and most amillennial works.[4] However, as we shall see, it requires a strained interpretation of 2 Thessalonians 2.

2. All of the chapters refer to the coming of Christ in judgment upon Jerusalem. This position is rarely held, but it is gaining popularity among a small group of full preterists.[5] Its primary weakness is its interpretation of 1 Thessalonians 4.

3. All of the chapters except 2 Thessalonians 2 refer to the Second Coming. This appears to be the position of B. B. Warfield.[6] Its primary weakness is that it requires Paul to change the meaning of the phrase "day of the Lord" between the writing of 1 Thessalonians 5 and the writing of 2 Thessalonians 2. That seems unlikely, in light of the existing Thessalonian confusion about this "day."

4. All of the chapters except 1 Thessalonians 4 refer to the coming of Christ for judgment in A.D. 70. This is the position defended in the following pages.[7]

The interpretation of 1 Thessalonians 5 adopted in this study allows us to avoid the difficulties of the other interpretations, without resorting to strained exegetical maneuvers. It answers several of the questions that plague the other interpretations, while maintaining consistency within the context of these two books. Here is the evidence that Paul is speaking of two temporally separate events in 1 Thessalonians 4 and 5:

1. In 1 Thessalonians 4 and 5, Paul appears to be responding to several different questions that were brought to him by Timothy from the Thessalonian church (3:5–6). In 4:1–8, he deals with the subject of sexual immorality. In 4:9–12, he reminds these Christians of the need for love among the brethren. In 4:13–18, he answers their apparent concern for believers who have died. In 5:1–8, using the same phrase to change the subject that he used in 4:9, he answers their question regarding the timing of the day of the Lord. And in 5:9–11, he summarizes his arguments. In other words, the immediate context allows for the possibility that Paul changes the subject in chapter 5.

2. The subject of 1 Thessalonians 4:13–18 is our future bodily resurrection, while the subject of 5:1–8 is the destruction that will come upon at least some unbelievers. Chapter 5 seems to be dealing with the same subject as the one discussed in 2:16, namely, the time when the Jews who are persecuting this church will be judged (cf. Acts 17:5). This difference in subject matter does not in itself necessitate a difference in the time of fulfillment, but it does seem to indicate that Paul is answering a separate question.

3. The language used in 1 Thessalonians 5 is also used in passages describing the coming of Christ for judgment in A.D. 70. We have already mentioned that the term "day of the Lord" (5:2) is used in 2 Thessalonians 2 in a passage that refers to A.D. 70. Another interesting parallel is found in verse 3, where the coming of this destruction is compared to "birth pangs." The same phrase is used in Matt. 24:8 to describe the judgments leading up to the destruction of Jerusalem in A.D. 70.

4. Finally, if Paul taught in 1 Thessalonians 5 that the day of the Lord would occur at the same time as the bodily resurrection and the "catching up" into the air of all living believers (chapter 4), then why would anybody have believed that that day had already come (2 Thess. 2:2)?

We conclude, therefore, that Paul is answering two separate questions in 1 Thessalonians 4:13–18 and 5:1–8. In answering the first question, regarding those Christians who have died, Paul assures them of their future bodily resurrection at the second coming of Christ. In response to an apparent question about the timing of God's judgment upon their persecutors, Paul reminds them that the day of the Lord will come like a thief in the night upon those unbelievers. Although Paul does not specifically distinguish between the time of this judgment and the time of the bodily resurrection at this point, nothing in the context forbids it, and 2 Thessalonians seems to demand it. Perhaps the fact that Paul did not specifically distinguish between the time of these two events in 1 Thessalonians explains the confusion over the timing of the day of the Lord which he addresses in 2 Thessalonians.

2 Thessalonians

In Paul's second epistle to the Thessalonians, we find a church which has become incredibly confused about the timing of the day of the Lord. Someone has been teaching them that the day of the Lord has already come (2:2). In order to correct this false teaching and instruct them on several other matters, Paul wrote a second epistle to the Thessalonian church.

Judgment on Those Who Afflict You

In the first chapter of 2 Thessalonians, Paul offers comfort to this group of persecuted believers, assuring them that Christ will come to judge those who are afflicting them. Since Scripture uses the word "coming" to refer to a number of different events, the question we must answer is whether the coming of Christ spoken of in this context is the coming of Christ in judgment in A.D. 70 or the personal coming of Christ at the consummation of His kingdom.

There are several pieces of evidence that indicate a fulfillment in A.D. 70:

1. The language of impending judgment and destruction by God links this chapter conceptually to 1 Thessalonians 5 (cf. 2 Thess. 1:6–9; 1 Thess. 5:3).
2. The text itself speaks of God's coming judgment upon those who are afflicting them at the time of the writing of the letter (1:6).
3. Those who are in fact afflicting them are the Jews (Acts 17:5–9), whom Jesus explicitly declared would be judged within one generation of his death (Matt. 24:34; Mark 13:30; Luke 21:32).
4. There is a distinct parallel between the language of 2 Thessalonians 1:7–9 and the prophecies of Daniel 7:9–12 and Joel 2–3, in which a fiery judgment is intimately connected with events that are known now to have occurred in the first century, namely, the rule of the fourth kingdom (the Roman Empire) and the outpouring of the Holy Spirit on the Day of Pentecost. Joel, in fact, refers to this judgment as the day of the Lord (Joel 3:14).

5. There is a distinct parallel between the language of 2 Thessalonians 1:7–9 and Matthew 16:27–28, which describes a coming of the Son of Man for judgment within the lifetime of some of His disciples.

On the basis of this evidence, we conclude that the coming of Christ for judgment in 2 Thessalonians 1 is the same as the coming of Christ for judgment revealed in the Olivet discourse and elsewhere.[8]

The Man of Lawlessness

Interpreting 2 Thessalonians 2 is one of the most difficult tasks facing any student of Scripture. Commentators and theologians disagree about the meaning of virtually every statement in the chapter, and some do not even attempt to interpret it at all.[9] We enter an examination of this passage, therefore, with due caution and humility. We do not, however, despair of gaining at least a basic understanding of the main points of the chapter. God gave us His written word, not to confuse us, but in order to communicate to us. We believe, therefore, that the main points of this chapter can be understood even if debate over certain details remains.

One of the primary causes for the extraordinary confusion surrounding the interpretation of this chapter is the assumption of most commentators that Paul is referring in this chapter to events surrounding the second coming of our Lord. The assumption is usually made for two reasons. First, it is assumed that 1 Thessalonians 4 and 1 Thessalonians 5 are speaking about the same event. And since 1 Thessalonians 4 refers to the second coming of our Lord, then the "day of the Lord" in both 1 Thessalonians 5 and 2 Thessalonians 2 must also refer to His second coming. Second, because there are many striking parallels between 2 Thessalonians 2 and Matthew 24, and because it is assumed that Matthew 24 is a prophecy of our Lord's second coming, it is concluded that 2 Thessalonians 2 is also a prophecy of His second coming.

Once an exegete assumes that 2 Thessalonians 2 is referring to our Lord's second coming, the difficulties of interpretation become overwhelming.[10] There are a large number of such difficulties, but we shall mention only three:

1. As in the case of 1 Thessalonians 5, no commentator who approaches this text under the assumption that it refers to the events surrounding the Second Coming has ever been able to offer an even remotely plausible explanation for the belief of the Thessalonian Christians that the day of the Lord had already come. If we grant the assumptions of these commentators, then Paul has already told them in his first epistle that this event would involve the bodily resurrection of the dead and the "catching up" in the air of those who would still be alive to be with the Lord forever. Unless one concludes that the Thessalonian Christians were profoundly oblivious to reality, there is no explanation for why they would have believed that this had already taken place.

2. Futurist interpreters have also failed to offer a plausible explanation of Paul's argumentation in 2 Thessalonians 2. If the "coming" of Christ, our "gathering" to Him, and the day of the Lord in *this* chapter refer to the Second Advent, the Rapture, and the bodily resurrection of the dead, then it is necessary to explain Paul's method of proving that these things had not yet occurred. Why would Paul have tried to convince a group of believers that the Rapture and the bodily resurrection of all believers had not yet occurred by arguing that the apostasy and revelation of the man of lawlessness must come first? If this chapter is referring to the Second Advent, the Rapture, and the bodily resurrection of the dead, the proof that these things had not yet happened would have been far more simple and obvious. The entire argument of 2 Thessalonians 2 could have been reduced to the single question, "Are you still here?"

3. The third major difficulty facing futurist interpreters of 2 Thessalonians 2 is the large number of references within the chapter itself which indicate a first-century fulfillment. Whoever the man of lawlessness is, Paul refers to him as being restrained "now" (2:6). In other words, the man of lawlessness was being restrained at the time when Paul wrote this letter. Again, in verse 7, Paul tells his readers that "the mystery of lawlessness is already at work." Also in verse 7,

the restrainer of the man of lawlessness "now" restrains him. Finally, the numerous parallels between this chapter and the Olivet discourse, which is clearly tied to a first-century fulfillment, indicate a first-century fulfillment of this chapter, too. Some of these parallels are:

a. a coming of our Lord (2 Thess. 2:1; cf. Matt. 24:27, 30),
b. a gathering together to Him (2 Thess. 2:1; cf. Matt. 24:31),
c. apostasy (2 Thess. 2:3; cf. Matt. 24:5, 10–12),
d. the mystery of lawlessness (2 Thess. 2:7; Matt. 24:12),
e. satanic signs and wonders (2 Thess. 2:9–10; cf. Matt. 24:24),
f. a deluding influence on unbelievers (2 Thess. 2:11; cf. Matt. 24:5, 24).

The evidence that 2 Thessalonians 2 points to a first-century fulfillment is overwhelming. With this in mind, we shall summarize the main points of the chapter.

In 2 Thessalonians 2:1–2, Paul tells the church not be disturbed by a message that they have apparently received to the effect that the day of the Lord has come. Paul ties two events together with this day of the Lord, namely, the "coming of our Lord Jesus Christ" and "our gathering together to Him." The "coming" of our Lord Jesus, as we have seen, could refer to several things (e.g., His ascension, His coming in judgment in A.D. 70, or His second coming at the consummation of all things). The context of the passage must be studied in order to determine which meaning is intended.

The word translated "gathering together" in verse 1 is the Greek word *episynagoge*. In the New Testament, this verb is used only here and in Hebrews 10:25. But the context in Hebrews is not eschatological and therefore does not help us to interpret 2 Thessalonians. There are, however, two indications that the "gathering together" of 2 Thessalonians 2 refers to something which at least began in the first century.

1. The verb *episynagoge* ("gathering together") in 2 Thessalonians 2:1 is not the same word or concept used in 1 Thessalonians 4:17. At the Second Coming, those who are alive

will be "caught up." This phrase in 1 Thessalonians 4 translates the Greek verb *harpazo*, which means literally "to suddenly and vehemently snatch or seize." Therefore, we should not automatically assume that 1 Thessalonians 4:17 and 2 Thessalonians 2:1 are speaking of the same thing.

2. Although *episynagoge*, as used in 2 Thessalonians 2:1, is found elsewhere in only one, noneschatological text (Heb. 10:25), the cognate verb *episynago* (which closely corresponds in meaning to *episynagoge*) is found in texts which do shed light on our understanding. It is used, for example, in both Matthew 24:31 and Mark 13:27 in connection with the coming of the Son of Man for judgment in A.D. 70.

When the time indicators within the chapter itself are also taken into consideration, there seems to be no compelling reason to understand the "coming" and "gathering together" of 2 Thessalonians 2 to be referring to anything other than the same first-century "coming" and "gathering" described in Matthew 24, which were not the final coming of Christ and the bodily resurrection of believers described in 1 Thessalonians 4.

In 2 Thessalonians 2:3, Paul explains to the church why they should not be disturbed. He tells them that the day of the Lord will not come until two things occur. First, the apostasy must occur. Second, the man of lawlessness must be revealed. The word translated "apostasy" simply means "rebellion" and can refer to either political or religious rebellion.[11] Kenneth Gentry argues:

> A good case can be made in support of the view that it speaks of the Jewish apostasy/rebellion against Rome. Josephus certainly speaks of the Jewish War as an *apostasia* against the Romans (Josephus, *Life* 4). Probably Paul merges the two concepts of religious and political apostasy here, although emphasizing the outbreak of the Jewish War, which was a result of their apostasy against God. The emphasis must be on the revolt against Rome because it is *future and datable*, whereas the revolt against God is ongoing and cumulative. Such is necessary to dispel the deception that Paul is concerned with.[12]

As a matter of historical fact, the Jews did "apostatize" against Rome within twenty years of the writing of the second epistle to the Thessalonians.

The second event that must occur before the day of the Lord comes is the revelation of the man of lawlessness. Contrary to much current eschatological speculation, the one thing that is certain about this man of lawlessness is that he was alive when Paul wrote this letter.[13] In verse 6, Paul says that the man of lawlessness is being restrained "now." There are several clues to the identity of this man:

1. He is one "who opposes and exalts himself above every so-called god or object of worship, so that he takes his seat in the temple of God, displaying himself as being God" (2:4). In the Old Testament prophets, language virtually identical to this is used to condemn several political rulers: (1) the king of Babylon in Isaiah 14:4–21 (esp. vv. 13–14), (2) the king of Tyre in Ezekiel 28:2–19 (esp. v. 2), and (3) Antiochus Epiphanes in Daniel 11:36. Thus, the language of 2 Thessalonians 2 points to a mighty and evil political ruler.
2. He is alive, yet restrained at the time Paul wrote this letter in A.D. 51–52 (v. 6).
3. His "restrainer" is known to the Thessalonians (v. 6).
4. During his reign, there will be an abundance of false signs and satanic wonders (v. 9; cf. Matt. 24:24).
5. He is characterized by extraordinary wickedness and lawlessness (vv. 3–4, 9–10).
6. He is "slain" by God in connection with the events surrounding the coming of Christ for judgment (v. 8). This kind of language is also used by the prophets to describe judgments upon kings and kingdoms. In Isaiah 30:27–33, this kind of language is used to describe God's impending judgment upon Assyria.

There was only one person in the first century who fit these descriptions, and that was Nero. At the time Paul wrote 2 Thessalonians, Nero was not yet emperor. His step-father, Claudius, sat on the throne. However, shortly after the writing of Paul's epistle, Claudius was "taken out of the way"—murdered by Nero's mother, Agrippina.

The "mystery of lawlessness" may therefore refer to Agrippina's ongoing plotting and scheming to get her son on the throne. It is also a matter of historical record that Nero's reign was characterized by lawlessness, wickedness, and cruelty that repulsed even pagan Romans. Significantly, he was the first of the emperors to persecute Christians relentlessly. Finally, his death occurred during the midst of God's judgment upon Jerusalem. He died in A.D. 68, in the midst of the Jewish War. The main point of 2 Thessalonians 2, then, would be that the day of the Lord would not come until the Jewish rebellion occurred and Nero ascended to the imperial throne. The Thessalonians would recognize these events after the fact and know that the coming of Christ for judgment was very near.

Summary

We conclude that in 1 Thessalonians, Paul answers several distinct questions asked by the Thessalonian church. In the process of doing so, he discusses the bodily resurrection of all believers at the second coming of Christ (1 Thess. 4) and the coming day of the Lord, God's temporal judgment upon those persecuting the Thessalonians, which would come upon the persecutors like a thief in the night (1 Thess. 5). Within a few short months after receiving this letter, however, the Thessalonians became confused about when this "day of the Lord" would occur. They were probably concerned that they had not been "alert and sober" (cf. 1 Thess. 5:6), and that the day of the Lord had come. This seems to have left them wondering why their persecutors, who were to be judged on the day of the Lord, were still persecuting them. Paul reassures them in 2 Thessalonians 1 that God will in fact judge their persecutors on the day of the Lord, and then in chapter 2 he proceeds to give them specific reasons why they should not think that this day has already come.

A Brief Critique of Full Preterism

Because this study has advocated a preterist interpretation of a large number of biblical texts, a word must be said about an eschatological position known as full preterism. This understanding of eschatology is gaining popularity in some circles due to the reprinting of such works as James Stuart Russell's *The Parousia* and the publication of books, pamphlets, and papers by such men as Max King, Edward Stevens, Don Preston, Timothy James, Richard and Janice Leonard, and Ron McRay.

What Is Full Preterism?

The first thing that must be noted about full preterism is that it is not a monolithic movement. There are disagreements over the interpretation and application of key texts and concepts among the advocates of full preterism. Thus, some of the following comments and criticisms will probably not apply to all full preterists. With that in mind, we will briefly delineate the primary points of full preterism.

The essential defining doctrine of full preterism is that all eschatological events, such as the Second Coming and the Last Judgment, took place by the time of the destruction of Jerusalem in A.D. 70. Edward Stevens lists seventeen propositions which summarize the full-preterist position:

1. The kingdom has arrived.
2. The kingdom is spiritual.

3. The kingdom must be entered and dwelt in through spiritual means.

4. All things written about Christ in the Old Testament have been fulfilled (Luke 21:22).

5. The Great Commission has been fulfilled (Matt. 28:18–20).

6. All things have been made new (Rev. 21:5).

7. The scheme of redemption has been consummated.

8. The old heavens and earth have passed away, and the new heavens and earth are here (Matt. 5:17–20).

9. The time of reformation has occurred (Heb. 9:10).

10. Christ has returned.

11. The "perfect" has come (1 Cor. 13:10; Eph. 4:13).

12. The Bridegroom has returned.

13. The first covenant became obsolete and disappeared (Heb. 8:13).

14. The mystery is finished (Rom. 16:25–26; 1 Cor. 2:6–8; Eph. 3:4–10; Rev. 10:7).

15. Death and hades have been thrown into the lake of fire (Rev. 20:13–14).

16. All things have been "restored" (Acts 3:21).

17. Armageddon is past.[1]

It should also be noted that some full preterists, such as Stevens himself, maintain that although these events were fulfilled in the past, they have ongoing application for men and women today. Stevens explains:

> The resurrection and judgment at A.D. 70 were once-for-all events like the Cross and Christ's resurrection. They are never to be repeated. But, like the Cross, they have ongoing benefits and implications for all Christians for the rest of eternity.[2]

Stevens believes that those who label his position "hyper-preterism" fail to take into account his concept of eschatology "accomplished and applied." According to Stevens, however, there are some full preterists who do not see any application of these eschatological events after A.D. 70. He writes:

If the term "hyper-preterist" is valid at all, it would only apply to those rare extreme preterists who take everything in the Bible as past in fulfillment with no ongoing fulfillments or contemporary applications. Such would be subject to the charge of "post-everythingism." These folks would see the church as a temporary transitional phase of the Kingdom, with its phase-out in A.D. 70. These folks would also see baptism, the Lord's Supper and other such physical expressions of our ongoing covenant relationship with God as being no longer valid in the post-70 Kingdom. This is certainly an extreme "hyper" preterist position, and very few have taken that route.[3]

The Arguments Used by Full Preterists

Full preterists have taken a two-pronged approach to promoting their position. First they point out with some success the inconsistency and confusion that has characterized Christian eschatology for centuries. They point out the repeated failure and embarrassment of futurist expositors who have applied prophecies of the last days to their own generation. They suggest that perhaps all of this confusion has been due to a fundamental flaw in our approach to eschatology.

The primary argument of full preterism, however, rests upon the language of imminence in the New Testament. James Stuart Russell's full-preterist book *The Parousia*, for example, is a massive exegetical study of every New Testament text that is even remotely related to the coming of Christ. Based upon such studies, full preterists have come to the conclusion that the apostles expected all of the eschatological events prophesied in the New Testament to occur within a short time after the death and resurrection of Christ. They find no warrant for reinterpreting the imminence passages to allow for a postponed fulfillment. Nor do they find any reason to place some of those events in the apostles' near future while relegating others to the distant future.[4]

The Strengths of Full Preterism

The primary strength of full preterism is the strong desire of its proponents to maintain the veracity of Jesus and the apostles. They realize that if Jesus was a false prophet, then Christianity is a false religion. They demand an interpretation of the Bible which takes the language of imminence seriously and which strives for consistency. Another strength of full preterism is the constant push for exegetical answers to perplexing biblical questions. It is not enough, argue full preterists, simply to respond with pat answers that do not really get to the heart of the matter. Full preterists recognize that eschatology has been a source of confusion, complacency, and extremism, and they are pushing churches to reexamine their conflicting beliefs.

The Weaknesses of Full Preterism

To date, only a few responses to the full-preterist position have been published.[5] A comprehensive evaluation and critique of full preterism would require a book.[6] The comments offered here are quite limited.

Attacks upon the Creeds of the Church

One of the most serious weaknesses of full preterism is the almost hostile antagonism that some of its more vocal proponents express toward the orthodox creeds of Christianity. In an unpublished paper, Edward Stevens responds to critics of his position who have suggested that it falls outside the bounds of creedal orthodoxy:

> Even if the creeds were to clearly and definitively stand against the preterist view (which they don't), it would not be an overwhelming problem since they have no real authority anyway. They are no more authoritative than our best opinions today, but they are valued because of their antiquity.[7]

Elsewhere he adds:

> We must not take the creeds any more seriously than we do the writings and opinions of men like Luther, Zwingli, Calvin, the Westminster Assembly, Campbell, Rushdoony, or C. S. Lewis. The opinions of such wise and godly men all have much value, but not Biblical authority.[8]

In his response to Kenneth Gentry's critique of full preterism, Stevens explains why he feels this way about the creeds:

> Since when did the label "heterodox" (different doctrine) get re-defined in terms of conformity with the creeds? The Reformers were very careful to define "orthodoxy," "heterodoxy," and "heresy" in terms of conformity or non-conformity with Scripture.[9]

There are a number of serious flaws in this line of reasoning.[10] Stevens indicates throughout his attack on the creeds a complete failure to distinguish between the ecumenical creeds (e.g., the Nicene Creed) and denominational confessions (e.g., the Westminster Confession of Faith). He also betrays a serious misunderstanding of the Reformation doctrine of *sola Scriptura*.[11] As Andrew Sandlin points out, "*Sola Scriptura* means that the Bible in the context of Christian orthodoxy is the sole, ultimate touchstone for faith and practice."[12] But why is this true? Why did the Reformers continue to maintain that Scripture must be interpreted within the boundaries of creedal orthodoxy?

If creedal orthodoxy is not maintained as a boundary, biblical interpretation necessarily sinks into the sea of subjectivity and thereby loses any claim to absolute authority. It becomes impossible to declare anything to be heresy. Unitarianism, Arianism, Pelagianism, and a host of other false doctrines become viable alternatives within Christianity once again.

If we do not believe that God providentially guided the church to establish a basic rule of faith (the creed), then there is no such thing as Christian orthodoxy. There are only individual Christian orthodoxies, each as authoritative as the next. No doctrine may ever be declared heretical as long as its adherents claim biblical support for it. Their opinion is no more and no less authoritative than that of any other reader of Scripture. Even if every other Christian for two thousand years has believed that their interpretation is wrong, it is possible, as full preterists are fond of saying, that every other Christian has been wrong. A progressive growth in understanding Scripture is actually destroyed, not enhanced, by throwing out creedal orthodoxy.

Pelagius claimed to be teaching only what the Bible taught. Arius claimed to be teaching only what the Bible taught. Jehovah's Witnesses claim to teach only what the Bible teaches. As Samuel Miller pointed out in the early nineteenth century,

> Many who call themselves Christians, and profess to take the Bible for their guide, hold opinions, and speak a language as foreign, nay, as opposite, to the opinions and languages of many others, who equally claim to be Christians, and equally profess to receive the Bible, as the east is to the west.[13]

Full preterists must seriously reckon with the fact that their position has never been the Christian position, Protestant or otherwise. The most zealous opponents of the creeds have always been cults and heretics. Interpreting Scripture outside the boundaries of creedal orthodoxy does not lead merely to theological anarchy and subjectivity, but to the complete overthrow of Christianity itself.

Eternal Sin

A second weakness of full preterism is its understanding of sin and evil. According to full preterism, the destruction of sin and evil was accomplished at the Cross. Like many others, full preterists argue that this destruction is progressively worked out in the present age. The problem with that view, however, is that this progressive conquest of sin and evil never ends. As Kenneth Gentry explains,

> Hyper-preterists eternalize time, by allowing history to continue forever. This not only goes against express statements of Scripture, but also has God dealing with a universe in which sin will dwell forever and ever and ever.[14]

Strangely, in his lengthy response to Gentry's brief critique, Edward Stevens never actually answers this particular criticism. He announces his intention to give a response, but never provides one. The question is simple. Does the Bible really teach that God is going to allow rebellion against His sovereign authority (i.e., sin) to continue forever? Full preterists have not answered this particular question adequately.

The Millennium

A third weakness of full preterism is its doctrine of the Millennium. According to many full preterists, the Millennium was the transitional period between A.D. 30 and A.D. 70. But according to others, this interpretation is unlikely. They argue that the only two plausible alternatives for the time of the Millennium are from 70 (the destruction of Jerusalem) to 73 (the fall of Masada) or from 70 to 132 (the revolt of Bar Kochba).

There are a number of serious problems with all three of these full-preterist options. The most serious problem is that their "Millennium" is too short (forty, three, or sixty-two years). Full preterists chide futurists for not taking seriously biblical language that denotes a short period of time. But in this case full preterists are not taking seriously biblical language that indicates a long period of time. It is conceivable that "a thousand years" could literally mean one thousand years or could symbolically mean a long period of time. But it could hardly be symbolic of no more than sixty-two years. We must take all time indicators seriously—those which indicate short periods of time and those which indicate long periods of time.

The two post–A.D. 70 alternatives have an added problem, since either one creates a self-contradiction within the full-preterist eschatological system. According to full preterists, all biblical prophecy was fulfilled by A.D. 70 (Luke 21:22). But if the Millennium prophesied in Revelation 20 began in 70, then there is at least one biblical prophecy (Rev. 20:1–10) that finds its primary fulfillment after 70. This is especially true of the events that are prophesied to occur at the conclusion of the Millennium.

Another difficulty with placing the Millennium after 70 is that it establishes a second transitional period—something which full preterists criticize in other systems. In the full-preterist system, A.D. 30–70 is the only transitional period. Full preterists who accept either of the post–A.D. 70 suggestions must explain what the difference is before and after 73 or before and after 132. What is the difference between the millennial reign of Christ (70–73 or 70–132) and the present kingdom age?

Progressive Victory

Full preterists often argue that such texts as Matthew 13, Daniel 2, and Ezekiel 47 apply to the present age. Edward Stevens, for example, believes that these texts picture "the victorious conquest of the kingdom over all cultures and nations. This is an ongoing process."[15]

To many, this may sound like postmillennialism, but there is one glaring difference: the "ongoing process" never ends.[16] The obvious problem with this position is that all of these texts which speak of gradual growth and victory also explicitly or implicitly speak of a point in time when the goal of that conquest will be achieved. Consider the following passages:

- Ezekiel 47:1–12 pictures a small stream of water growing gradually until it becomes a huge river. There is progress toward a goal (becoming a river, not an ocean), and the goal is achieved.
- Daniel 2:35, 44: "But the stone that struck the statue became a great mountain and *filled* the whole earth. . . . And in the days of those kings the God of heaven will set up a kingdom which will never be destroyed, . . . it will *crush* and *put an end* to all these kingdoms, but it will itself endure forever."
- Matthew 13:31–32: "The kingdom of heaven is like a mustard seed, which a man took and sowed in his field; and this is smaller than all other seeds; but when it is *full grown*, it is larger than the garden plants, and becomes a tree."
- Matthew 13:33: "The kingdom of heaven is like leaven, which a woman took, and hid in three pecks of meal, *until it was all leavened.*"
- First Corinthians 15:25: "For He must reign *until He has put all His enemies* under His feet."

Full preterists profess to believe in Christ's completed victory, but their teaching actually implies an eternally *incomplete* application of that victory. The point is that while Scripture surely speaks of the progressive growth and victory of Christ's kingdom during the present age, it also speaks of a consummation to that growth and an end to the fight. A battle of conquest that continues forever is not a victory. It is a stalemate.

Other Questions

Because full preterism claims to be a valid Christian option, it is incumbent upon full preterists to answer some other important questions.

If Christ arose in the same body that was crucified (even granting changes in it), where is that body now? Did it return in 70? If not, then in what sense did Christ return? What is the difference between the constant "presence" of His divine nature and the Parousia? Is Christ's resurrection body still in heaven, or is it here? Did Christ "shed" his glorified human body and thus cease to be fully man? Or did His human nature cease to be a truly human nature by acquiring the divine attribute of omnipresence?

If Christians receive their resurrection bodies at the point of death, where do those resurrection bodies go? Do Christians go to be with Christ here on earth, or do they go to heaven? Do Christians wander around with Christ in their incorporeal resurrection bodies forever?

In light of the full-preterist rejection of creedal authority, we must ask whether the creeds contain errors about such doctrines as the Trinity and the deity of Christ. If not, then are the creeds without error on these points? Is it not possible for a merely human document to be inerrant as a matter of fact without implying that its authors are incapable of error? Is there not a difference between claiming that someone "did not err" and claiming that he "cannot err"?

If the "perfect" has come and we now see face-to-face rather than in a glass darkly (1 Cor. 13:10, 12), why do we have to grow in our understanding of doctrine? In the full-preterist system, it seems that the transitional period when Christ was away was more doctrinally stable than the present perfect age when Christ is here in fullness. Why did the coming of Christ in 70 lead to such rapid doctrinal decay and confusion?

Pastorally, how does one tell the middle-aged mother of three whose body is riddled with cancer that in the present age there is no longer any death; that there is no longer any mourning, or crying, or pain; that all these things have passed away? How does one tell her little boy, who only wants his mother to come home, that there is no more pain, that God has wiped away every tear?

Evaluation

What then is our response to full preterism? First, we must note that the problem of individualism faces both sides in the debate. Many (such as full preterists) seem to believe that it is the right of the individual to decide what aspects of orthodoxy are truly orthodox. Other Christians have sometimes fallen into the trap of believing that it is the right of the individual Christian to decide what aspects of theology are truly orthodox. In both cases, the true (although subordinate) authority of the creeds and the church are subverted by the presumed authority of the individual. Every reader of this book who is a member of any denomination, who holds to any particular view of the sacraments or any view of eschatology is on at least one Christian's heretic list. The real question is, who has the authority to decide what is and is not orthodoxy, what is and is not heresy? The individual or the church as a whole?

The attack upon the creeds and the naive claim to be teaching "nothing but what the Bible teaches" are widespread in American Christianity,[17] but they are not in and of themselves necessarily indicative of heterodoxy. They are, however, highly irresponsible, illogical, and very dangerous. All Christians must come to a better understanding of the relationship between the final authority of Scripture and the subordinate but necessary authority of the creeds.

The real question that must be asked regarding full preterism is whether or not it is a viable option within the boundaries already established by the church as a whole. A number of writers have recently written excellent critiques of full preterism, in which they describe it as heresy, outside the bounds of orthodox Christianity.[18] This criticism appears to be valid because the fundamental tenets of orthodox eschatology have always included belief in the future visible coming of Jesus for the judgment of all men and the future bodily resurrection of all men. Full preterists firmly deny these doctrines, thereby placing themselves outside of historic Christianity.

All branches of the visible church—Catholic, Orthodox, and Protestant—have always understood the Scriptures to teach that Christ is presently seated at the right hand of God and that He will return to judge the living and the dead. Neither of these propositions allows for any version of full preterism. Let us briefly examine what the church as a whole has said on this subject.

Patristic and Medieval Era

The Old Roman Creed (late second century). This ancient confession states that Christ "ascended into heaven, and *sits* [present tense] at the right hand of the Father, from thence he *shall come* [future tense] to judge the quick *and* the dead." We see here that one of the earliest creeds of the church declares that Christ is presently seated at the Father's right hand. In other words, he has yet to return. But what is the significance of the phrase "and the dead"? According to full preterism, all who have died have already been judged. Everybody who died prior to A.D. 70 was judged in a corporate judgment in that year, and everybody who has died since 70 has been judged at the point of their death. There is no future judgment of the living *and* the dead in any version of full preterism, and Christ is not presently seated at the right hand of God in any version of full preterism. Therefore, no version of full preterism can be harmonized with these doctrinal statements. The citations below will illustrate that this was the uniform testimony of the early Christian church.

The "Regula Fide" of Tertullian (c. 200). Tertullian writes that Jesus Christ, "having been raised up by the Father and taken back into heaven, *sits* at the right hand of the Father and *will come* to judge the quick *and* the dead."

Interrogatory Creed of Hippolytus (c. 215). "Do you believe in Christ Jesus, the Son of God, Who . . . ascended into the heavens, and sat down on the right hand of the Father, and *will come* to judge the living *and* the dead?"

Creed of Caesarea (325). This Eastern creed declares of Jesus, "He suffered, and rose the third day, and ascended to the Father, and *will come* again in glory to judge the living *and* the dead."

The Nicene Creed (325). This ecumenical creed bears witness to the following truth about Jesus: "He ascended to heaven and *is seated* at the right hand of the Father. He *will come* again with glory to judge the living *and* the dead."

Creed of Marcellus (c. 340). "I believe . . . in Jesus Christ . . . who rose from the dead on the third day, ascending to the heavens and taking his seat at the Father's right hand, whence He *shall come* to judge both living *and* dead."

Creed of Rufinus (c. 404). "He ascended to heaven, where He *sits* at the Father's right hand and from whence He *will come* to judge both living *and* dead."

Athanasian Creed (c. 500). "He ascended to heaven; he *is seated* at the Father's right hand; from there he *will come* to judge the living *and* the dead. At his coming *all people* will arise *bodily* and give an accounting of their own deeds."

Apostles' Creed (c. 700). "I believe in . . . Jesus Christ, His only Son, our Lord, who . . . ascended to heaven and *is seated* at the right hand of God the Father almighty. From there he *will come* to judge the living *and* the dead."

This confession was not only the testimony of the early church, but has also been explicitly or implicitly included in the creeds and confessions of every branch of Christendom. Presented below are some of the confessions in which these fundamental tenets of Christian orthodoxy have been reaffirmed.

Lutheran

The Augsburg Confession (1530). Chapter 3: "The same Christ . . . ascended into heaven, and sits on the right hand of God. . . . The same Lord Christ will return openly to judge the living and the dead, as stated in the Apostles' Creed." Chapter 17: "It is also taught among us that our Lord Jesus Christ will return on the last day for judgment and will raise up all the dead."

Reformed

The Belgic Confession (1561). Article 37: "Finally we believe, according to God's Word, that when the time appointed by the Lord is come . . . our Lord Jesus Christ will come from heaven bodily and visibly, as he ascended, with great glory and majesty, to declare himself the judge of the living and the dead."

The Westminster Confession of Faith (1646). Chapter 8: "On the third day He arose from the dead, with the same body in which he suffered, with which also He ascended into heaven, and there sitteth at the right hand of His Father, making intercession, and shall return, to judge men and angels, at the end of the world."

Anglican

The Thirty-nine Articles (1563). Article 4: "Christ did truly rise again from death, and took again his body, with flesh, bones, and all things appertaining to the perfection of Man's nature; wherewith he ascended into Heaven, and there sitteth, until he return to judge all Men at the last day."

Mennonite

The Dordrecht Confession (1632). Article 4: "Further, we believe and confess that [Christ] . . . rose again from the dead on the third day, and ascended into heaven, where He now sits at the right hand of the Majesty of God on high; from whence He will come again to judge the living and the dead."

Baptist

The London Confession (1644). Chapter 19: "Touching his Kingdome, Christ being risen from the dead, ascended into heaven, sat on the right hand of God the Father." Chapter 20: "This Kingdome shall then be fully perfected when he shall the second time come in glory to reigne amongst his Saints."

The 1689 Confession. Chapter 8, section 4: "On the third day he arose from the dead with the same body in which he suffered, with which he also ascended into heaven, and there sitteth at the right hand of his Father, making intercession, and shall return to judge men and angels at the end of the world."

The New Hampshire Confession (1833). Chapter 18: "[We believe] . . . that at the last day, Christ will descend from heaven, and raise the dead from the grave."

The Baptist Faith and Message (1925). Chapter 16: "He now exists in his glorified body at God's right hand. There will be a resurrection of the righteous and the wicked." Chapter 17: "The New Testament teaches in many places the visible and personal return of Jesus to this earth."

Roman Catholic

Catechism of the Catholic Church (1994). Article 6:665: "Christ's ascension marks the definitive entrance of Jesus' humanity into God's heavenly domain, whence he will come again." Article 7:681: "On Judgment Day at the end of the world, Christ will come in glory to achieve the definitive triumph of good over evil which, like the wheat and the tares, have grown up together in the course of history."

Methodist

Articles of Religion (1784). Chapter 3: "Christ did truly rise again from the dead, and took again his body, with all things appertaining to the perfection of Man's nature, wherewith he ascended into heaven, and there sitteth until he return to judge all men at the last day."

The church as a whole for almost two thousand years has steadfastly proclaimed that the Scriptures teach a future second coming of Christ, at which time all men will be raised for judgment. There have been a number of disagreements over secondary eschatological issues, but these fundamental doctrines have remained as boundaries of orthodoxy. Full preterism falls outside of the boundaries of Christianity's own definition of itself. It stands with Arianism, Pelagianism, and Gnosticism as a doctrine which cannot be reconciled with the uniform testimony of the Holy Spirit to the Christian church.

Endnotes

Introduction

1. Kenneth L. Gentry, Jr., *He Shall Have Dominion: A Postmillennial Eschatology* (Tyler, Tex.: Institute for Christian Economics, 1992), 79.

Chapter 1: Presuppositions and Definitions

1. Dan McCartney and Charles Clayton, *Let the Reader Understand* (Wheaton: Victor Books, 1994), 16–17.
2. Kenneth L. Gentry, Jr., *He Shall Have Dominion* (Tyler, Tex.: Institute for Christian Economics, 1992), 15.
3. For a concise defense of propositional revelation, see Ronald Nash, *The Word of God and the Mind of Man* (Phillipsburg, N.J.: P&R, 1982).
4. A fine exposition of the doctrine of Scripture may be found in E. J. Young, *Thy Word Is Truth* (Grand Rapids: Eerdmans, 1957). For a more contemporary discussion, see Norman L. Geisler, ed., *Inerrancy* (Grand Rapids: Zondervan, 1980).
5. Quoted in Wayne Grudem, *Systematic Theology* (Grand Rapids: Zondervan, 1994), 1204. Emphasis added.
6. See John M. Frame, *The Doctrine of the Knowledge of God* (Phillipsburg: P&R, 1987).
7. Creed of Chalcedon (A.D. 451).
8. Moisés Silva, ed., *Foundations of Contemporary Interpretation: Six Volumes in One* (Grand Rapids: Zondervan, 1996), 15.
9. The difficulty of a strictly literalistic hermeneutic may be observed by comparing Malachi's prophecy of the coming of Elijah (Mal. 4:5–6) with Jesus' declaration of its fulfillment (Matt. 17:10–13).
10. For those seeking a basic introduction to the principles of hermeneutics, see McCartney and Clayton, *Let the Reader Understand*. For a good introduction to the importance of the canonical context in hermeneutics, see Joseph Braswell, "Interpreting Prophecy: The Canonical Principle," *Chalcedon Report*, No. 384, July 1997, 26–28.
11. Braswell, "Interpreting Prophecy," 28.
12. See J. N. D. Kelly, *Early Christian Doctrines*, rev. ed. (San Francisco: HarperCollins, 1978), 29–79; Alister McGrath, *Reformation Thought: An Introduction*, 2d ed. (Cambridge: Blackwell, 1993), 135–36, 144–47; Heiko Oberman, "Quo

vadis, Petre? Tradition from Irenaeus to *Humani Generis,*" in *The Dawn of the Reformation: Essays in Late Medieval and Early Reformation Thought,* by Heiko A. Oberman (Edinburgh: T. & T. Clark, 1986), 269–96.

13. It should be noted that among adherents of each millennial position, and especially among amillennialists, there are differences of opinion on various subjects. The definitions are by no means comprehensive. They are merely intended to provide a framework for understanding the following discussion. For those seeking fuller explanations of each position, see the footnotes following the definitions of them.

14. The most able defender of historic premillennialism in this century was George E. Ladd. He defended this position in *The Gospel of the Kingdom* (Grand Rapids: Eerdmans, 1959) and *The Presence of the Future* (Grand Rapids: Eerdmans, 1974).

15. The dispensational premillennial position is defended in the following books: Lewis Sperry Chafer, *Systematic Theology,* 8 vols. (Dallas: Dallas Seminary Press, 1947); J. Dwight Pentecost, *Things to Come* (Grand Rapids: Zondervan, 1958); Charles C. Ryrie, *The Basis of the Premillennial Faith* (Neptune, N.J.: Loizeaux Brothers, 1953); John F. Walvoord, *The Millennial Kingdom* (Grand Rapids: Zondervan, 1959); Donald K. Campbell and Jeffrey L. Townsend, *A Case for Premillennialism* (Chicago: Moody Press, 1992).

16. Amillennialism is most ably set forth in the following works: William Hendriksen, *The Bible on the Life Hereafter* (Grand Rapids: Baker, 1959); Anthony Hoekema, *The Bible and the Future* (Grand Rapids: Eerdmans, 1979); Herman Ridderbos, *The Coming of the Kingdom,* trans. H. de Jongste, ed. Raymond O. Zorn (Philadelphia: Presbyterian and Reformed, 1962).

17. The postmillennial position is explained in the following works: Loraine Boettner, *The Millennium,* rev. ed. (Phillipsburg: P&R, 1984); John Jefferson Davis, *The Victory of Christ's Kingdom* (Moscow, Idaho: Canon Press, 1996); Gentry, *He Shall Have Dominion.*

Chapter 2: Covenant Theology

1. Douglas M. Jones III, "Back to the Covenant," in *Back to Basics,* ed. David G. Hagopian (Phillipsburg, N.J.: P&R, 1996), 67.

2. Some of the most well-known dispensationalist authors are Hal Lindsey, Grant Jeffrey, Dave Hunt, Tommy Ice, C. I. Scofield, Charles Ryrie, and John Walvoord.

3. Keith A. Mathison, *Dispensationalism: Rightly Dividing the People of God?* (Phillipsburg: P&R, 1995), 21.

4. Charles Ryrie, *Dispensationalism,* rev. ed. (Chicago: Moody Press, 1995), 28.

5. Ibid.

6. Charles Ryrie, *Dispensationalism Today* (Chicago: Moody Press, 1965), 62.

7. See, for example, Charles Hodge, *Systematic Theology* (Grand Rapids: Eerdmans, 1989 [1871–1873]), 2:373–377.

8. For an extended critique of the dispensational doctrine of the church, see my *Dispensationalism,* 25–42.

9. See, for example, J. Dwight Pentecost, *Thy Kingdom Come* (Wheaton: Victor,

1990), 323. It appears that Pentecost has added a third method of structuring biblical history. In addition to dispensations and covenants, he has stages of the theocratic kingdom on earth. The way these three fit together, however, is not altogether clearly explained in his book.

10. Although this chapter has dealt with dispensationalism in its classic form, it must be noted that there is a small but growing number of dispensationalists who have recognized many of the flaws inherent in this system. In what they term "progressive dispensationalism," they offer a method of structuring redemptive history which has discarded many of the errors of classical dispensationalism, including the radical distinction between the people of God in the Old Testament and the people of God in the New Testament. However, in discarding this distinction they seem to have discarded dispensationalism altogether. For an explanation of progressive dispensationalism, see Craig A. Blaising and Darrell L. Bock, eds., *Dispensationalism, Israel and the Church: The Search for Definition* (Grand Rapids: Zondervan, 1992); Robert L. Saucy, *The Case for Progressive Dispensationalism* (Grand Rapids: Zondervan, 1993); Craig A. Blaising and Darrell L. Bock, *Progressive Dispensationalism* (Wheaton: Victor, 1993). For a classical dispensationalist response to progressive dispensationalism, see the chapters by Charles C. Ryrie, John F. Walvoord, and Elliott E. Johnson in Wesley R. Willis and John R. Master, eds., *Issues in Dispensationalism* (Chicago: Moody Press, 1994), and Ryrie, *Dispensationalism,* 161–81. For a Reformed response to progressive dispensationalism, see the chapters by Willem Van Gemeren and Bruce Waltke in Blaising and Bock, eds., *Dispensationalism, Israel and the Church.*

11. Jones, "Back to the Covenant," 72. Jones's discussion and explanation of covenant theology is an outstanding introduction to this crucial topic.

12. Ibid.

13. Westminster Larger Catechism, Q. 22. For a discussion of the various interpretations of Romans 5:12ff., see John Murray, *The Imputation of Adam's Sin* (Philadelphia: Presbyterian and Reformed, 1959).

14. Westminster Confession of Faith, VII.3.

15. O. Palmer Robertson, *Christ of the Covenants* (Phillipsburg: Presbyterian and Reformed, 1980), 93.

16. Jones, "Back to the Covenant," 82.

17. Ibid., 85.

18. Ibid., 93–94.

19. For an excellent discussion of the way in which Jesus fulfilled the promises, see David Holwerda, *Jesus and Israel: One Covenant or Two?* (Grand Rapids: Eerdmans, 1995).

Chapter 3: Patristic and Medieval Eschatology

1. Athanasius, *On the Incarnation* (Crestwood, N.Y.: St. Vladimir's Orthodox Theological Seminary, 1982), sec. 55.

2. For helpful summaries of the eschatology of the early church, see J. N. D. Kelly, *Early Christian Doctrines,* rev. ed. (New York: HarperCollins, 1978), 459–489; Jaroslav Pelikan, *The Christian Tradition: A History of the Development of Doc-*

trine, vol. 1, *The Emergence of the Catholic Tradition (100–600)* (Chicago: University of Chicago Press, 1971), 123–32; Stanley J. Grenz, *The Millennial Maze* (Downers Grove, Ill.: InterVarsity Press, 1992), 37–44. For an in-depth study of the eschatology of the early church fathers, see Charles Hill, *Regnum Caelorum: Patterns of Future Hope in Early Christianity* (Oxford: Oxford University Press, 1992). For more detailed information on each of the church fathers, see Johannes Quasten, *Patrology*, 4 vols. (Allen, Tex.: Christian Classics, n.d. [1950–1977]).

3. The term *amillennialism*, for example, apparently did not begin to be used as a separate eschatological term until the late nineteenth or early twentieth century, despite the fact that the essential teaching of modern amillennialism had already existed for centuries.

4. Kelly, *Early Christian Doctrines*, 462.

5. Unless otherwise indicated, excerpts from the patristic sources in this chapter are from the 10-volume set *Ante-Nicene Fathers*, ed. Alexander Roberts and James Donaldson (Grand Rapids, Eerdmans, 1950).

6. Grenz, *The Millennial Maze*, 41.

7. Kelly, *Early Christian Doctrines*, 462.

8. Pelikan, *The Christian Tradition*, 125.

9. Geoffrey W. Bromiley, *Historical Theology: An Introduction* (Grand Rapids: Eerdmans, 1978), 24.

10. Hill, *Regnum Caelorum*, 178.

11. Ibid., 179.

12. Ibid., chap. 2. Hill also points out that in the subsequent history of the church, there has often (but not always) been a connection between chiliasm and the denial of an "immediate experience of heaven at death." He notes that at the time of the Reformation, psychopannychism (or soul sleep) was promulgated by certain Anabaptists who also revived the doctrine of chiliasm. In the nineteenth century, several chiliastic sects (e.g., Mormonism, Seventh-Day Adventism, and Jehovah's Witnesses) were also noted for their doctrine of soul sleep (pp. 180–81).

13. Kelly, *Early Christian Doctrines*, 469.

14. Alister McGrath, *Christian Theology: An Introduction* (Cambridge: Blackwell, 1994), 467.

15. Ibid.

16. Again we note that although it is anachronistic to use this term, the eschatological position of Augustine, when viewed as a whole, would best be described as undeveloped amillennialism.

17. Pelikan, *The Christian Tradition*, 129.

18. See, for example, John Walvoord, *The Millennial Kingdom* (Grand Rapids: Zondervan, 1959), 120–21.

19. Hill, *Regnum Caelorum*, 189.

20. Ibid., 191.

21. Ibid.

22. See also Alan Patrick Boyd, "A Dispensational Premillennial Analysis of the

Eschatology of the Post-Apostolic Fathers" (Th.M. thesis, Dallas Theological Seminary, 1977).

23. The Nicene Creed was originally formulated at the Council of Nicaea (325), but additions were made at the Council of Constantinople (381). Its present form was finally adopted at the Council of Chalcedon (451). The *filioque* clause was added by the Western church centuries later.

24. Grenz, *The Millennial Maze*, 45.

25. Ibid.

26. Alister McGrath, *Reformation Thought*, 2d ed. (Cambridge: Blackwell, 1993), 221.

27. For an in-depth discussion of the eschatology of Joachim, see Marjorie Reeves, *Joachim of Fiore and the Prophetic Future* (New York: Harper & Row, 1977).

28. McGrath, *Christian Theology*, 468.

29. Grenz, *The Millennial Maze*, 47–48.

30. E.g., purgatory and limbo.

Chapter 4: Reformation and Modern Eschatology

1. John Calvin, "Prefatory Address to King Francis I of France," in *Institutes of the Christian Religion*, Library of Christian Classics, trans. Ford Lewis Battles, ed. John T. McNeill (Philadelphia: Westminster, 1960), 1:12.

2. E. H. Klotsche, *The History of Christian Doctrine* (Burlington, Iowa: Lutheran Literary Board, 1945), 187.

3. Paul Althaus, *The Theology of Martin Luther* (Philadelphia: Fortress, 1966), 419.

4. Ibid., 420. See also Richard Kyle, *The Last Days Are Here Again: A History of the End Times* (Grand Rapids: Baker, 1998), 55, 60–62.

5. See Stanley J. Grenz, *The Millennial Maze* (Downers Grove, Ill.: InterVarsity Press, 1992), 50.

6. John M. Headley, *Luther's View of Church History* (New Haven: Yale University Press, 1963), 198.

7. Avihu Zakai, *Exile and Kingdom: History and Apocalypse in the Puritan Migration to America* (Cambridge: Cambridge University Press, 1992), 20–21.

8. Althaus, *The Theology of Martin Luther*, 419.

9. Grenz, *The Millennial Maze*, 49–51.

10. For a good discussion of the eschatology of John Calvin, see David E. Holwerda, "Eschatology and History: A Look at Calvin's Eschatological Vision," in *Exploring the Heritage of John Calvin*, ed. David E. Holwerda (Grand Rapids: Baker, 1976).

11. Cf. Francois Wendel, *Calvin: Origins and Development of His Religious Thought*, trans. Philip Mairet (Durham, N.C.: The Labyrinth Press, 1963), 251–52.

12. Calvin, *Institutes*, 3.20.42. For further examples of the optimistic thread in Calvin's eschatological thought, see his commentaries on the following texts: Pss. 2:8; 21:8, 17; 45:16; 47:2–3, 7–8; 72; 110 (intro.); Isa. 2:2–4; 9:7; 49:6; 60:3–4, 16; 65:17; 66:19; Zech. 9:10; Mal. 1:11; 2 Thess. 2:8.

13. As we noted in the previous chapter, it is difficult and often anachronistic to use twentieth-century terms and categories to characterize earlier eschatologi-

cal teaching. Because amillennialism and postmillennialism were not clearly distinguished at this point in history, we are searching, not for pure representatives or forerunners of these modern schools of thought, but for the key elements that were later developed into modern amillennialism and postmillennialism. With this in mind, we recall that the essential element in all forms of premillennialism is the coming of Christ immediately prior to His establishment of a one-thousand-year earthly kingdom. The essential doctrine of modern postmillennialism is the overwhelming visible growth of Christ's present "millennial" kingdom and the ultimate worldwide success of the gospel. The essential doctrine of modern amillennialism is the spiritual or heavenly nature of Christ's present "millennial" kingdom and the corresponding rejection of the essential doctrines of both premillennialism and postmillennialism.

14. James A. DeJong, *As the Waters Cover the Sea: Millennial Expectations in the Rise of Anglo-American Missions 1640–1810* (Kampen: J. H. Kok, 1970), 9.

15. See Peter Toon, ed., *Puritans, the Millennium and the Future of Israel: Puritan Eschatology 1600–1660* (Cambridge: James Clark, 1970).

16. James Leo Garrett, Jr. *Systematic Theology: Biblical, Historical, and Evangelical,* vol. 2 (Grand Rapids: Eerdmans, 1995), 751. See also Richard Kyle, *The Last Days Are Here Again,* 58–60.

17. Grenz, *The Millennial Maze,* 51.

18. De Jong, *As the Waters Cover the Sea,* 37. See also Iain Murray, *The Puritan Hope* (Carlisle, Pa.: Banner of Truth, 1971), 223; Greg L. Bahnsen, "The *Prima Facie* Acceptability of Postmillennialism," *The Journal of Christian Reconstruction* 3, no. 2 (1976–77): 68.

19. For an in-depth discussion of Brightman's eschatological position, see Zakai, *Exile and Kingdom,* 46–55.

20. See Murray, *The Puritan Hope,* 45–46.

21. Thomas Goodwin, *Works of Thomas Goodwin* (Eureka, Calif.: n.p., 1996), 12:72.

22. John Owen, *The Works of John Owen,* ed. William H. Goold (Carlisle: Banner of Truth, 1991), 9:507.

23. Ibid., 8:334 ff.

24. Again we must note that at this time in history, amillennialism was not a separate school of thought. However, Reformed eschatology at this time may be generally classified as postmillennial simply because of its strong eschatological optimism, the absence of which is one of the hallmarks of modern amillennialism. Of course, not every Reformed preacher and teacher at that time shared this eschatological optimism, just as not every Reformed theologian in the twentieth century has held to the generally accepted amillennial eschatology.

25. For an overview of the eschatological theories of liberal and neoorthodox theologians, see Alister McGrath, *Christian Theology: An Introduction* (Cambridge: Blackwell, 1994), 469–73; Millard J. Erickson, *Contemporary Options in Eschatology* (Grand Rapids: Baker, 1977), 17–51; Anthony Hoekema, *The Bible and the Future* (Grand Rapids: Eerdmans, 1979), 288–316.

26. See, for example, John F. Walvoord, *The Millennial Kingdom* (Grand Rapids: Zondervan, 1959), 7.

27. See DeJong, *As the Waters Cover the Sea*, 83; Murray, *The Puritan Hope*, xxiii; Bahnsen, "The *Prima Facie* Acceptability of Postmillennialism," 68.

28. However, even these futuristic elements were present in unsystematized form in the writings of Brightman and many other Puritans. See Murray, *The Puritan Hope*.

29. Jonathan Edwards, *Apocalyptic Writings*, ed. Stephen J. Stein (New Haven: Yale University Press, 1977), 337.

30. Grenz, *The Millennial Maze*, 56.

31. Jonathan Edwards, *The Works of Jonathan Edwards* (Carlisle, Pa.: Banner of Truth, 1974), 1:609.

32. Ibid., 1:604–611.

33. Charles Hodge, *Systematic Theology* (Grand Rapids: Eerdmans, 1970), 3:859.

34. In an unpublished paper, "Princeton and the Millennium: A Study of American Postmillennialism," Kim Riddlebarger takes postmillennialists such as J. Marcellus Kik and Greg Bahnsen to task for not discussing Hodge's "moderating comments" along with his more militantly postmillennial statements. Riddlebarger argues that in one passage (*Systematic Theology*, 3:811), Hodge "qualifies his millennial views, by carefully mitigating the secular nature of any aspect of [the] kingdom of God." However, these "moderating comments" are specifically directed at the crass literalism of premillennial interpreters who expect a restoration of national Israel to the land of Palestine along with their restoration to a place of preeminence in the kingdom of God. There is no tension between these "moderating comments" directed at premillennialism and Hodge's postmillennialism.

35. Hodge, *Systematic Theology*, 3:803.

36. A. A. Hodge, *Outlines of Theology* (Carlisle: Banner of Truth, 1972), 568.

37. James Henley Thornwell, *Collected Writings of James Henley Thornwell* (Carlisle: Banner of Truth, 1974), 2:48–49.

38. Grenz, *The Millennial Maze*, 59.

39. For an excellent summary of the history of dispensationalism, see Richard Kyle, *The Last Days Are Here Again: A History of the End Times* (Grand Rapids: Baker, 1998), 73–74, 99–137.

40. Benjamin B. Warfield, "The Millennium and the Apocalypse" [1904], in *The Works of Benjamin B. Warfield*, vol. 2, *Bible Doctrines* (Grand Rapids: Baker, 1991 [1929]), 662.

41. Benjamin B. Warfield, "The Gospel and the Second Coming," in *Selected Shorter Writings of Benjamin B. Warfield*, vol. 1, ed. John E. Meeter (Nutley, N.J.: Presbyterian and Reformed, 1970), 355.

42. Herman Bavinck, *Our Reasonable Faith*, trans. Henry Zylstra (Grand Rapids: Baker, 1956), 561. Also see Bavinck, *The Last Things*, trans. John Vriend, ed. John Bolt (Grand Rapids: Baker, 1996).

43. Geerhardus Vos, *The Pauline Eschatology* (Phillipsburg, N.J.: P&R, 1991).

44. Ibid., 37 ff.

45. See, for example, Anthony Hoekema, *The Bible and the Future* (Grand Rapids: Eerdmans, 1979), 238, n. 15.

46. Oswald T. Allis, "Foreword" to Roderick Campbell, *Israel and the New Covenant* (Philadelphia: Presbyterian and Reformed, 1954), ix.

47. Louis Berkhof, *Systematic Theology* (Grand Rapids: Eerdmans, 1941), 708.

48. Compiled from Anthony Hoekema, "Amillennialism," in *The Meaning of the Millennium: Four Views*, ed. Robert G. Clouse (Downers Grove: InterVarsity Press, 1977), 177ff.

49. See Loraine Boettner, *The Millennium*, rev. ed. (Phillipsburg, N.J.: P&R, 1984); Roderick Campbell, *Israel and the New Covenant* (Philadelphia: Presbyterian and Reformed, 1954).

50. The main points of Christian Reconstructionism are set forth in the following works: Rousas J. Rushdoony, *The Institutes of Biblical Law* (Phillipsburg: P&R, 1973); Greg L. Bahnsen, *Theonomy in Christian Ethics*, expanded ed. (Phillipsburg: P&R, 1984); Gary North and Gary DeMar, *Christian Reconstructionism: What It Is, What It Isn't* (Tyler, Tex.: Institute for Christian Economics, 1991).

51. Rousas J. Rushdoony, *God's Plan for Victory: The Meaning of Postmillennialism*, 2d ed. (Vallecito, Calif.: Chalcedon Foundation, 1997).

52. J. Marcellus Kik, *An Eschatology of Victory* (Phillipsburg: P&R, 1971).

53. Greg L. Bahnsen, "The *Prima Facie* Acceptability of Postmillennialism," 48–105.

54. Kenneth L. Gentry, Jr., *He Shall Have Dominion* (Tyler, Tex.: Institute for Christian Economics, 1992).

55. John Jefferson Davis, *The Victory of Christ's Kingdom: An Introduction to Postmillennialism* (Moscow, Idaho: Canon Press, 1996).

56. Gary DeMar, *Last Days Madness: Obsession of the Modern Church* (Atlanta: American Vision, 1994).

57. R. C. Sproul, *The Last Days According to Jesus* (Grand Rapids: Baker, 1998). See also R. C. Sproul, "A Journey Back in Time," *Tabletalk*, vol. 23, no. 1 (Jan. 1999): 6.

58. There is a small but growing number of so-called "hyper-preterists," who deny both of these essential truths of Christianity. Although this work adopts a moderately preterist position on certain passages of Scripture, this is not to be confused with hyper-preterism.

Chapter 5: The Pentateuch and the Historical Books

1. Kenneth Gentry, *He Shall Have Dominion* (Tyler, Tex.: Institute for Christian Economics, 1992), 182 (emphasis added).

2. Gordon J. Wenham, *Genesis 1–15*, Word Biblical Commentary (Waco: Word, 1987), 32.

3. Geerhardus Vos, *Biblical Theology: Old and New Testaments* (Grand Rapids: Eerdmans, 1948), 42.

4. Ibid., 45.

5. Wenham, *Genesis 1–15*, 275.

6. Douglas M. Jones III, "Back to the Covenant," in *Back to Basics*, ed. David G. Hagopian (Phillipsburg, N.J.: P&R, 1996), 72.

7. Vos, *Biblical Theology*, 23.

8. For an excellent discussion of the promise of the land and its fulfillment, see

David Holwerda, *Jesus and Israel: One Covenant or Two?* (Grand Rapids: Eerdmans, 1995), 85–112.

9. John Jefferson Davis, *The Victory of Christ's Kingdom* (Moscow, Idaho: Canon Press, 1996), 24.

10. Wenham, *Genesis 1–15*, 332.

11. Vos, *Biblical Theology*, 90.

12. Ibid.

13. Ibid., 131.

14. For an insightful exposition of the Jubilee and its New Testament fulfillment, see Gordon J. Wenham, *The Book of Leviticus*, New International Commentary on the Old Testament (Grand Rapids: Eerdmans, 1979), 313–24.

15. See, for example, Richard B. Gaffin, Jr., "Theonomy and Eschatology: Reflections on Postmillennialism," in *Theonomy: A Reformed Critique*, ed. William S. Barker and W. Robert Godfrey (Grand Rapids: Zondervan, 1990), 220–24.

16. Vos, *Biblical Theology*, 267.

17. Holwerda, *Jesus and Israel*, 63.

Chapter 6: The Psalms

1. John Jefferson Davis, *The Victory of Christ's Kingdom* (Moscow, Idaho: Canon Press, 1996), 28.

2. There are many hermeneutical issues that are unique to Hebrew poetry in general and to the Psalms in particular. For a good introduction to these issues, see Tremper Longman III, *How to Read the Psalms* (Downers Grove, Ill.: InterVarsity Press, 1988); Gordon D. Fee and Douglas Stuart, *How to Read the Bible for All Its Worth*, 2d ed. (Grand Rapids: Zondervan, 1993), 187–205; Grant R. Osborne, *The Hermeneutical Spiral* (Downers Grove: InterVarsity Press, 1991), 174–90.

3. Derek Kidner, *Psalms 1–72*, Tyndale Old Testament Commentaries (Downers Grove: InterVarsity Press, 1973), 105.

4. Marvin E. Tate, *Psalms 51–100*, Word Biblical Commentary (Waco: Word, 1990), 159.

5. Quoted ibid.

6. For a fuller explanation of this concept, see David Holwerda, *Jesus and Israel: One Covenant or Two?* (Grand Rapids: Eerdmans, 1995).

7. Derek Kidner, *Psalms 73–150*, Tyndale Old Testament Commentaries (Downers Grove: InterVarsity Press, 1975), 393.

Chapter 7: The Prophets

1. The interpretation of the prophetic books presents the Christian with special challenges. For a good overview of the principles of prophetic interpretation, see Patrick Fairbairn, *The Interpretation of Prophecy* (reprint, Carlisle, Pa.: Banner of Truth, 1993); Willem A. VanGemeren, *Interpreting the Prophetic Word* (Grand Rapids: Zondervan, 1990); David E. Holwerda, *Jesus and Israel: One Covenant or Two?* (Grand Rapids: Eerdmans, 1995).

2. Because of the sheer volume of material in Isaiah, we must limit our discussion

to a handful of texts. Of course, such a selection is necessarily subjective, and the author is aware of several texts that are used as evidence against postmillennialism. These texts and others will be discussed more fully in the chapters dealing with the objections to postmillennialism.

3. J. Alec Motyer, *The Prophecy of Isaiah* (Downers Grove, Ill.: InterVarsity Press, 1993), 103.

4. Ibid., 120.

5. Ibid., 125, and J. A. Alexander, *Commentary on the Prophecies of Isaiah* (reprint, Grand Rapids: Zondervan, 1974), 253–55.

6. Motyer, *The Prophecy of Isaiah*, 125.

7. This is not difficult to comprehend from a postmillennial perspective, because postmillennialism sees Christ gradually putting all enemies under His feet *before* His second coming (1 Cor. 15:25). Then all things are subjected to the Father (1 Cor. 15:28), and the final state is ushered in. In the postmillennial understanding, the change between the two states is not as catastrophic as it is in amillennialism or premillennialism, which would explain the similarity and overlap of the prophetic description.

8. Motyer, *The Prophecy of Isaiah*, 540.

9. While this Old Testament passage alone uses the term "new covenant," there are related passages in other prophets that include the concept (e.g., Ezek. 37:15–28).

10. O. Palmer Robertson, *The Christ of the Covenants* (Phillipsburg, N.J.: P&R, 1980), 277.

11. E.g., John F. Walvoord, *The Millennial Kingdom* (Grand Rapids: Zondervan, 1959), 309ff.

12. E.g., Patrick Fairbairn, *An Exposition of Ezekiel* (Evansville, Ind.: Sovereign Grace Publishers, 1960), 431ff.

13. Ibid., 436ff.

14. Dispensationalists recognize that if these atoning sacrifices were to be literally instituted, they would undermine Christianity. So they almost unanimously interpret them figuratively as "memorial" sacrifices. See, for example, J. Dwight Pentecost, *Things to Come* (Grand Rapids: Zondervan, 1958), 517ff.; Walvoord, *The Millennial Kingdom*, 311–15; Charles C. Ryrie, *The Basis of the Premillennial Faith* (Neptune, N.J.: Loizeaux Brothers, 1953), 152–53. But this is inconsistent with the dispensationalist hermeneutic, which demands that prophecies be interpreted literally as history written in advance. Thus, Ezekiel leaves us a choice between the once-for-all atoning sacrifice of Christ and dispensationalism.

15. See Holwerda, *Jesus and Israel*, 75ff.

16. E. J. Young, *The Prophecy of Daniel: A Commentary* (Grand Rapids: Eerdmans, 1949), 78.

17. Ibid., 143–50.

18. See Walvoord, *The Millennial Kingdom*, 267.

19. See, for example, Raymond Dillard, "Joel," in *The Minor Prophets*, vol. 1, ed. Thomas Edward McComisky (Grand Rapids: Baker, 1992).

20. Although dispensationalists and some others insist that such language must refer

to the end of the world, their view is invalidated by two facts. First, this kind of language is commonly used in the Prophets to describe judgments against nations that were carried out long ago (cf. Isa. 13:10; 34:4; Ezek. 32:7; Amos 8:9). Second, Peter tells us that it was being fulfilled on the Day of Pentecost (Acts 2:16).

Chapter 8: The Gospels and Acts

1. The best study of the nature of "fulfillment" in the New Testament is David E. Holwerda, *Jesus and Israel: One Covenant or Two?* (Grand Rapids: Eerdmans, 1995).
2. Because of the nature of the Gospels, the focus of our attention will be on the book of Matthew; our discussions of Mark, Luke, and John will be limited to their distinctive eschatological contributions.
3. Holwerda, *Jesus and Israel*, 43.
4. See also Isa. 49:1–13; 50:4–9; 52:13–53:12.
5. Holwerda, *Jesus and Israel*, 43.
6. Ibid., 48.
7. Ibid., 131–32.
8. R. T. France, *Matthew*, Tyndale New Testament Commentaries (Downers Grove, Ill.: InterVarsity Press, 1985), 228.
9. William Hendriksen, *Exposition of the Gospel of Matthew*, New Testament Commentary (Grand Rapids: Baker, 1973), 496, 649.
10. Geerhardus Vos, *Biblical Theology: Old and New Testaments* (Grand Rapids: Eerdmans, 1948), 400.
11. I am gratefully indebted to the exegesis of Kenneth Gentry, Jr., J. Marcellus Kik, and R. T. France, which has profoundly shaped my understanding of this often difficult passage.
12. See Josephus, *Antiquities*, 20.8.5, 6.
13. Kenneth L. Gentry, Jr. "The Gospel of the Kingdom in All the World," in *Dispensationalism in Transition*, vol. 4, no. 9 (September 1991).
14. Expositors who agree that Matthew 24:3–35 refers to the coming of Christ in judgment upon Jerusalem are divided in their interpretation of Matthew 24:36–25:46. Many see 24:36 as a transition, where Jesus changes the subject from His coming in judgment on Jerusalem to His visible second coming. Others see no transition and understand the remainder of the discourse as also referring to the events of A.D. 70. For a defense of the view that sees a transition at 24:36, see R. T. France, *Matthew*, and J. Marcellus Kik, *An Eschatology of Victory* (Phillipsburg, N.J.: P&R, 1971). For a defense of the view that there is no transition, see John Gill, *An Exposition of the New Testament*, 2 vols. (London: W. H. Collingridge, 1852–53 [1744]), and John L. Bray, *Matthew 24 Fulfilled* (Lakeland, Fla.: John L. Bray Ministry, 1996).
15. For a fuller explanation of these verses, see Kenneth L. Gentry, Jr., *The Greatness of the Great Commission* (Tyler, Tex.: Institute for Christian Economics, 1990).

Chapter 9: The Epistles

1. There are a wealth of excellent commentaries on Romans. E.g., John Murray, *The Epistle to the Romans*, New International Commentary on the New Testa-

ment, 2 vols. (Grand Rapids: Eerdmans, 1968); Charles Hodge, *A Commentary on Romans* (Carlisle, Pa.: Banner of Truth, 1972 [1864]); C. E. B. Cranfield, *Romans: A Shorter Commentary* (Grand Rapids: Eerdmans, 1985); Douglas Moo, *The Epistle to the Romans*, New International Commentary on the New Testament (Grand Rapids: Eerdmans, 1996).

2. Cranfield, *Romans: A Shorter Commentary*, 215.

3. Murray, *The Epistle to the Romans*, 2:xiv. See also Moo, *The Epistle to the Romans*, 553–54; Hodge, *A Commentary on Romans*, 352.

4. Moo, *The Epistle to the Romans*, 554. See also Cranfield, *Romans: A Shorter Commentary*, xvi.

5. Moo, *The Epistle to the Romans*, 719–20.

6. Ibid., 720. For the time reference, see also Cranfield, *Romans: A Shorter Commentary*, 282.

7. Hodge, *A Commentary on Romans*, 371. The same inclination is found among modern Reformed commentators who hold this position. Because of the prevalence of dispensational eschatology, with its extreme emphasis upon ethnic Israel, the tendency is to move to the opposite extreme by removing ethnic Israel from the picture altogether.

8. Ibid., 374.

9. Willem VanGemeren, "Introduction to the Book of Isaiah," in *New Geneva Study Bible* (Nashville: Nelson, 1995), 1020–21.

10. See Philip Edgcumbe Hughes, *A Commentary on the Epistle to the Hebrews* (Grand Rapids: Eerdmans, 1977); F. F. Bruce, *The Epistle to the Hebrews*, rev. ed. (Grand Rapids: Eerdmans, 1990).

11. The evidence for the Jewish-Christian character of the original recipients and for the pre-70 date of composition is presented in the commentaries by Hughes and Bruce mentioned in the previous footnote.

12. See P. W. L. Walker, *Jesus and the Holy City* (Grand Rapids: Eerdmans, 1996), 201–34.

13. Hughes, *A Commentary on the Epistle to the Hebrews*, 388–89.

14. Walker, *Jesus and the Holy City*, 212.

15. Ibid., 219.

16. Ibid., 220.

Chapter 10: The Book of Revelation

1. Unfortunately, the book of Revelation is where many new Christians begin their study of the Scriptures rather than where they conclude it. Many such Christians, frustrated with the language and symbolism, give up trying to understand this book altogether, while others, equally unable to grasp its meaning, rely on one or more of the popular "prophecy experts" to decipher the hidden "codes." Much of the frustration and speculation surrounding the interpretation of the book of Revelation could be avoided if Christians would first commit themselves to an in-depth study of the rest of the Bible.

2. For a good examination of these positions, see C. Marvin Pate, ed., *Four Views*

of the Book of Revelation (Grand Rapids: Zondervan, 1998), and Steve Gregg, ed., *Revelation: Four Views* (Nashville: Nelson, 1997).

3. John F. Walvoord, *The Revelation of Jesus Christ: A Commentary* (Chicago: Moody Press, 1966), 18.

4. W. J. Grier, *The Momentous Event* (London: Banner of Truth, 1945), 88.

5. Readers interested in a full discussion of the date when Revelation was written are urged to read Kenneth L. Gentry, Jr., *Before Jerusalem Fell: Dating the Book of Revelation* (Tyler, Tex.: Institute for Christian Economics, 1989). This book presents an exhaustive and compelling case for the pre-70 composition of the book of Revelation.

6. Quoted in Gentry, *Before Jerusalem Fell,* 46–47. The quotation is found in *Against Heresies,* 5.30.3.

7. See Gentry, *Before Jerusalem Fell,* 47ff.

8. See for example, the evidence in the Muratorian Canon, the Syriac versions of the Revelation, and Tertullian, presented in Gentry, *Before Jerusalem Fell,* 86–109.

9. Ibid., 121–256.

10. "Tribes" in the New Testament most frequently refers to Jews, and this is made certain by the reference in Rev. 1:7 to "those who pierced Him." According to the New Testament, this refers to the wicked generation of Jews who rejected Christ (cf. Matt. 26:4, 14–15, 47; 27:1–12, 24–25, 59–66; John 11:53; Acts 2:22–23, 36; 3:13–15; 5:30; 7:52).

11. In Hebrew, Nero Caesar was spelled *NRWN QSR.* The numerical value of the letters in his name are: N=50, R=200, W=6, N=50, Q=100, S=60, and R=200. The sum of these numbers is 666. For a thorough explanation of the evidence for the theory that "666" is a veiled reference to Nero, see Kenneth L. Gentry, Jr., *The Beast of Revelation* (Tyler: Institute for Christian Economics, 1989).

12. F. F. Bruce, *New Testament History* (New York: Doubleday, 1969), 382.

13. For a detailed exposition of Revelation, see David S. Clark, *The Message from Patmos* (Grand Rapids: Baker, 1989); Greg L. Bahnsen, *The Book of Revelation: An Exposition,* audiotapes (Texarkana, Ark.: Covenant Media Foundation, 1977–78); Kenneth L. Gentry, Jr., *Revelation: A Tale of Two Cities* (Atlanta: American Vision, 1999).

14. An interesting contradiction within the dispensational interpretation of Revelation and eschatology is found in their historicist interpretation of these two chapters. Dispensationalists usually understand these letters to the seven churches to be a symbolic prophecy of seven stages of church history, extending from the first century to the last day. See, for example, John F. Walvoord, *The Revelation of Jesus Christ: A Commentary* (Chicago: Moody Press, 1966), 50–100. But how could the pretribulation Rapture have been "imminent" all along, as dispensationalists insist it has been, if the church had to go through these seven stages before Christ could return?

15. This passage is used by many dispensationalists as a proof-text for the pretribulation Rapture theory. However, a rapture is nowhere mentioned or implied in

these verses, and the hour of testing that *is* mentioned was "about to come" when this was written.

16. For a helpful chart of the parallels, see David Chilton, *The Days of Vengeance: An Exposition of the Book of Revelation* (Fort Worth: Dominion Press, 1987), 182.

17. Milton S. Terry, *Biblical Hermeneutics* (Grand Rapids: Zondervan, 1974 [1885]), 352.

Chapter 11: Reformed Theology and Eschatology

1. John Jefferson Davis, *The Victory of Christ's Kingdom* (Moscow, Idaho: Canon Press, 1996), 45.

2. Readers interested in the classic statement of the orthodox doctrine of the Trinity are encouraged to read the Athanasian Creed and Augustine's *On The Trinity*.

3. The Scriptures used to support this doctrine will be examined in detail in the last section of this book.

4. The truth about hell has been ably defended in a recent work by Robert A. Peterson, *Hell on Trial: The Case for Eternal Punishment* (Phillipsburg: P&R, 1995). The argument in this section is not meant in any way to deny any aspect of the truth of eternal punishment. But it is meant to question the often implied assumption that one of the primary reasons why God created man was to populate the place of torment. For further study, see Benjamin B. Warfield, "Are They Few That Be Saved?" in *Biblical and Theological Studies* (Philadelphia: Presbyterian and Reformed, 1952), 334–50.

5. Thomas Watson, *Body of Divinity* (Grand Rapids: Baker, 1979), 112.

6. Charles Hodge, *Systematic Theology* (reprint, Grand Rapids: Eerdmans Publishing Co., 1989), II:637–638.

7. Charles Ryrie, *Dispensationalism*, rev. ed. (Chicago: Moody Press, 1995), 28.

8. One of the key scholars to initiate thinking along these lines was Geerhardus Vos. See his *The Pauline Eschatology* (reprint, Phillipsburg, N.J.: P&R, 1991).

9. For an outstanding study of the person and work of the Holy Spirit, see Sinclair B. Ferguson, *The Holy Spirit*, Contours of Christian Theology (Downers Grove, Ill.: InterVarsity Press, 1996).

10. We are speaking here not of the regenerating work of the Spirit, which has necessarily been constant in all ages, but of His ministry of empowerment.

11. Ferguson, *The Holy Spirit*, 59–60.

12. For further study of Reformed soteriology, see, for example, James Buchanan, *The Doctrine of Justification* (reprint, Carlisle, Pa.: Banner of Truth, 1961); Anthony Hoekema, *Saved by Grace* (Grand Rapids: Eerdmans, 1989); John Murray, *Redemption: Accomplished and Applied* (Grand Rapids: Eerdmans, 1955); John Owen, *The Death of Death in the Death of Christ* (reprint, Carlisle: Banner of Truth, 1989).

13. See, for example, Louis Berkhof, *Systematic Theology* (Grand Rapids: Eerdmans, 1941), 331–43.

14. W. G. T. Shedd, *Calvinism: Pure and Mixed* (Carlisle: Banner of Truth, 1986).

15. Ferguson, *The Holy Spirit*, 249–50.

16. Emphasis added.

17. Anthony Hoekema, *The Bible and the Future* (Grand Rapids: Eerdmans, 1979), 180.

Chapter 12: The Inadequacy of Premillennialism and Amillennialism

1. Oswald T. Allis, "Foreword" to Roderick Campbell, *Israel and the New Covenant* (Philadelphia: Presbyterian and Reformed, 1954), ix.

2. For a full critique of premillennialism, see David Brown, *Christ's Second Coming: Will It Be Premillennial?* (Edmonton, Alta.: Still Waters Revival Books, 1990 [1882]).

3. I have dealt extensively with the dispensational version of premillennialism in *Dispensationalism: Rightly Dividing the People of God?* (Phillipsburg, N.J.: P&R, 1995).

4. This does not mean that God has to repeat Himself before we are to believe something He reveals. It does mean that we have to understand correctly what He has revealed before we can believe it. When a difficult text like Revelation 20 is interpreted in such a way that it conflicts with a large number of clearer texts, then we are forced to conclude either that Scripture contradicts itself or that the interpretation is wrong.

5. Premillennialists expect that large numbers of people will be saved in the millennial kingdom. See, for example John F. Walvoord, *The Millennial Kingdom* (Grand Rapids: Zondervan, 1959), 316–17; Charles Ryrie, *The Basis of the Premillennial Faith* (Neptune, N.J.: Loizeaux Brothers, 1953), 150.

6. There have been postmillennialists who would disagree with the position taken in this study that the Millennium spans the entire period between Christ's first and second advents. These postmillennialists argue that the Millennium refers to either the last thousand years of the present age or to a long period of time immediately preceding the Second Coming.

7. See, for example, Anthony Hoekema, *The Bible and the Future* (Grand Rapids: Eerdmans, 1979), 173–74; William E. Cox, *Amillennialism Today* (Phillipsburg, N.J.: P&R, 1966), 70–71.

8. Anthony Hoekema, *The Bible and the Future*, 180.

9. See, for example, Lewis Neilson, *Waiting for His Coming* (Cherry Hill, N.J.: Mack, 1975), 351.

10. See chapters 5–10.

11. Richard B. Gaffin, Jr., "Theonomy and Eschatology: Reflections on Postmillennialism," in *Theonomy: A Reformed Critique*, ed. William S. Barker and W. Robert Godfrey (Grand Rapids: Zondervan, 1990), 223.

12. A strong case can be made for considering the conquest of Canaan to be the primary metaphor of the present age. Paul, for example, uses the imagery of warfare and conquest quite often in his epistles (cf. Rom. 13:12; 1 Cor. 15:25; 2 Cor. 6:7; 10:3–5; Eph. 6:12–17; Phil. 2:25; 1 Thess. 5:8; 2 Tim. 2:3–4; Philem. 2). For an in-depth study of the theme of God as the divine warrior and its application to Christ and the New Testament church, see Tremper Longman III and Daniel G. Reid, *God Is a Warrior* (Grand Rapids: Zondervan, 1995).

13. We have already dealt with a number of these texts in some detail. We shall deal with several others in the last section of this book.

14. Hoekema, *The Bible and the Future*, 178.

15. This debate, of course, will have to continue on a text-by-text basis. But in view of the hermeneutical chaos caused by futurist and historicist interpretations, the preterist interpretations of these passages should be given serious scholarly attention.

16. Gaffin, "Theonomy and Eschatology," 210–11 (emphasis added).

17. For a full critique of this argument, see Kenneth L. Gentry, Jr., "Whose Victory in History?" in *Theonomy: An Informed Response*, ed. Gary North (Tyler, Tex.: Institute for Christian Economics, 1991), 219–30.

Chapter 13: The Answer of Postmillennialism

1. Loraine Boettner, *The Millennium*, rev. ed. (Phillipsburg, N.J.: P&R, 1984), 29.

2. John F. Walvoord, *The Millennial Kingdom* (Grand Rapids: Zondervan, 1959), 35.

3. J. Dwight Pentecost, *Things To Come* (Grand Rapids: Zondervan, 1958), 386.

4. It should be noted that dispensationalists commonly level this same accusation against amillennialism, and it is entirely false in this case, too.

5. Charles C. Ryrie, *The Basis of the Premillennial Faith* (Neptune, N.J.: Loizeaux Brothers, 1953), 13–14.

6. Floyd E. Hamilton, *The Basis of Millennial Faith* (Grand Rapids: Eerdmans, 1952), 33.

7. W. J. Grier, *The Momentous Event* (London: Banner of Truth, 1945), 13.

8. Geerhardus Vos, *Biblical Theology: Old and New Testaments* (Grand Rapids: Eerdmans, 1948), 379.

9. John R. Muether, "The Theonomic Attraction," in *Theonomy: A Reformed Critique*, ed. William S. Barker and W. Robert Godfrey (Grand Rapids: Zondervan, 1990), 258.

10. Ibid.

Chapter 14: Theological and Practical Objections

1. William Symington, *Messiah the Prince or, The Mediatorial Dominion of Jesus Christ* (Edmonton, Alta.: Still Waters Revival Books, 1990 [1884]), 187.

2. Joseph P. Braswell, "Interpreting Prophecy: The Canonical Principle," *Chalcedon Report*, No. 384 (July 1997), 28.

3. Ibid.

4. John F. Walvoord, *The Millennial Kingdom* (Grand Rapids: Zondervan, 1959), 203. Emphasis Walvoord's.

5. Richard B. Gaffin, Jr., "Theonomy and Eschatology: Reflections on Postmillennialism," in *Theonomy: A Reformed Critique*, ed. William S. Barker and W. Robert Godfrey (Grand Rapids: Zondervan, 1990), 202.

6. Charles Hodge, *Systematic Theology* (reprint, Grand Rapids: Eerdmans, 1989), 3:221.

7. George Eldon Ladd, "An Historic Premillennial Response," in *The Meaning of the Millennium: Four Views*, ed. Robert G. Clouse (Downers Grove, Ill.: Inter-Varsity Press, 1977), 143.

8. For example, see D. James Kennedy, *What If Jesus Had Never Been Born?* (Nashville: Nelson, 1993).
9. Walvoord, *The Millennial Kingdom*, 35.
10. J. Dwight Pentecost, *Things to Come* (Grand Rapids: Zondervan, 1958), 386.
11. See, for example, Rodney Clapp, "Democracy as Heresy," *Christianity Today* 31, no. 3 (February 20, 1987):17–23. For a full response to this article, see Gary North, *Westminster's Confession* (Tyler, Tex.: Institute for Christian Economics, 1991), 317–41.
12. The phrase "separation of church and state" is not found in the U.S. Constitution, but even if it were, Christians would not be doctrinally bound by it.
13. Richard B. Gaffin, Jr., "Theonomy and Eschatology," 218.
14. Ibid., 219.
15. Oswald T. Allis, *Prophecy and the Church* (Philadelphia: Presbyterian and Reformed, 1947), 169.
16. The historicist method of interpreting Revelation, for example, which was widely used by Reformed believers, automatically precludes the doctrine of imminence. Historically, Reformed Christians have believed that there are signs which will necessarily precede the coming of the Lord.
17. John Murray, "The Last Things," *Collected Writings of John Murray*, vol. 2, *Select Lectures in Systematic Theology* (Carlisle, Pa.: Banner of Truth, 1977), 407.
18. Morton H. Smith, *Systematic Theology* (Greenville, S.C.: Greenville Seminary Press, 1994), 2:801. Emphasis added.
19. Allis, *Prophecy and the Church*, 168.
20. For a fuller argument against the doctrine of imminence, see Allis, *Prophecy and the Church*, 167–75.
21. Smith, *Systematic Theology*, 2:801.
22. Allis, *Prophecy and the Church*, 169.
23. Ibid.

Chapter 15: Biblical Objections

1. Benjamin B. Warfield, "Are They Few That Be Saved?" in *Biblical and Theological Studies* (Philadelphia: Presbyterian and Reformed, 1952), 349.
2. Ibid., 338.
3. Ibid.
4. Floyd E. Hamilton, *The Basis of Millennial Faith* (Grand Rapids: Eerdmans, 1952), 33.
5. Anthony Hoekema, *The Bible and the Future* (Grand Rapids: Eerdmans, 1979), 178.
6. Millard J. Erickson, *Contemporary Options in Eschatology* (Grand Rapids: Baker, 1977), 72.
7. See the section in chapter 8 on the Olivet discourse. Also see R. T. France, *Matthew*, Tyndale New Testament Commentaries (Downers Grove, Ill.: InterVarsity Press, 1985); J. Marcellus Kik, *An Eschatology of Victory* (Phillipsburg, N.J.: P&R, 1971).
8. Hoekema, *The Bible and the Future*, 153.
9. Ibid., 154.

10. The same objection is also raised against amillennialism.
11. Erickson, *Contemporary Options in Eschatology*, 72.

Conclusion
1. Quoted in Ned B. Stonehouse, *J. Gresham Machen: A Biographical Memoir* (Carlisle, Pa.: Banner of Truth, 1987), 187.

Appendix 1: The Seventy Weeks
1. For a fuller exposition of this passage from a dispensationalist perspective, see John F. Walvoord, *Daniel: The Key to Prophetic Revelation* (Chicago: Moody Press, 1971), 216–37.
2. See E. J. Young, *The Prophecy of Daniel: A Commentary* (Grand Rapids: Eerdmans, 1949); Sinclair B. Ferguson, *Daniel* (Waco: Word, 1988).

Appendix 2: 1 and 2 Thessalonians
1. The difficulty of interpreting these chapters is universally acknowledged by commentators, and the conclusions to which one comes do not significantly affect the millennial question. However, these chapters are eschatologically significant, and they offer a number of insights into God's redemptive work. But because of the difficulties of interpretation, the interpretation offered in this study is by no means dogmatic. It is offered for the consideration of God's people in the hope that it will encourage others to reexamine some of the assumptions that are commonly brought to these texts.
2. There are some "full preterists" who assign a first-century fulfillment to this text (and to all other eschatological texts). However, this text must refer to a yet future resurrection of believers, since at the resurrection, death is finally destroyed and we receive glorified bodies that cannot perish or die (cf. 1 Cor. 15:51–55). But that is not our situation now.
3. See, for example, F. F. Bruce, *1 and 2 Thessalonians*, Word Biblical Commentary (Waco: Word, 1982); Leon Morris, *The First and Second Epistles to the Thessalonians*, New International Commentary on the New Testament (Grand Rapids: Eerdmans, 1959).
4. Ibid.
5. The most important full-preterist work is James Stuart Russell's *The Parousia* (Bradford, Pa.: Kingdom Publications, 1996 [1878]). Most full preterists teach that all biblical prophecy has already been fulfilled. Their view should not be confused with the partial preterist position advocated in this book, which teaches that some prophecies have already been fulfilled, while others await fulfillment at the consummation of the kingdom.
6. See Benjamin B. Warfield, "The Prophecies of St. Paul," in *The Works of Benjamin B. Warfield*, vol. 2, *Biblical Doctrines* (Grand Rapids: Baker, 1991 [1929]), 601–40.
7. See also Gary DeMar, *Last Days Madness* (Atlanta: American Vision, 1994).
8. This interpretation is by no means certain, and the coming of Christ in this chapter could be interpreted as the second coming of Christ, without causing the

enormous hermeneutical problems that misinterpretation of the other three chapters has caused.

9. For a list of some of the many laments by commentators, see DeMar, *Last Days Madness*, 312–13.

10. This is demonstrated by the history of the interpretation of this chapter.

11. Morris, *The First and Second Epistles to the Thessalonians*, 218.

12. Kenneth L. Gentry, Jr., *He Shall Have Dominion* (Tyler, Tex.: Institute for Christian Economics, 1992), 388–89.

13. Some deny that the phrase "man of lawlessness" refers to an individual, but this does not change the fact that this person or thing existed at the time of Paul's writing.

Appendix 3: A Brief Critique of Full Preterism

1. See Edward Stevens, "Doctrinal Implications of Preterist Eschatology," unpub. paper. Note that not all of these propositions are unique to full preterism.

2. Edward Stevens, *What Happened in A.D. 70?* (Bradford, Pa.: Kingdom Publications, 1997), 33.

3. Edward Stevens, *Response to Gentry's Analysis of the Full Preterist View* (Bradford: Kingdom Publications, 1997), 2. The "hyper-preterists" to whom Stevens refers would probably accuse full preterists like him of inconsistent preterism, using the same arguments that he uses to charge the moderate preterists with inconsistency. Stevens asks partial preterists where Luke 21:22 speaks of future fulfillments; "hyper-preterists" would ask him where Luke 21:22 speaks of "ongoing fulfillments."

4. See such full-preterist works as Max R. King, *The Cross and the Parousia of Christ* (Warren, Ohio: Parkman Road Church of Christ, 1987); J. Stuart Russell, *The Parousia* (Grand Rapids: Baker, 1983 [1887]); Edward E. Stevens, *What Happened in A.D. 70?*; Timothy A. James, *The Messiah's Return* (Bradford: Kingdom Publications, 1991).

5. See, for example, the following articles in the July 1997 issue of *Chalcedon Report*: Andrew Sandlin, "Hymenaeus Resurrected"; Jim West, "The Allurement of Hymenaean Preterism: The Rise of Dispensable Eschatology"; Kenneth L. Gentry, Jr., "A Brief Theological Analysis of Hyper-Preterism."

6. For an exhaustive critique, see Kenneth L. Gentry, Jr., *The Triumph of Death: A Critique of Hyper-Preterism* (Tyler, Tex.: Institute for Christian Economics, forthcoming).

7. Edward Stevens, "Creeds and Preterist Orthodoxy," unpub. paper.

8. Ibid.

9. Edward Stevens, *Response to Gentry's Analysis of the Full Preterist View*, 8.

10. See Andrew Sandlin, "Hymenaeus Resurrected," for an excellent response.

11. For more information on the Reformation understanding, see Alister McGrath, *Reformation Thought: An Introduction*, 2d ed. (Oxford: Blackwell, 1993), 134–57; Richard A. Muller, *Post-Reformation Reformed Dogmatics* (Grand Rapids: Baker, 1993), 2:358–88; Heiko A. Oberman, "Quo vadis, Petre? Tradition from Irenaeus to *Humani Generis*," in *The Dawn of the Reformation: Essays in Late Medieval and Early Reformation Thought* (Edinburgh, T. & T. Clark, 1986), 269–96.

12. Sandlin, "Hymenaeus Resurrected," 8.

13. Samuel Miller, *The Utility and Importance of Creeds and Confessions* (Greenville, SC: A Press, 1991 [1839]), 4.

14. Gentry, "A Brief Theological Analysis of Hyper-Preterism," 24.

15. Stevens, *What Happened in A.D. 70?* 33.

16. This also raises the interesting question of how one can measure "progress" against an endless background. Toward what are we "progressing"?

17. For an explanation of how this view became so widespread in American Christianity, see Nathan O. Hatch, *The Democratization of American Christianity* (New Haven: Yale University Press, 1989).

18. See the articles by Sandlin, West, and Gentry in the July 1997 issue of *Chalcedon Report*.

For Further Reading

Hermeneutics

Fee, Gordon D., and Douglas Stuart. *How to Read the Bible for All Its Worth.* 2d ed. Grand Rapids: Zondervan Publishing House, 1993. A useful introduction to the interpretation of the various types of literature found in Scripture.

McCartney, Dan, and Charles Clayton. *Let the Reader Understand.* Wheaton, Ill.: Victor Books, 1994. An outstanding intermediate-level hermeneutics textbook. Provides valuable information on the importance of understanding hermeneutical presuppositions.

Osborne, Grant. *The Hermeneutical Spiral.* Downers Grove, Ill.: InterVarsity Press, 1991. A comprehensive textbook on biblical hermeneutics.

Silva, Moisés, ed. *Foundations of Contemporary Interpretation: Six Volumes in One.* Grand Rapids: Zondervan Publishing House, 1996 [1987–94]. A very helpful volume that introduces the reader to the hermeneutical contributions of several fields of study, including linguistics, history, science, and theology.

Scripture and Tradition

Jones, Douglas, III. *The Shape of Sola Scriptura.* Moscow, Idaho: Canon Press, forthcoming.

McGrath, Alister E. *Reformation Thought: An Introduction.* 2d ed. Oxford: Blackwell Publishers, 1993. The chapter on the return to Scripture provides a helpful historical overview of the church's understanding of tradition.

Oberman, Heiko A. "*Quo vadis, Petre?* Tradition from Irenaeus to *Hu-*

mani Generis." In *The Dawn of the Reformation: Essays in Late Medieval and Early Reformation Thought*, 269–96. Edinburgh: T. & T. Clark, 1986.

Reformed Theology

Berkhof, Louis. *Systematic Theology.* Grand Rapids: Wm. B. Eerdmans Publishing Co., 1939. A standard Reformed systematic theology.

Calvin, John. *Institutes of the Christian Religion.* Library of Christian Classics, vols. 20–21. Translated by Ford Lewis Battles. Edited by John T. McNeill. Philadelphia: Westminster Press, 1960. Reformed classic.

Hagopian, David, ed. *Back to Basics.* Phillipsburg, N.J.: P&R Publishing Company, 1996. One of the more helpful introductions to Reformed theology available. The section on covenant theology is excellent.

Hodge, A. A. *Outlines of Theology.* 2d ed. Carlisle, Pa.: The Banner of Truth Trust, 1972. A very helpful introduction to Reformed theology written in question-and-answer format.

Turretin, Francis. *Institutes of Elenctic Theology.* Translated by George Musgrave Giger. Edited by James T. Dennison, Jr. 3 vols. Phillipsburg, N.J.: P&R Publishing Co., 1992–97. An almost exhaustive treatment of systematic theology from a Reformed perspective.

Westminster Confession of Faith and Catechisms. One of the greatest Reformed confessions of faith.

Covenant Theology

Jones, Douglas, III. "Back to the Covenant." In *Back to Basics,* ed. David G. Hagopian, 65–140. Phillipsburg, N.J.: P&R Publishing Co., 1996.

Robertson, O. Palmer. *The Christ of the Covenants.* Phillipsburg, N.J.: P&R Publishing Co., 1980. A comprehensive yet readable treatment of covenant theology. A standard text.

Witsius, Herman. *The Economy of the Covenants Between God and*

Man: Comprehending a Complete Body of Divinity. 2 vols. Reprint, Escondido, Calif.: The den Dulk Christian Foundation, 1990. A lengthy exposition of a covenantal approach to Scripture by one of its earliest proponents.

History

Bahnsen, Greg L. "The *Prima Facie* Acceptability of Postmillennialism." *The Journal of Christian Reconstruction* 3, no. 2 (1976–77): 48–105. A good introduction to the history of postmillennialism with an emphasis on Reformed theologians.

Boyd, Alan Patrick. "A Dispensational Premillennial Analysis of the Eschatology of the Post-Apostolic Fathers." Th.M. thesis, Dallas Theological Seminary, 1977. A dispensational reevaluation and critique of the common claim that premillennialism was the historic faith of the early church.

DeJong, James A. *As the Waters Cover the Sea: Millennial Expectations in the Rise of Anglo-American Missions 1640–1810.* Kampen: J. H. Kok N.V., 1970. A helpful overview of the history of different millennial positions from the seventeenth to the nineteenth century.

Hill, Charles. *Regnum Caelorum: Patterns of Future Hope in Early Christianity.* Oxford: Oxford University Press, 1992. An in-depth, scholarly study of the eschatology of the early church fathers.

Kyle, Richard. *The Last Days Are Here Again: A History of the End Times.* Grand Rapids: Baker Books, 1998. A fascinating history of apocalyptic speculation in the church.

Murray, Iain. *The Puritan Hope.* Carlisle, Pa.: Banner of Truth Trust, 1971. An outstanding study of the eschatology of the Puritans.

Old Testament Issues

Fairbairn, Patrick. *The Interpretation of Prophecy.* Carlisle, Pa.: Banner of Truth Trust, 1993. A classic Reformed study of this difficult subject.

LaRondelle, Hans K. *The Israel of God in Prophecy.* Berrien Springs, Mich.: Andrews University Press, 1983. Although written by a

Seventh-Day Adventist, there are a number of helpful insights in this book.

Longman, Tremper, III. *How to Read the Psalms*. Downers Grove, Ill.: InterVarsity Press, 1988.

Pratt, Richard. *He Gave Us Stories*. Phillipsburg, N.J.: P&R Publishing Co., 1990. A useful introduction to the interpretation of historical narratives.

Strom, Mark. *The Symphony of Scripture*. Downers Grove, Ill.: InterVarsity Press, 1990. A great book to help the reader grasp the overall message and structure of the Bible.

VanGemeren, Willem A. *Interpreting the Prophetic Word*. Grand Rapids: Zondervan Publishing House, 1990.

VanGroningen, Gerard. *Messianic Revelation in the Old Testament*. Grand Rapids: Baker Book House, 1990. An exhaustive study of the messianic prophecies and promises of the Old Testament.

Vos, Geerhardus. *Biblical Theology: Old and New Testaments*. Grand Rapids: Wm. B. Eerdmans Publishing Co., 1948. A standard Reformed text on the progressive revelation of Scripture.

New Testament Issues

Bruce, F. F. *New Testament History*. Garden City, N.Y.: Doubleday & Company, 1971. Very useful background information for New Testament studies.

Campbell, Roderick. *Israel and the New Covenant*. Philadelphia: Presbyterian and Reformed Publishing Company, 1954. Good discussion of the working out of the new covenant in the present age.

Feinberg, John S., ed. *Continuity and Discontinuity: Perspectives on the Relationship Between the Old and New Testaments*. Wheaton, Ill.: Crossway Books, 1988. Dispensationalist and Reformed theologians dialogue on a number of crucial issues.

Gentry, Kenneth L., Jr. *The Greatness of the Great Commission*. Tyler, Tex.: Institute for Christian Economics, 1990. Very helpful treatment of the scope of Christ's commission to His church.

Gentry, Kenneth L., Jr., and Thomas D. Ice. *The Great Tribulation: Past or Future?* Grand Rapids: Kregel Publications, 1999. A debate over the interpretation of the Olivet discourse.

Holwerda, David E. *Jesus and Israel: One Covenant or Two?* Grand Rapids: Wm. B. Eerdmans Publishing Co., 1995. This book is the most helpful discussion available of the relationship between Jesus, the people of God in the Old Testament, and the people of God in the New Testament. Very highly recommended.

Kik, J. Marcellus. *An Eschatology of Victory.* Phillipsburg, N.J.: P&R Publishing Co., 1971. Helpful exegesis of Matthew 24 and Revelation 20.

Ridderbos, Herman. *The Coming of the Kingdom.* Translated by H. de Jongste. Edited by Raymond O. Zorn. Phillipsburg, N.J.: P&R Publishing Co., 1962. An outstanding dissertation on the kingdom of God in the New Testament by a Dutch amillennialist. Develops the "already–not yet" theme at length.

———. *Paul: An Outline of His Theology.* Translated by John Richard DeWitt. Grand Rapids: Wm. B. Eerdmans Publishing Co., 1975.

Symington, William. *Messiah the Prince.* Edmonton: Still Waters Revival Books, 1990 [1884]. A brilliant dissertation on the kingship of Christ over the church and the nations. Examines the necessity, nature, and universal extent of Christ's dominion. There is nothing else in print like this book.

Vos, Geerhardus. *The Pauline Eschatology.* Reprint, Phillipsburg, N.J.: P&R Publishing Co., 1991. Standard Reformed amillennialist discussion. Helpful on many texts.

Walker, P. W. L. *Jesus and the Holy City: New Testament Perspectives on Jerusalem.* Grand Rapids: Wm. B. Eerdmans Publishing Co., 1996. Significant treatment of the New Testament understanding of the city of Jerusalem and the temple.

Eschatological Studies

Allis, Oswald T. *Prophecy and the Church.* Phillipsburg, N.J.: P&R Publishing Co., 1945. The classic Reformed critique of dispensationalism.

Bahnsen, Greg L. *The Book of Revelation: An Exposition.* Texarkana, Ark.: Covenant Media Foundation, forthcoming. A verse-by-verse commentary on the book of Revelation from a preterist, postmillennial perspective.

Bahnsen, Greg L., and Kenneth L. Gentry, Jr. *House Divided: The Break-up of Dispensational Theology.* Tyler, Tex.: Institute for Christian Economics, 1989.

Blaising, Craig A., and Darrell L. Bock. *Progressive Dispensationalism.* Wheaton, Ill.: Victor Books, 1993. The most thorough and clear presentation of the view held by a small but growing number of dispensationalists.

Bock, Darrell L., ed. *Three Views of the End of History and Beyond.* Grand Rapids: Zondervan Publishing House, 1999. Dialogue and debate between proponents of amillennialism, premillennialism, and postmillennialism.

Boettner, Loraine. *The Millennium.* Rev. ed. Phillipsburg, N.J.: P&R Publishing Co., 1984. Defense of postmillennialism.

Brown, David. *Christ's Second Coming: Will It Be Premillennial?* Edmonton: Still Waters Revival Books, 1990. A thorough critique of premillennialism.

Campbell, Donald K., and Jeffrey L. Townsend. *A Case for Premillennialism.* Chicago: Moody Press, 1992. Expository defense of premillennialism.

Cox, William E. *Biblical Studies in Final Things.* Nutley, N.J.: P&R Publishing Co., 1967. Introductory explanation of amillennial eschatology.

Davis, John Jefferson. *The Victory of Christ's Kingdom.* Moscow, Idaho: Canon Press, 1996. Brief explanation and defense of postmillennialism.

DeMar, Gary. *Last Days Madness.* Rev. ed. Atlanta: American Vision, 1994. Excellent analysis of the hysteria often associated with dispensational speculations about the end of the world.

Erickson, Millard J. *Contemporary Options in Eschatology.* Grand Rapids: Baker Book House, 1977. Examines the four millennial positions and several views of the Rapture from a historic premillennialist perspective. Good discussion of modern liberal and neoorthodox eschatological views.

Gentry, Kenneth L., Jr. *He Shall Have Dominion: A Postmillennial Eschatology.* 2d ed. Tyler, Tex.: Institute for Christian Economics, 1997. The most exhaustive defense of postmillennialism available. Highly recommended.

———. *Perilous Times: A Study in Eschatological Evil.* Bethesda, Md.:

Christian Universities Press, 1998. A thorough study of Dan. 9:24–27; Matt. 24; 2 Thess. 2; Rev. 13, 17.

Grenz, Stanley. *The Millennial Maze*. Downers Grove, Ill.: InterVarsity Press, 1992. The most accurate and helpful explanation of the different millennial positions. Very good introductory text.

Grier, W. J. *The Momentous Event*. London: Banner of Truth Trust, 1945. Introduction to amillennial eschatology.

Hendriksen, William. *The Bible on the Life Hereafter*. Grand Rapids: Baker Book House, 1959. Good discussion of individual and cosmic eschatology from a Reformed, amillennial perspective.

Hoekema, Anthony. *The Bible and the Future*. Grand Rapids: Wm. B. Eerdmans Publishing Co., 1979. The best and most comprehensive explanation of amillennialism in print.

Ladd, George E. *The Presence of the Future*. Grand Rapids: Wm. B. Eerdmans Publishing Co., 1974. The best defense of historic premillennialism available.

Mathison, Keith A. *Dispensationalism: Rightly Dividing the People of God?* Phillipsburg, N.J.: P&R Publishing Co., 1995. A Reformed critique of dispensationalism.

North, Gary. *Rapture Fever: Why Dispensationalism Is Paralyzed*. Tyler, Tex.: Institute for Christian Economics, 1993. A study of the religious and societal consequences of total preoccupation with the Rapture.

Pate, C. Marvin, ed. *Four Views of the Book of Revelation*. Grand Rapids: Zondervan Publishing House, 1998. A dialogue and debate between proponents of four approaches to interpreting the book of Revelation: preterism, idealism, progressive dispensationalism, and classical dispensationalism.

Peterson, Robert A. *Hell on Trial*. Phillipsburg, N.J.: P&R Publishing Co., 1995. The best defense available of the traditional orthodox doctrine of eternal punishment.

Rushdoony, R. J. *God's Plan for Victory: The Meaning of Postmillennialism*. 2d ed. Vallecito, Calif.: Chalcedon Foundation, 1997. Excellent introduction to postmillennialism. Includes a good discussion of the implications of eschatological positions.

Sandlin, Andrew. *A Postmillennial Primer*. Vallecito, Calif.: Chalcedon Foundation, 1997. A very helpful overview of the essential features of biblical postmillennialism.

Index of Scripture